VMware vSphere® 5 Administration

Instant Reference

VMware vSphere® 5 Administration
Instant Reference

Christopher Kusek

Van V. Van Noy

Andy Daniel

John Wiley & Sons, Inc.

Acquisitions Editor: Agatha Kim
Development Editor: Stef Jones
Technical Editor: Jason Boche
Production Editor: Christine O'Connor
Copy Editor: Alexa Murphy
Editorial Manager: Pete Gaughan
Production Manager: Tim Tate
Vice President and Executive Group Publisher: Richard Swadley
Vice President and Publisher: Neil Edde
Book Designer: Chris Gillespie, Happenstance Type-O-Rama
Proofreaders: Paul Sagan and Sheilah Ledwidge, Word One New York
Indexer: Robert Swanson
Project Coordinator, Cover: Katherine Crocker
Cover Designer: Ryan Sneed

Dear Reader,

Thank you for choosing *VMware vSphere 5 Administration Instant Reference*. This book is part of a family of premium-quality Sybex books, all of which are written by outstanding authors who combine practical experience with a gift for teaching.

Sybex was founded in 1976. More than 30 years later, we're still committed to producing consistently exceptional books. With each of our titles, we're working hard to set a new standard for the industry. From the paper we print on, to the authors we work with, our goal is to bring you the best books available.

I hope you see all that reflected in these pages. I'd be very interested to hear your comments and get your feedback on how we're doing. Feel free to let me know what you think about this or any other Sybex book by sending me an email at nedde@wiley.com. If you think you've found a technical error in this book, please visit http://sybex.custhelp.com. Customer feedback is critical to our efforts at Sybex.

Best regards,

Neil Edde
Vice President and Publisher
Sybex, an Imprint of Wiley

To my wife Courtney, who provides me endless inspiration and whom I can always count on to have limitless patience when my head is in the clouds.

—Andy

I dedicate this book to my son Alexander and my godson Erehwon. They are the future of technology and will be the recipients of all of the gifts we imbue within the clouds from here and forever.

—Christopher

I dedicate this book to my wife Laurie and my two kids Henry and Avabella. They are the reason I get up every day and push myself to do more and be better than the day before.

—Van

Acknowledgments

I'd like to thank all those at Wiley for the opportunity to participate in the writing of this book. Agatha Kim and Stef Jones, thank you for your patience as I struggled to squeeze yet another item into my schedule. Many thanks to my coauthors, Christopher Kusek and Van V. Van Noy, for their dedication to this project, and to Jason Boche for his keen eye on the technical details. I'd like to thank all of my colleagues and customers with whom I've had the pleasure of "breaking stuff" (and fixing some, too) over the years. A very special thanks to Charlie Gautreaux. Without you, my words would not be here. I'd also like to thank my family. First, my parents, who have always taught by example. It is their tireless work ethic that I mimicked from an early age that has taken me far. Finally, my wife, Courtney, who always has patience for "just a few more minutes," and who never fails to encourage my ambition. I can't imagine success without you by my side.

—Andy

No man is an island (except for the Isle of Man) and this book would not have been possible without everyone involved! I'd like to thank the team at Wiley for making this book a reality—especially Agatha Kim, Stef Jones and Christine O'Connor. To my coauthors Van V. Van Noy and Andy Daniel, you guys were a blast to work with, and your candid natures will take you great distances. I personally want to thank John Troyer, a rock star in his own right and well deserving of all thanks he receives. Without Joseph DAngelo, I'd never have gotten through the legal wrangling of internal protocol! My contribution to this book would have never been possible if not for the motivation and inspiration given to me by Shanley Kane: you helped drive me towards great things. It goes without saying, but the vExpert community was a great source of inspiration and perspective to help produce a book that is technically accurate and current. I'd like to thank those Starbucks baristas and staff who tolerated me writing while sipping on vanilla red rooibos tea and wearing cat ears. I am also grateful for my family and my son Alexander, who understood that sometimes I needed to focus on my writing and could tolerate this dedication. And last but not least, I'd like to thank the VMware community. Without your dedication to using and making these technologies better, we wouldn't have a reason to write books to help spread the good word of virtualization. You are truly our future and the reason we write what we do, whether in blogs, books, or tweets. Keep inspiring us to do better and keeping us honest to improve ourselves.

—Christopher

I would like to first thank Wiley for inviting me to be part of this project—it's been quite the adventure. I am truly honored. Thanks to Christopher Kusek and Andy Daniel for all of their hard work and time on their parts of the book. I know you are as proud of this book as I am. Thanks to Agatha Kim, Stef Jones, and Christine O'Connor. You were a tremendous help to me along the way. I would also like to thank Jason Boche for making sure that everything is technically accurate. Without John Troyer and Matt Graybiel from VMware, I would not have been able to be part of this book. Finally, I want to thank my family. My father, Bill, for taking care of things around the house that I was too busy to get to. My mother, Fran, for reading through drafts of chapters, ensuring that everything made sense and was stated clearly. And finally and most importantly, thanks to my wife and kids for the time missed over the past six months. Thank you for always allowing me to pursue my passions.

—Van

About the Authors

Andy Daniel is a Senior IT Engineer at TIAA-CREF, specializing in virtualization, networking, and IP-based storage area networks. He is VCAP-DCA #29, and before joining TIAA-CREF, he worked as a Senior VMware Consultant where he architected and provided pre-sales support for VMware solutions utilizing Cisco UCS servers, Nexus 1kv, 2k, 5k switches, and NetApp FAS storage systems. Andy has designed, implemented, and managed multisite, multitenant virtual environments and large multisite VMware SRM-protected vSphere deployments. He's an avid blogger at his site, vnephos.com, and is leader of the Richmond, Virginia VMware User Group.

Christopher Kusek is the Global Virtualization Lead for EMC, where he leads a global team of Cloud and Virtualization Professionals. Personally, he has a hardened focus on Virtualization, Applications, Security, and Cloud, both from an overarching strategic standpoint as a technology evangelist, as well as a practical and tactical standpoint with a direct focus on customers. Christopher is founder of multiple user groups and maintains an active role within the technical communities, both locally and globally. Working with x86 Virtualization going back to VMware's roots, Christopher also has been actively involved with Citrix and Microsoft Virtualization solutions over the past 15 years. Recognized as a VMware vExpert, Christopher maintains an active profile on both where Virtualization is from a here-and-now strategy but also looking forward years in advance to the future of IT. Two common misconceptions are that Christopher doesn't sleep and that he is a cat. Only one of those statements is correct. Maintaining an industry active social profile, Christopher is also an official EMC Blogger posting on EMC and Industry at his blog, PKGuild.com, and has heavy interaction within social media and Twitter via @CXI. A frequent presenter at conferences, he is comfortable leading the vision from high with the executives while also earning the respect of the troops deep in the trenches.

Van V. Van Noy has worked for over 16 years with a variety of different operating systems, including more than six years experience working with

VMware in an enterprise IT environment. He is currently a Systems Engineer for one of the nation's largest department store chains and consults for other businesses during his free time. In 2009 and 2010, Van was awarded VMware's vExpert Award for his work in Arkansas promoting VMware. Van is the chair of the Central Arkansas VMware User Group and continues to promote VMware whenever possible.

Contents

Introduction

For those of us who have been working in the virtualization industry since its earliest days, it's hard to imagine what datacenters were like without virtualization. Still, there are some organizations that have yet to adopt virtualization within their datacenter. With the release of VMware vSphere 5, VMware's flagship enterprise-class virtualization solution, VMware aims to change that reality.

However, even though virtualization has many benefits—not the least of which include reducing your hardware footprint, enabling faster server provisioning, and simplifying disaster recovery—some people feel that virtualization also has a steep learning curve. IT professionals who want to become more familiar with virtualization need to learn about terms like vMotion, vSphere Distributed Switch, vSphere Fault Tolerance, and VMkernel interfaces. All these new terms and new technologies can seem confusing to someone not familiar with how all the pieces fit together.

In addition, virtualization sometimes forces IT professionals to think differently about how to solve old challenges. The "traditional" way of doing things often isn't the best way of handling something after you've virtualized your datacenter.

This book is intended to help address these concerns. For administrators who might be new to virtualization, this book explains how virtualization works, what the components are, and how these components fit together—in a hands-on, how-to approach. We believe this approach will help new vSphere administrators get up to speed quickly.

For administrators who are familiar with previous versions of VMware's virtualization product suite but not VMware vSphere 5, this book will fill in the gaps through the step-by-step review of vSphere's new features and functionality—such as vSphere Web Client Server.

While this book isn't an in-depth, highly technical view of VMware vSphere—that's what you'll find in *Mastering VMware vSphere 5*, also from Sybex—it is a comprehensive reference guide for finding information quickly, just when you need it. We hope that it will earn its place on your reference bookshelf as a book to which you can return when you need a little extra guidance on how something works or how to perform a task within VMware vSphere.

What Is Covered in This Book

This book is written as a blend of explanatory text and "cookbook-style" recipes that are intended to help administrators become more familiar with installing, configuring, managing, and monitoring a virtual environment using the VMware vSphere product suite. We start by introducing the vSphere product suite and all of its great features. After introducing all the bells and whistles, this book details how to install the product, including considerations and steps you should take to upgrade to VMware vSphere 5. After showing you how to install vSphere, we move on to configuring VMware vSphere to meet your specific needs. This includes configuring VMware vSphere's extensive networking and storage functionality. Next, the book moves into virtual machine creation and management, importing and exporting virtual machines, security, and finally monitoring and resource management.

You can read this book from cover to cover to gain an understanding of the vSphere product suite in preparation for a new virtual environment, but you might find it more useful as a reference work to which you can refer when you're stuck and can't remember exactly how something works. If you're an IT professional who is new to virtualization with VMware vSphere, this book is intended to help you hit the ground running.

Here is a glance at what's in each chapter:

Chapter 1: Introduction to vSphere　Chapter 1 takes a look at the features of VMware vSphere 5. This includes vSphere's "legacy" features—those features that were also present in earlier versions of VMware's enterprise virtualization products—as well as the new features specific to VMware vSphere 5. This feature overview should provide you with some idea of how VMware vSphere can address business problems.

Chapter 2: Installing and Configuring ESXi　VMware ESXi is the foundation of the vSphere product suite, and Chapter 2 provides information on how to install and configure VMware ESXi.

Chapter 3: Installing and Configuring vCenter Server　Many of the advanced features within the VMware vSphere product suite are only present when you also have vCenter Server, the management server for VMware ESXi. Chapter 3 describes how to install and configure vCenter Server and vCenter Server Appliance to manage your ESXi hosts and your virtual machines.

Chapter 4: Understanding Licensing VMware vSphere 5 continues use of an integrated licensing mechanism. How to install licenses, how to assign and manage licenses, and how to review current license usage are all covered in Chapter 4.

Chapter 5: Upgrading to vSphere 5 Perhaps you already use vSphere 4 but are looking to upgrade to VMware vSphere 5. This chapter provides information on the upgrade process, including which tasks should come first, and the various methods for upgrading the different components.

Chapter 6: Creating and Managing Virtual Networking Chapter 6 provides information and procedures for creating and configuring VMware vSphere's virtual networking features. This includes vSphere Standard Switches as well as vSphere Distributed Switches.

Chapter 7: Configuring and Managing Storage Storage is an essential part of every virtualization implementation, so Chapter 7 covers the different types of storage that are supported by VMware vSphere 5 and how to configure each of them.

Chapter 8: High Availability and Business Continuity Chapter 8 discusses the different ways that administrators can configure VMware vSphere to provide high availability for virtual machines. Features like vSphere High Availability, VM failure monitoring, and vSphere Fault Tolerance are all covered.

Chapter 9: Managing Virtual Machines Managing virtual machines is a pretty broad topic, but Chapter 9 attempts to cover it by discussing the most frequently performed tasks. Tasks such as creating virtual machines, adding or removing hardware from virtual machines, managing virtual machine power state, and managing virtual hardware versions are all covered in this chapter.

Chapter 10: Importing and Exporting Virtual Machines Creating new virtual machines sometimes means converting physical systems to virtual machines. This type of migration, a physical-to-virtual migration, is one of a couple of different types of imports discussed in Chapter 10. This chapter also provides information on how to export VMs out of VMware vSphere for use with other VMware virtualization products.

Chapter 11: Configuring Security Chapter 11 covers security-related aspects of VMware vSphere, such as role-based access controls and how to harden vSphere 5.

Chapter 12: Managing Resources and Performance   Chapter 12 covers the important topics of resource management and performance, two areas that are closely related. This chapter discusses how to allocate resources, how to modify resource allocation behaviors, and how to identify performance concerns related to resource allocation.

Appendix: Fundamentals of the Command-Line Interface To help build your proficiency with command-line tasks, this online appendix focuses on navigating through the Direct Console User Interface and performing management, configuration, and troubleshooting tasks. You can find the appendix online at www.sybex.com/go/vsphere5instantref.

Who Should Buy This Book

This book is for IT professionals looking to strengthen their knowledge of constructing and managing a virtual infrastructure on VMware vSphere 5. Although the book can be helpful for those new to IT, we assume the target reader has the following:

- A basic understanding of networking architecture

- Experience working in a Microsoft Windows environment

- Experience managing the domain name system (DNS) and Dynamic Host Configuration Protocol (DHCP)

- A basic understanding of how virtualization differs from traditional physical infrastructures

- A basic understanding of hardware and software components in standard x86 and x64 computing

How to Contact the Authors

We welcome feedback from you about this book or about books you'd like to see from us in the future.

You can contact Andy Daniel by messaging @vnephos on Twitter, by writing to adaniel@vnephos.com, or by visiting his blog at http://vnephos.com.

You can contact Christopher Kusek by messaging @CXI on Twitter, by email to christopher.kusek@pkguild.com, or via his blog http://pkguild.com.

You can contact Van V. Van Noy by writing to van@triplevpc.com or by visiting his blog at http://triplevpc.com.

PART I

Building a VMware vSphere Environment

IN THIS PART ⊙

1

Introduction to vSphere

IN THIS CHAPTER, YOU WILL LEARN TO:

- Enhancements in VMFS-5 (Page 16)
- Enhancements in Storage vMotion (Page 17)
- Virtual Machine Scalability (Page 17)
- vCenter Improvements (Page 18)
- Fault Tolerance (Page 18)
- Networking Enhancements (Page 19)
- VMware vShield 5 Suite (Page 19)

V Sphere 5 is here! With this fifth-generation release, the VMware Virtual Datacenter operating system continues to transform x86 IT infrastructure into the most efficient shared on-demand utility, with built-in availability, scalability, and security services for all applications and simple, proactive automated management.

Administrators who have been around for a while may think of the new product as the fifth generation, or simply VMware Infrastructure 5. However, this release better aligns the new product with the direction that virtual datacenters are taking. It introduces many new features that promise to continue to revolutionize the infrastructure of the modern and evolving datacenter, making this release even bigger than the VI4 release. The most sought-after three features—vMotion, Distributed Resource Scheduler (DRS), High Availability (HA)—have been improved and are better than ever.

Understand the Legacy Features of vSphere

Welcome to the legacy features of vSphere. They serve as the foundation that brings tremendous flexibility to managing an x86 environment. There are many legacy features, but we'll be covering the top three here:

- vMotion, which offers the ability to relocate a running virtual machine or server from one physical location to another without any downtime.

- Distributed Resource Scheduler, which you use to make sure that your servers are balanced, getting the resources they deserve.

- High Availability, which ensures you'll never have to rush into the office to address bad hardware.

vMotion

vMotion remains one of the most powerful features of virtualization today. With vMotion, you can perform work on underlying hosts during business hours rather than having to wait until the wee hours of the morning or weekends to upgrade BIOS or firmware or do something as simple as add more memory to a host. vMotion requires that each underlying host have a CPU that uses the same instruction set, because, after all, moving a running virtual machine (VM) from one physical host to another without any downtime is a phenomenal feat. VMware

VMs run on top of the Virtual Machine File System (VMFS) or NFS. Windows still runs on New Technology File System (NTFS), but the underlying file system is VMFS-5 or VMFS-3. VMFS allows for multiple access, and that is how one host can pass a running VM to another host without downtime or interruptions. It is important to realize that even momentary downtime can be critical for applications and databases. Zero downtime when moving a VM from one host to another physical host is crucial.

Unfortunately, there is no way to move from Intel to AMD, or vice versa. In the past, there were even issues going from an older Intel CPU to a newer Intel CPU, which were somewhat mitigated by Enhanced vMotion Compatibility (EVC).

VMware has several years of experience mastering virtualization while the competitors are playing catch-up. Furthermore, VMware has explored many approaches to virtualization and has seen firsthand where some approaches fall short and where some excel.

vMotion technology requires shared storage, but the virtual machine files do not move from that shared storage during the logical transition. If, for example, you have to change the virtual machine's physical location, you must first power down the VM and then "migrate" it from one logical unit number (LUN) or hard drive to another LUN or hard drive. Or you can use Storage vMotion, allowing the virtual machine to move between hosts and storage.

A caveat to vMotion is that traditional Intrusion Detection Systems (IDS) and Intrusion Prevention Systems (IPS) may not work as originally designed. Part of the reason for this is that the traffic of VMs that are communicating with one another inside a host never leaves the host and therefore cannot be inspected. Virtual appliances are being developed to address this concern. They have the ability to run side-by-side VMs.

Since uptime is important, VMware developed Storage vMotion so that the physical location of a running VM can be changed, again without any downtime and without losing any transactional information. Obviously, Storage vMotion is very exciting because one of the reasons that virtualization is the hottest technology in IT today is the flexibility it brings to the datacenter (compared with running servers the old-fashioned way in a physical environment).

There are other ways to leverage the technology. Virtual machines can be moved on the fly from shared storage to local storage if you need to perform maintenance on shared storage or if LUNs have to be moved to other hosts. Imagine moving a physical server with no downtime or sweat on your part by simply clicking on a new rack in your datacenter and then clicking OK. Wouldn't that ability be useful for a variety of needs and tasks every day?

VMware Cluster

A VMware cluster allows you to pool the resources of several physical hosts and create logical and physical boundaries within a virtual infrastructure or datacenter. Some organizations may want to create several clusters in their vCenter (formerly VMware Virtual Center) based on functionality—for example, a demilitarized zone (DMZ) cluster or an application cluster. You may want to create a VMware cluster based on the type of LUNs, their speed, their size, or the type of appliance they represent—for example, EMC VNX versus Left Hand Networks. Networking teams may not always want to present all networks to all hosts in the cluster. By creating pools of resources, you can manage these assets and work may be performed on individual clusters rather than the entire infrastructure.

What resources are pooled? CPU, memory, networking bandwidth, storage, and physical hosts are all shared by the VMs that are defined on the specific cluster.

A good rule of thumb is to have sufficient capacity to run extra VMs in the event that one or more ESXi hosts go down. For example, a cluster with three hosts that runs at 50 percent of resources on each host could probably handle one host failure; the remaining two hosts would then take on 25 percent of the load from the failed host and the cluster would be running at 75 percent of resources. In this scenario, a second host failure would overwhelm the remaining host and some virtual machines would not be able to start on the last host. Obviously, you should plan for extra capacity when designing clusters if failover is important.

Distributed Resource Scheduler

Distributed Resource Scheduler (DRS) helps you load-balance workloads across a VMware cluster. Advanced algorithms constantly analyze the cluster environment and even use vMotion to move a running server or VM from one host to another without any downtime. You can specify that DRS performs these actions automatically. Say, for instance, that a VM needs more CPU or memory and the host it is running on lacks those resources. With the automatic settings you specify, DRS will use vMotion to move the VM to another host that has more resources available. DRS can be set to automatically make needed adjustments any time of the day or night or to issue recommendations instead. Two circumstances that often trigger such events are when an Active Directory server is used a lot in the morning for logins and when backups are run. A DRS-enabled cluster shares all the CPU and memory bandwidth as one unified unit for the VMs to use.

DRS is extremely important because in the past, VMware administrators had to do their best to analyze the needs of their VMs, often without a lot of quantitative information. DRS changed the way the virtualization game was played and revolutionized the datacenter. You can now load VMs onto a cluster and the technology will sort out all the variables in real time and make necessary adjustments. DRS is easy to use, and many administrators boast about how many vMotions their environments have completed since inception.

For example, let's say an admin virtualizes a Microsoft Exchange server, a SQL Server, an Active Directory server, and a couple of heavily used application servers and puts all of them on one host in a cluster. The week before, another admin virtualized several older NT servers that were very lightweight; because those servers didn't use very much CPU, memory, network, or disk input/output (I/O), the admin put those servers on another host. At this point, the two hosts are off balance based on their workloads. One host has too little to do because its servers have low utilization, and the other host is getting killed with heavily used applications. Before DRS, a third admin would have had to look at all the servers running on these two hosts and determine how to distribute the VMs evenly across the hosts. Admins would have had to use a bit of ingenuity—along with trial and error—to figure out how to balance the needs of each server with the underlying hardware. DRS analyzes these needs and moves VMs when they need more resources so that you can attend to other, more pressing issues.

High Availability

When CIOs and management types begin learning about virtualization, one of their most common fears is "putting all their eggs in one basket." "If all our servers are on one host, what happens if that host fails?" This is a smart question to ask, and one that VMware prepared for when they revealed the HA, or High Availability, feature of VI3. A virtual infrastructure is controlled by vCenter, which is aware of all the hosts that are in its control and all the VMs that are on those hosts. vCenter installs and configures HA but at that point, the ESXi hosts monitor heartbeats and initiate failovers and VM startup. This is fundamentally important to understand because vCenter can be one of the VMs which has gone down in an outage and HA will still function, providing a primary HA host, aka failover coordinator, is still available.

VMware recommends a strategy referred to as *N+1* (as a minimum, not an absolute), dictated by architectural requirements. This simply means that your cluster should include enough hosts (*N*) so that if one fails, there is enough capacity to restart the VMs on the other host(s). Shared storage among the hosts is a requirement of HA. When a host fails and HA starts, there is a small window of downtime—roughly the same amount that you might expect from a reboot. If the organization has alerting software, a page or email message might be sent indicating a problem, but at other times, this happens so quickly that no alerts are triggered. The goal of virtualization is to keep the uptime of production servers high: hosts can go down, but if servers keep running, you can address the challenge during business hours.

> **NOTE**   vMotion is not utilized in a High Availability failover scenario.

VMware vCenter Converter

If your organization is new to virtualization, VMware vCenter Converter is handy. It's a plug-in to vCenter in the Enterprise version, but there is also a free stand-alone download that lets you convert physical servers into the virtual infrastructure without downtime—thanks to a technology that enables incremental changes to be captured during the physical to virtual (P2V) conversion process. This application works extremely well. You can use it to convert a single server or multiple servers, move a VM from a workstation or another virtual infrastructure, resize hard drives, or work with partitions. Organizations are choosing virtualization because it gives them the flexibility to convert already-built working servers, or if the need exists, rebuild a server from a known good build. Both Windows and Linux servers can be virtualized, and there is interoperability with other third-party formats, such as Norton Ghost, Acronis, and Windows Virtual PC (a feature of Windows 7).

VMware vSphere Update Manager

A second plug-in that has proved to be invaluable is VMware vSphere Update Manager. This feature allows for a baseline creation that represents a security standard. A baseline, for example, would be one host or virtual machine that has been configured to be the golden image; it has all the right patches and all other hosts or VMs should have this level of configuration. You can then apply this baseline to all hosts or select Microsoft and Linux virtual machines, and the technology will remediate updates and apply them to the infrastructure, saving you valuable time. The technology will automatically place one host in a cluster in maintenance mode, migrate the VMs to another host, update the host, reboot, exit maintenance mode, and move to the next host to continue the process. You can remediate one host at a time to achieve a fine level of control in environments or organizations that have high visibility or special needs, or you can remediate an entire cluster and sit back to watch it happen.

Another outstanding feature of VMware vSphere Update Manager is its ability to patch offline virtual machines. Obviously not possible with physical servers, this feature offers a level of security compliance far superior to datacenters without virtual infrastructure.

Although this may not sound like a breakthrough in technology, in the old days, administrators would have to go to the VMware site; download several patches with long, cryptic names; copy the patches to each host; clear off the virtual machines; open the command line; run an even more cryptic command to work with each file on each ESXi host; reboot—and do the same thing over on each and every host. Now, with the click of a mouse, VMware vSphere Update Manager does all these steps quickly and efficiently. Furthermore, since a baseline is utilized, each host receives exactly the same build. No longer will you need to worry whether you applied every patch to every host. The technology handles this task for you.

NOTE   It is important to know that VMware is discontinuing support of patching inside guests via VUM.

64-Bit

With the release of vSphere 5, ESXi continues with 64-bit technology for the Direct Console User Interface (DCUI). The difference between 32- and 64-bit is that with 64-bit, you can achieve higher consolidation ratios (VMs per host) and a better return on investment (ROI) on your hardware. Most likely, only the largest organizations will approach those top ends, but either way, the infrastructure just became more robust.

The downside is that many organizations will have no choice but to purchase new hardware for their infrastructure. With prior versions of VMware, organizations had the option of virtualizing some of their newer servers, and then turning around and using that hardware as their next ESXihost.

VMware Capacity Planner

A third plug-in we'll look at is VMware Capacity Planner. When tasked with virtualizing a physical datacenter, this tool enables you to gather quantitative data from physical servers to better understand which servers are the best candidates for virtualization. Of course, the underlying premise of virtualizing is that on average, most physical servers use significantly less than 10 percent of the resources available on a server; it only makes sense to take a handful of those servers and place them on a host to achieve better utilization of the company's hardware. VMware Capacity Planner analyzes how much CPU, memory, disk I/O, and network bandwidth a server uses over time, and how much it isn't using. As any tenured VMware administrator will attest, VMs need less CPU and less memory than their physical counterparts. Capacity Planner is your quantitative friend in the virtualization journey.

Host Profiles

Host profiles are similar in notion to a template or a golden image used to consistently replicate new desktops or virtual machines. Prior to this feature, you either rebuilt each host from scratch or used some kind of automated build process and then did your best to create consistency across all hosts. Host profiles greatly reduce configuration management by allowing you to build a golden image once and then "plug it into" any new hosts, thus ensuring standards across the infrastructure.

Every organization and administrator chooses how they want to configure their hosts. Some manually build each one; some use scripting to create exact copies. These approaches each have their merits. However, host profiles will allow an administrator to create a golden image and then apply those settings to any new or replaced ESXi hosts.

vCenter Linked Mode

vCenter Linked Mode creates a simplified approach to management in large environments by allowing you to use a single interface for multiple vCenter servers. If there is more than one vCenter server in your environment, they can be interconnected in a mode that allows you to share management roles across the infrastructure, licensing, and other related tasks. This reduces the amount of work associated with setting up the same configurations on multiple vCenter servers.

Distributed Power Management

Distributed Power Management (DPM) is the ability of the system to identify when there is enough extra capacity to either automatically shut down hosts or make recommendations to reduce power consumption (think holidays, evenings, and weekends!).

You don't have to be "green" to appreciate this feature. Studies by many industry analysts point out how fast energy costs have gone up in the past few years, and those costs now account for a significant portion of operating costs. The ability to reduce unneeded capacity during the course of a fiscal year can add up to a bigger bonus at year-end. And as any business student will point out, cutting costs adds directly to the bottom line.

VMware states on their website that power and cooling costs can be cut by up to 20 percent in the datacenter during low-utilization time periods. Distributed Resource Scheduler (DRS) helps to accomplish the task. During a weekend or holiday, vCenter recognizes extra CPU capacity and/ or memory in a cluster and uses DRS to migrate VMs off a designated ESXi host. Once all systems are off the host, that host can be powered off or put in standby mode to conserve energy and lower costs. If the need for capacity starts to increase, that host will be powered back up and VMs will migrate back onto it to take advantage of all cluster resources.

Enhanced vMotion Compatibility

The Enhanced vMotion Compatibility (EVC) feature will add more flexibility when you are configuring vMotion between CPUs from the same manufacturer. As noted earlier, vMotion is not always compatible between older and newer CPU generations. However, the EVC feature allows the hypervisor to mask or hide certain differences (CPU instruction sets) so that compatibility between generations is more relaxed. This works for both Intel and AMD.

VMware Data Recovery

A virtual infrastructure would not be complete without a backup solution. VMware introduced its Data Recovery feature in vSphere 4. The traditional approach to backing up virtual machines (agent-based backups) utilizes a lot of system resources from a host. Data Recovery relieves that unnecessary pressure by providing a centralized and agent-free process to back up virtual machines. A separate physical server or servers that have access to the shared storage will pull the data through their own network instead of through the ESX/ESXi host, thereby reducing the load on the hosts and allowing the host to provide its resources for performance instead of backups.

> **NOTE** ESXi hosts are both bare-metal enterprise-class hypervisors that function as hosts for virtual machines.

VMware Data Recovery can be integrated with backup tools and technologies that are already part of your organization's datacenter. Full and incremental file-level backups are much easier to perform in this release. Changed block tracking functionality allows incremental backups to be even more efficient.

vSphere Client

One of many areas where VMware excels over its competitors is its management features. There are several ways to interact with a VMware infrastructure, chief among them vSphere Client. (The other methods, vSphere Web Access and DCUI [ESXi's command-line interface], are discussed in upcoming sections.) You can use vSphere Client to connect to vCenter or directly to a host. However, we recommend that you use vCenter as the central administrative unit for the infrastructure. vSphere

Building a VMware vSphere Environment

PART I

Client is installed on a Windows machine and with it, you can do such tasks as the following:

- Configure vCenter.
- Create virtual machines.
- Monitor, manage, and adjust settings for hosts, VMs, and vCenter.

vSphere Client is not a tool for end users. It's intended for VMware administrators only. As tools go, this is a great one. The user interface is intuitive and the features are easy to navigate. You can open up your favorite browser, enter the server name of vCenter or any ESXi hostname, and download the client.

VMkernel Protection

The new VMkernel Protection technology helps protect the hypervisor by ensuring that the integrity of the VMkernel is not compromised and/or changed by either common attacks or software loaded on the host. The VMkernel modules are now digitally signed and validated during each reboot so that nothing is overwritten, and they use memory integrity for protection from buffer overflow. When you combine this technology with VMware VMsafe (which is used to protect VMs by including an Application Programming Interface [API] for third-party developers to create security products), you'll see that security has been enhanced yet again.

VMkernel Protection is somewhat similar to what Microsoft did to try to eliminate the "Blue Screen of Death": they created digitally signed device drivers. Before this, third-party vendors created all sorts of software that interacted with Windows operating systems. Sometimes, that software was coded well and played nicely. Other times, it blue-screened the operating system. Microsoft did not have control over outside companies, so they did the next best thing by introducing digitally signed drivers. In a similar manner, VMkernel Protection ensures that the kernel is not modified, ensuring the long-term stability of the VMware platform.

Virtual Disk Thin Provisioning

In the storage realm, there is a feature called *virtual disk thin provisioning*. SAN storage is more expensive than direct attached disk. Therefore, administrators are careful to properly provision each new VM with the right amount of GBs on their drives. Virtual disk thin provisioning allows you to overprovision valuable shared storage while at the same time allowing the VM to grow into its allocated hard drives. This technology would not be complete without the underlying reporting and notifications that ensure proper maintenance of the storage, and that is well taken care of on the management side in vCenter Server. This feature reduces the need for SAN storage, helping keep costs low and under control.

Take a moment to imagine a virtual infrastructure that has, say, 255 virtual machines in version 3.5, update 2. If, on average, each VM has between 1 and 5 GB of unused space on just the C: drive, that means between 255 GB and 1.2 TB of SAN storage is unused. If each VM has two hard drives, almost 2 TB of space could be reclaimed if this feature is utilized. Now, that is valuable.

VMware DCUI

The Direct Console User Interface, or ESXi DCUI, is an interface used to configure, manage, and monitor an ESXi host from a command-line level. The DCUI is in essence the first virtual machine on an ESXi, and it serves as a communication device between the administrator and the hypervisor. Recently, admins have begun using PowerShell to configure and manage the infrastructure. This will open up many powerful opportunities for scripting.

NOTE A hypervisor is a high-speed scheduler and hardware abstraction layer. It hands out resources (CPU, memory, network, disk) to the virtual machines asking for them, very quickly.

---

vSphere Web Client

The final interface is the vSphere Web Client, formally vSphere Web Access. The vSphere Web Client is a fully-extensible, platform-independent implementation of the vSphere client based on Adobe Flex. This tool enables full virtual machine management, including creation of virtual machines, deployment from templates, and even client-side USB device access. This new feature of the vSphere 5 family finally solves the age-old challenge of management access from non-Windows clients.

Understand the New Features of vSphere

The list of new features is a lot longer than what we will introduce here, but the following sections detail some of the most exciting ones.

Enhancements in Storage

Storage by far has had some of the greatest investment in the release of VMware vSphere 5, with features and enhancements responding to the needs of customers worldwide. At a glance, the feature set enhancements are:

- Storage DRS (SDRS)
- Policy-driven storage delivery
- VMFS-5
- iSCSI UI enhancements
- Storage IO Control (SIOC) NFS Support
- Storage APIs - Array Integration (VASA) : Thin Provisioning
- Swap to SSD
- 64-TB LUN and pRDM support
- FCoE Software Initiator
- Storage vMotion snapshot and linked-clone support

Storage DRS

Carrying the torch of DRS throughout the stack, Storage DRS delivers the benefits of resource aggregation, automated initial placement, and bottleneck avoidance with storage. Because storage is aggregated into a logical management point, administrators are able to manage it as pools as they do compute. Storage DRS enables smart and rapid placement of new virtual machines and virtual disk drives while load-balancing existing workloads.

Enhancements in VMFS-5

Of the changes associated with VMFS-5, the ones you will find most life-changing are 64-TB device support, unified block size (1 MB), and an improved sub-block mechanism. Supporting a non-disruptive upgrade from VMFS-3 to VMFS-5 will enable you to take advantage of these features immediately in your infrastructure! It should be noted that the in-place upgrade will maintain existing block sizes >1 MB, so consider that in your migration strategy. With datastore scaling enhancements, you can reach higher-density virtual machine allocation (64 TB on a single extent) and up to 30,000 sub-blocks of 8 KB can be allocated for files such as virtual machine metadata and log files.

> **NOTE**   Not all new features are supported after performing a VMFS-3 to VMFS-5 in-place upgrade so plan accordingly.

Enhancements in Storage vMotion

With vSphere 5, there have been numerous enhancements to improve performance and supportability with Storage vMotion. Migration of virtual machines is supported with vSphere snapshots and Linked Clones! The Mirror Mode feature increases efficiency with single-pass block copies being sent to source disk and destination disk by mirroring I/Os of copied blocks providing a direct impact on improving Storage vMotion. These enhancements make it easier to plan while reducing the time elapsed during a migration.

Virtual Machine Scalability

Virtual machine scalability has increased! 32-way virtual symmetric multiprocessing (SMP) supports even more demanding workloads; 1 TB of RAM can be assigned to VMs; and 3D graphics support Windows Aero and Basic 3D applications. USB 3.0 support and UEFI virtual BIOS allow booting from Unified Extended Firmware Interfaces.

Usability enhancements enable you to configure the number of virtual CPU cores per socket in Virtual Machine properties via the vSphere Web Client and vSphere client (previously only configurable through advanced settings). Virtual Machines can connect to locally attached USB devices, including support for smart card readers.

VMware vSphere 5 further enhances the datacenter with support for Apple MAC OSX Server 10.6 as a guest. Host-side UEFI boot support enables booting from hard drives, CD-ROM, or USB media.

Taking scale to the next level, VMware vSphere 5 supports up to 512 virtual machines with a maximum of 2048 virtual CPUs per host. Larger system scale supports 160 logical CPUs and up to 2 TB of RAM. These advances allow you to scale up as well as scale out as your virtual infrastructure matures with your business.

vCenter Improvements

New with VMware vCenter Server is the vCenter Server Appliance. This preconfigured Linux-based virtual appliance reduces setup time and provides a low-cost alternative to the traditional Windows server–based vCenter host.

The next-generation browser-based vSphere client is a fully-extensible, platform-independent implementation of the vSphere client based on Adobe Flex. The browser-based client includes a subset of the functionality available in the Windows-based client—primarily related to inventory display, virtual machine deployment, and configuration.

With inventory extensibility, vCenter Server will become the unified console to manage your virtualized datacenter. This is enabled through extensions created by VMware partners in the form of inventory, agents, graphical user interface enhancements, and more!

You'll find solutions installation and management to be simplified with vCenter Solutions Manager and vSphere ESXi Agent Manager. Solutions Manager provides a simpler installation, configuration, and monitoring interface for managing your virtual infrastructure. vSphere ESXi Agent Manager takes this a step further, enabling you to deploy, update, and monitor your vSphere agents on ESXi hosts. This is independent of the maintenance mode and distributed power management features of vSphere.

System messaging logging can now deliver all messages generated to local and remote syslog servers with support for multiple remote log servers via TCP or securely over SSL. Log messages from different sources can be configured to go to different logs for convenience or role separation. This helps with the process of troubleshooting errors in your organization. Configuring message logging is enabled via esxcli or the vSphere client.

Fault Tolerance

VMware High Availability has reached new levels of fault tolerance with the introduction of Fault Domain Manager. VMware HA is now more reliable, more scalable, and able to protect and provide better uptime than ever before! Instead of an active/passive configuration strategy, all hosts in the cluster can be primary nodes using shared storage as a channel for host-side heartbeat detection. This enables VMware HA to more efficiently and accurately react to host failures, allowing the cluster to transform into a cloud-optimized platform.

Networking Enhancements

VMware vSphere 5 builds upon network enhancements in vSphere 4. Enhanced Network I/O Control (NIOC) allows control leveraging user-defined network resource pools, enabling true multitenancy deployments, and bridging virtual and physical infrastructure QoS with per resource pool 802.1 tagging.

vNetwork Distributed Switches were introduced in vSphere 4. vSphere 5 improves visibility into virtual machine traffic through Netflow. Monitoring and troubleshooting are enhanced through the use of SPAN and LLDP.

Taking protection to the next level, the ESXi 5.0 management interface is protected with a service-oriented stateless firewall with ESXi Firewall. Configurable with vSphere Client, command line, or the esxcli interface, this new engine eliminates iptables and rule set–defined port rules for services. Remote hosts can be configured to be accessible via specific IP addresses or ranges of IP addresses.

These three features combined allow greater levels of granularity, management, and control of your virtual infrastructure at the network layer. They help alleviate some of the strain caused by network teams treating everything in the virtual infrastructure as a troubleshooting and support nightmare.

VMware vShield 5 Suite

The new VMware vShield 5 suite puts your virtual infrastructure on a par with physical isolation security. Included with this suite are VMware vShield App, VMware vShield App with Data Security, VMware vShield Edge, VMware vShield Endpoint, and VMware vShield Manager.

VMware vShield App enables you to secure the interior of your virtual infrastructure. This software-based solution is deployed as a virtual appliance, providing complete visibility and control of inter-virtual machine traffic. With vShield App, you can create virtual firewalls with unlimited port density, enabling multiple trust zones within an ESXi cluster. With protection at the hypervisor level, VMs are protected at layer 2 and layer 3, and enforced at the vNIC level. Governance, Risk, and Compliance have never been easier with vShield App's robust flow monitoring, logging, and auditing. vShield Data Security (vSDS) reduces risk of noncompliance with automated scans and assessment reporting on policy machines per virtual machine.

With vShield App protecting the inter-VM relationships, vShield Edge provides protection for the edge of the datacenter. The latest version includes static routing (instead of requiring NAT), certificate-based VPNs, and gateway services allowing isolation of virtual machines by port group. Commonly used to protect extranets, vShield Edge can also be used to secure multitenant environments—allowing perimeter security for each tenant's virtual datacenter.

Security is often considered an afterthought, but it can make or break your virtual or physical infrastructure. VMware vShield 5 suite allows you to secure and separate barriers without needing to physically isolate as you would have needed to in the past. The VMware vShield product protects such large installations as the New York Stock Exchange's own community cloud infrastructure. So whether you are a small shop managing a small virtual infrastructure or a major multitenant service provider, the VMware vShield 5 suite provides the single management framework to secure your hosts, network, applications, data, and endpoints!

2

Installing and Configuring ESXi

IN THIS CHAPTER, YOU WILL LEARN TO:

T hey say that when you build a house, one of the most important steps in that process is building the foundation, since everything will depend on its integrity. When deploying a virtual infrastructure, the underlying installation and its configuration are equally important. In this chapter, we are going to cover the most common approaches to deploying ESXi.

Prepare for Installation

With the release of vSphere 4, VMware signaled that the 32-bit era was nearing its "virtual" end. vSphere is now only available in 64-bit. While 64-bit hardware has been available for several years, some organizations may run a mix of classic ESX and vSphere until all their hardware has been upgraded so that it's capable of running vSphere. VMware is fully aware of this; the new version is capable of running and managing older versions as well as vSphere—in other words, a mix of the two. Some environments tend to keep it simple by deploying each host through the interactive installation method. There is no real problem with this—a host can be completely installed in 20 to 30 minutes by someone who knows what they're doing. Scripted installations can be carried out by creating a `ks.cfg` file and putting it on a CD, thumb drive, FTP site, or website.

There is a downside to manual installations: as the number of hosts that are to be manually installed increases, the likelihood of errors and inconsistencies in the builds and configurations across those hosts increases. It's important to have consistency across your builds, so implement a suitable deployment methodology. For example, without consistency in your datastore and networking setup, processes like vMotion may work inconsistently or not at all.

When planning to install ESXi version 5.0, it is important to know what hardware is required. The following lists are current as of the time of this writing. For the most up-to-date information, refer to the Hardware Compatability Guide (HCL) on the VMware website at the following URL:

`www.VMware.com/go/hcl`

Processor Types   The following 64-bit processor types are acceptable:

- 64-bit x86 CPUs.
- All AMD Opteron processors.

- Must have at least two cores.

- Supports only LAHF and SAHF CPU instructions.

- All Intel XEON 3000/3200, 3100/3300, 5100/5300, 5200/5400, 7100/7300, 7200/7400, 7500 processors.

RAM You need a minimum of 2 GB of RAM. Additional RAM is needed for each virtual machine added. We recommended that you start with 3 GB of RAM or more.

Network Adapters Follow these guidelines for network adapters:

- For best performance, select adapters with dedicated Gigabit Ethernet cards for VMs, such as Intel PRO/1000 adapters or better.

- For security purposes, keep the Management Network on its own virtual LAN (VLAN) or network interface card (NIC) (or use teamed NICs for redundancy).

- The more NICs you have on a virtual switch, the more redundancy there is in case of a failure.

- Broadcom NetXtreme 570x Gigabit controllers are acceptable.

Adapters and Controllers Keep the following in mind when selecting Fibre Channel adapters, SCSI adapters, or internal RAID controllers:

- Use only Fibre Channel Host Bus Adapter (HBA) cards as outlined in the Hardware Compatibility Guide.

- Basic SCSI controllers are Adaptec Ultra160 and Ultra320, LSI Logic's Fusion-MPT, and most NCR/Symbios controllers.

- RAID adapters supported include Dell PERC (Adaptec RAID and LSI MegaRAID), HP Smart Array, and most IBM (Adaptec) ServeRAID controllers.

- Supported serial-attached SCSI (SAS) controllers include LSI1068E (LSISAS3442E), LSI 1068 (SAS 5), IBM ServeRAID 8k SAS controller, Smart Array P400/256MB controller, and the Dell PERC 5.0.1 controller.

- Supported onboard Serial ATA (SATA) controllers include Intel ICH9, NVIDIA MCP55, and ServerWorks HT1000.

Installation and Storage Factors Here are the hardware requirements for installation and storage:

- You will need a SCSI disk, Fibre Channel LUN, or RAID LUN with unpartitioned space. In a minimum configuration, the disk or RAID is shared between the Service Console and the virtual machines.

- For hardware iSCSI, you will need a disk attached to an iSCSI controller, such as the QLogic QLA405x. Software iSCSI is not supported for booting or installing ESXi.

- Serial Attached SCSI (SAS) disk drives are supported for installing ESXi and for VMFS partitions.

- For Serial ATA (SATA), you will need a disk connected through supported SAS controllers or supported onboard SATA controllers. Only SATA disk drives connected behind supported SAS controllers or supported onboard SATA controllers are supported in ESXi hosts.

SATA Drives When installing ESXi on SATA drives, consider the following:

- Ensure that your SATA drives are connected through supported SAS controllers or supported onboard SATA controllers.

- Do not use SATA disks to create Virtual Machine File System (VMFS) datastores shared across multiple ESXi hosts.

Install ESXi

VMware has put together a list of prerequisites that you should be aware of before traveling down the virtualization highway. Take a moment to become familiar with this list. That way, you can avoid frustration down the road if something doesn't work the way you expect it to.

For a production environment, the most important thing is to make sure all hardware is listed in the Hardware Compatibility

Guide before you purchase it. Check specific pieces of hardware
like NICs and SAS and SATA controllers. If problems occur during
or after an installation, hardware compatibility is the last thing you
want to deal with. However, it is often the first thing support will
ask about.

Additionally, check to make sure that the hardware clock (in BIOS)
is set to coordinated universal time (UTC). If you're planning to build
multiple ESXi hosts, document the settings in BIOS for the CPU and
ensure they are the same on all hosts. If the settings in BIOS are not the
same on all hosts, you may not be able to move a virtual machine from
one host to another without having to power the virtual machine down.
With documentation, you won't have to guess what is and is not enabled
or disabled on other hosts.

TIP   Be careful when upgrading firmware and BIOS. Some
hosts may lose their settings in the BIOS after an upgrade. After
upgrading these software pieces, it is a good idea to double-
check and make sure the settings you originally had in place
have not changed.

TIP   There are circumstances where administrators are
required to know which physical NIC is which from inside the
operating system—for example, when troubleshooting. This is
not always easy to accomplish post-installation. One strategy
is to label the NICs at installation by plugging one cable in at a
time, labeling it, and repeating (look for the link light).

ESXi is the direction VMware has taken. They no longer provide
the ESX hypervisor platform. ESXi's configuration options have been
stripped down, making installing ESXi a small part of the overall
implementation. The installation of ESXi is extremely fast and easy,
partly because system, network, and storage devices as well as the IP
addressing (set to DHCP) are configured with defaults. In fact, you have
to configure only two things: which storage device to install on and the
root password.

NOTE Third-party drivers are available that integrate with the vSphere installation. However, if you are using a DVD to install vSphere, you must use that DVD drive to install the custom drivers as well. You will be required to remove the vSphere DVD and insert the custom driver's DVD, install the driver, and then replace the vSphere DVD to complete the installation. If you are using an International Organization for Standards (ISO) image to install vSphere, the custom drivers must also be on an ISO image. Unfortunately, if a USB device is the installation device, it *cannot be removed* for this process. If you forget to install custom drivers at this stage, you can install them later.

Install ESXi Manually

The interactive method is the most widely used method for installation. Administrators from novice to expert can use this method to get a host up quickly and easily. Follow these steps:

1. Insert the installation media into the appropriate drive and reboot.

2. The first screen is very generic, as you can see in Figure 2.1. The choices are ESXi Installer or Boot From Local Disk. Highlight the first option and press Enter.

Figure 2.1: Initial ESXi installation screen

3. The ESXi installer screen will appear. After a few moments of loading various modules, you will be presented with the Welcome screen. Press Enter to continue.

4. On the EULA screen, read the agreement and when you are ready, press F11 (Accept and Continue).

5. The Select A Disk screen (Figure 2.2) lists the available disks on the system. Highlight the drive you wish to install on and press Enter.

Figure 2.2: Selecting a disk on which to store EXSi

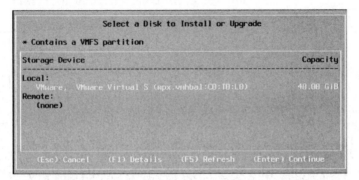

Building a VMware
vSphere Environment

PART I

Previously Formatted Drives

If you are installing on a drive that has a version of ESXi already installed, you will see a message asking what you want to do:

- Upgrade ESXi and preserve your VMFS datastore
- Install ESXi and preserve your VMFS datastore
- Install ESXi and overwrite your VMFS datastore

Consider your choices carefully. Remember, this list of storage devices could contain production data or virtual machine storage areas that are not physically located on the host and could be shared with other hosts. There might even be virtual machines running on these remotely attached hard drives. Smart administrators disconnect shared storage devices during an installation to avoid this potential issue. Don't be that admin who formatted production volumes and then had to restore or rebuild those deleted virtual machines!

As an extra check, make sure the size of the LUN matches expectations for the storage.

There are many ways to address attached storage. One of the best ways to handle this is to make sure the host is powered off and to simply unplug the fiber to the remote storage, or whatever physically connects the storage to the host. Another option is to ask the SAN administrator to disable the port(s).

The moral of the story is to be certain that when you go through the installation, there is no chance of deleting important storage.

6. Next, you will select your keyboard layout. Accept the default and press Enter to continue.

7. Now enter in your root password. Press the down-arrow button to highlight the Confirm Password field. Reenter your password, then press Enter to continue.

Password Guidelines

When you create a password, you should include a mix of characters from four character classes: lowercase letters, uppercase letters, digits, and special characters such as an underscore or dash.

Your password must meet the following length requirements:

- Passwords containing characters from one or two classes must be eight characters long.
- Passwords containing characters from three classes must be seven characters long.
- Password containing characters from all four classes must be six characters long.

An uppercase character that begins a password does not count toward the number of character classes used. A digit that ends a password does not count toward the number of character classes used.

8. At this point, a system scan begins, then you see a screen labeled Confirm Install (Figure 2.3). This message is a warning that the disk will be repartitioned. Press F11 to begin the install.

Figure 2.3: Warning about disk repartition

9. When you see the Installation Is Complete screen,
   remove your installation media and press Enter to reboot.
   The next screen will show the IP address and other system
   information.

While the physical part of the installation is finished, there are
still some tasks to complete before the ESXi host is ready to go into
production. See the "Configure Post-Install Options" section later in
this chapter.

Automate ESXi Installation

Automated installations are fast and useful way to build hosts. There
are times when a fast build is necessary—think disaster recovery.
Additionally, automated installations ensure all builds are exactly
the same. And most important, why spend unnecessary time doing
something that can be accomplished while you relax and watch the
process do what it is designed to do?

This section discusses several ways to automate ESXi installation:

- Installation script (ks.cfg file) on a USB device
- vSphere Auto Deploy
- vSphere ESXi Image Builder CLI

Perform a Scripted Installation Using a USB Device

A friend of mine says he does his best work while getting coffee (he
scripts everything). An installation script is nothing more than a text
file called ks.cfg. Essentially it is an answer file. The best approach to
scripting installs is to create a master script, and then make copies of it
for each ESXi host in your inventory, customized with the IP address,
hostname, and any other pertinent information needed. An added
benefit of this strategy is increased knowledge of the moving parts
encompassing an ESXi host.

Sample *ks.cfg* Script

The following code is an example of a ks.cfg file. This file is used to perform a scripted installation; it is the answer key. This is only an example—you can add to or subtract from it—but it is a good starting point for a scripted installation.

```
#
# Sample scripted installation file
#
# Accept the VMware End User License Agreement
vmaccepteula
# Set the root password for the DCUI and Tech Support Mode
rootpw mypassword
# Install on the first local disk available on machine
install --firstdisk --overwritevmfs
# Set the network to DHCP on the first network adapter
network --bootproto=dhcp --device=vmnic0
# A sample post-install script
%post --interpreter=python --ignorefailure=true
import time
stampFile = open('/finished.stamp', mode='w')
stampFile.write( time.asctime() )
```

Where can you find an install script? The default ks.cfg installation script is located in the initial RAM disk at /etc/vmware/weasel/ks.cfg. You can specify the location of the default ks.cfg file with the ks=file://etc/vmware/weasel/ks.cfg boot. Take a copy of what is in the ks.cfg file, use a program similar to Win32pad that produces a plain .txt file, save the file in Unix format, and then edit as necessary.

NOTE The ks.cfg file must be copied to the root directory of the USB drive. Only FAT16 and FAT32 file systems are supported.

Follow these steps to install via a script:

1. Insert the installation media and power on the host. The installation will boot from the CD/DVD and draw answers from the USB device.

2. When the ESXi installer screen appears, press Shift+O to edit boot options.

3. At the command prompt, type: **ks=usb**.

4. The process should take off. When complete, reboot as prompted.

Scripting the install of ESXi is a great step toward provisioning resources quickly. It is worth mentioning here the additional methods available to you.

A Bit About Cloud Computing

Imagine for a moment you needed more capacity in a VMware cluster. You could install an additional ESXi host and configure it with the same setup as all the other ESXi hosts in that cluster. But even if you script the build and everything is automated, the process can still take a few hours. Now imagine you have Host Profiles (a golden image or template) set up and working alongside vSphere Distributed Switch. You can take a host from one cluster that is underutilized, remove it, and place it into the other cluster that needs resources. You just apply the host profile and the switching, and the cluster then has more resources.

You could have spare hardware to put in place. Or you could perform a physical-to-virtual (P2V) conversion and then commandeer that hardware and install ESXi.

The two primary aspects of cloud computing you must consider are:

- How easy is it to add additional capacity and resources to the cloud?

- How easy is it to move applications or servers to and from different clouds?

Virtualization is moving toward a device-like host that is as simple as possible to plug into the virtual infrastructure so that additional resources (CPU, memory, network, storage) can be added with minimal effort.

Use vSphere Auto Deploy

By using vSphere Auto Deploy, system administrators can manage large vSphere deployments efficiently. Auto Deploy leverages a Pre-Boot Execution Environment (PXE) boot infrastructure to load the

ESXi image directly into the host memory and does not store ESXi state on the disk. The vCenter Server stores and manages ESXi patches and updates via the image profile. Optionally, you can specify the host profile to apply. Keep in mind that you will need to set up Dynamic Host Configuration Protocol (DHCP) and Trivial File Transfer Protocol (TFTP) servers if you do not already have these in your environment. You will need administrative privileges in order to configure these components to work with Auto Deploy.

Once you have the preliminaries in place, follow these steps to use vSphere Auto Deploy:

1. Install vSphere Auto Deploy.

NOTE   Auto Deploy can be installed on a vSphere server or a standalone Windows server. It comes preinstalled on the vCenter Server Appliance.

---

2. Connect the vSphere Client to the vSphere server that the Auto Deploy server registered with during the install.

3. Make sure you are on the home screen within the vSphere client. In the Administration section, select Auto Deploy. (See Figure 2.4.)

Figure 2.4: Auto Deploy icon

4. On the Auto Deploy page that appears, click Download TFTP Boot Zip.

5. Unzip the file and copy it to the directory where the TFTP server stores its files.

6. Configure the DHCP server to point to the TFTP server using option 66, sometimes referred to as *next-server*.

7. On the DCHP server, configure option 67, sometimes referred to as *boot-filename*, to point to the boot file name `undianly.kpxe.vmw-hardwired`.

8. Set the host to PXE boot.

9. Specify a host profile. You can create a new host profile, use an existing one, or save one from an already existing host.

10. Create rules to assign image profiles and optional host profiles to the host.

When the server is powered on, it will contact the DHCP server, which will direct it to Auto Deploy server to install the host.

> **NOTE**   Couple Auto Deploy with Image Builder CLI to create and deploy custom ESXi installs for your environment.

Use vSphere ESXi Image Builder CLI

ESXi Image Builder CLI is used to create ESXi installation images. These images can contain a customized set of updates, patches, and drivers. Additionally, Image Builder CLI can manage VMware Installation Bundle (VIB) and image profiles. VIBs are software packages. Image profiles define which VIBs to use.

> **NOTE**   Image Builder must be installed on a Windows server that has .NET 2.0 and PowerShell 1.0 or 2.0 installed.

Here are several different scenarios in which you could use Image Builder:

Auto Deploy   Create image profiles to auto-deploy new hosts.

Add custom drivers   Add third-party driver or extensions to an existing image profile.

Upgrade   Upgrade from 4.0 or 4.1 systems. Create an image profile that includes vSphere 5.0 base VIB and any custom extensions, and then export the profile to an ISO image.

Reduced footprint images   Use Image Builder CLI to clone your ESXi base image profile and remove VIBs.

Examples of Common Tasks within Image Builder

The following are examples of tasks that administrators would perform within Image Builder.

Clone an Image Profile   To clone an image profile, follow these steps:

1. From the PowerShell prompt, run the following command to add the depot that contains the profile you want to clone to the current session:

   ```
   Add-EsxSoftwareDepot -DepotUrl depot_url
   ```

2. Run the `New-EsxImageProfile` cmdlet to create the new profile and use the `-CloneProfile` parameter to specify the profile you want to clone.

   ```
   New-EsxImageProfile -CloneProfile Old_Profile -Name
   "Test Profile"
   ```

Add VIBs to an Image Profile   To add VIBs to an image profile, follow these steps:

1. From the PowerShell prompt, run the following command to add the depot that contains the profile you want to clone to the current session:

   ```
   Add-EsxSoftwareDepot -DepotUrl depot_url
   ```

2. To list all image profiles in all the currently visible depots, run the following command:

   ```
   Get-EsxImageProfile
   ```

3. To add a package to an image profile, run the following command:

   ```
   Add-EsxSoftwarePackage -ImageProfile My_Profile
   -SoftwarePackage partner-package
   ```

NOTE   An image profile is locked if it is assigned to one or more hosts. Clone the image profile and add the VIBs to the new profile.

Configure Post-Install Options

Once your ESXi installation is complete, there are still steps that need to be taken before you are ready to deploy Virtual Machines to the host.

1. Configure ESXi from the console.

2. Install the vSphere Client.

3. Configure ESXi from within the vSphere Client.

Configure ESXi from the Console

This section will cover additional steps needed to configure ESXi from the console. Some of the options available from the ESXi console can be configured from the vSphere Client once the server is up on the network. This will be covered in later chapters in the book.

Your first step is to configure the Management Network. Once the host has booted after the install, you will be presented with a gray and yellow screen (Figure 2.5) listing the version and build of ESXi you are running, some basic hardware information about the server it is running on, and the hostname of the server. Along the bottom of this screen, there are two options: (F2) Customize System/View Logs and (F12) Shutdown/Restart. Note that the F12 option is not shown in Figure 2.5.

Figure 2.5: ESXi has rebooted.

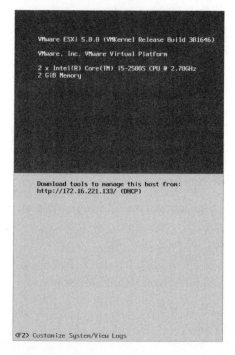

Building a VMware
vSphere Environment

PART I

1. Press F2 and the Authentication Required screen will appear. Log in as root.

2. Once logged in, you should see the System Customization screen. Use the down-arrow button to select Configure Management Network and press Enter.

3. The first option in the list is Network Adapters (Figure 2.6). Select this option, choose the network adapter that you want to use for the default management network, and press Enter.

Figure 2.6: Selecting multiple Network Interface Cards

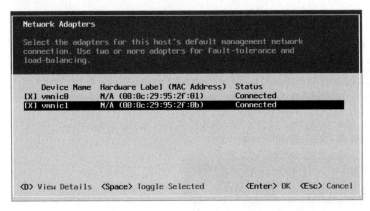

NOTE You can select more than one adapter for fault-tolerance and load-balancing configurations by highlighting each adapter you want to use and pressing the spacebar.

---

4. Now select the IP Configuration option and press Enter.

5. If you are using DHCP for the management network, then you should not have to change anything in the IP Configuration screen. You will configure the ESXi install with a static IP address. Select the Set Static IP Address And Network Configuration option and press the spacebar.

TIP   It is recommended that any production ESXi host be configured with a static IP address. Configuring the IP address statically reduces the chance for resolution issues later on.

6. The bottom portion of the screen (Figure 2.7) is now available to change. Enter the appropriate IP address, Subnet Mask, and Default Gateway. Press Enter.

Figure 2.7: IP Configuration screen

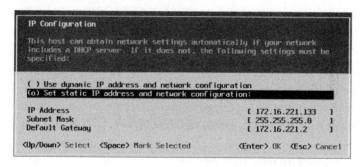

7. You should be back on the Configure Management Network screen. Now select DNS Configuration and press Enter.

8. Enter the addresses for the Primary DNS server and Alternate DNS server. Then enter the fully qualified domain name. Press Enter.

NOTE   Be sure to add a DNS entry for each host. Also, when adding hosts to vCenter, always use the fully qualified domain name (FQDN); features like High Availability (HA) and vMotion depend on this information. If your environment does not have DNS, you will want to add a host file after installation.

9. From the Configure Management Network screen, select Custom DNS Suffixes. Enter the DNS domain for your environment. This will be used to append to any short unqualified names for DNS

Building a VMware vSphere Environment

PART I

queries. Press Enter to return to the Configuration Management Network screen.

10. Press Esc to exit back to the System Customization screen.

11. You will be prompted to apply the network changes and restart the management network. Press Y to accept.

12. Select Test Management Network and press Enter.

13. A screen displaying the network settings assigned to the server appears. Review the information and then press Enter. This will test communication to the defined default gateway and DNS servers, and attempt to resolve the hostname with DNS. Press Enter to perform the test and Enter again once the test has completed.

14. At this point, the base install of ESXi is complete and you should be able to communicate with it on the network. Press Esc to quit the System Customization screen and return to the main ESXi screen. This will log you out of the console.

Install the vSphere Client

Follow these steps to install the vSphere Client on your computer. Doing so will allow you to use a graphical user interface (GUI) to access either vCenter or an ESX or ESXi host remotely.

1. Open your browser.

2. Note the IP address on the ESXi console window and enter your IP address into your web browser, like this:

```
http://172.16.231.133/
```

3. If the Choose A Digital Certificate window appears, click OK.

4. If the browser is Internet Explorer (IE), the next window to appear is a security certificate window; click Continue To This Website.

5. The Choose A Digital Certificate window may reappear; if so, click OK a second time.

6. The VMware ESXi Welcome browser page should load (see Figure 2.8). Click Download vSphere Client.

Figure 2.8: VMware ESXi Welcome page

Click here to download.

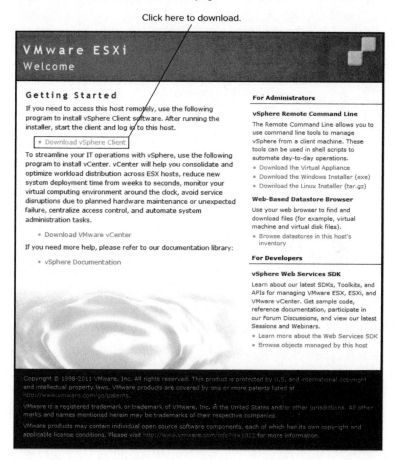

7. When the Do You Want To Run Or Save This File window opens, choose Run. Follow the prompts to finish the install.

Configure ESXi from within the vSphere Client

Now that you have the vSphere client installed, you will want to log in and perform a few more tasks before you start deploying virtual machines.

ESXi Licensing

Licensing can be entered via vCenter or through the host directly. We will cover licensing through the vCenter client.

To enter licensing on a standalone host:

1. Sign into the vSphere client. From the home screen, select Inventory. Click the Configuration tab; under Software, click Licensed Features.

2. In the top-right corner, click Edit and then click the radio button "Assign a new license key to this host."

3. Click the Enter Key button and type your license key (including the dashes), and click OK twice (see Figure 2.9).

Figure 2.9: Assigning a license

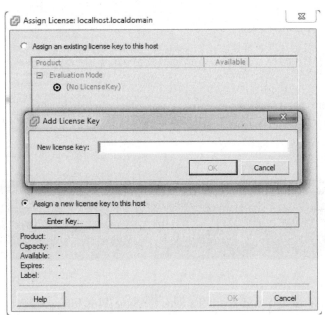

Add Datastores

VSphere 5 datastores support SCSI, iSCSI, Network File System (NFS), Fibre Channel, or Fibre Channel over Ethernet (FCoE) attached disks.

Naming Convention for Datastores

Datastores are essentially hard drives where you can store anything from virtual machines to templates to ISO files. They should be carefully named so that your infrastructure is easy to navigate and has intuitive organization. The characteristics of the storage can be used to name the datastores; for example, which clusters the storage belongs to, if the datastores are replicated for disaster recovery, if the datastore is a 15,000 RPM drive for databases, or the hexadecimal/decimal name of the LUN (if it is on a SAN).

For SAN storage, keep in mind that the way SAN administrators see LUNs and the way vCenter and ESXi see LUNs is not always the same (hexadecimal as opposed to decimal). Consider the example of a LUN named R003_DMZ_84_086a. A naming convention similar to the following will help not only the SAN team but also the administrators who manage the infrastructure:

R = Replicated storage

003 = Third LUN

84 = EMC DMX

086a = LUN device as seen by SAN administrators in hexadecimal format

Local storage, however, may not need such an elaborate naming convention.

Building a VMware vSphere Environment

PART I

To add datastores, follow these steps:

1. Sign in to the vSphere client. From the home screen, select Inventory. Click the Configuration tab. Under Hardware, click Storage.

2. In the upper-right section of the Storage screen, click Add Storage.

3. The Add Storage screen should open up. Select a storage type: Disk/LUN or Network File System. Choose Disk/LUN (see Figure 2.10) and click Next unless you want to add an NFS.

Figure 2.10: Selecting a disk for a new datastore

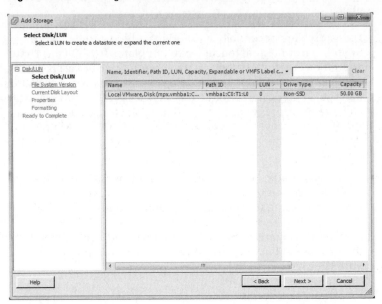

4. The next screen lists the available disks from which to select. Click the disk you want to use for the datastore. Click Next.

5. Select the file system version. If this is the first ESXi host in your environment, then you will want to go with VMFS-5. If you have existing ESX or ESXi hosts, then you will want to give your choice some consideration as it will dictate compatibility with existing hosts. For our purposes, we assume this is your first ESXi host and we will select VMFS-5 and click Next.

6. Now, you should be presented with the Review the Current Disk Layout Screen. Click Next.

7. You are now ready to name your datastore. Enter a descriptive name and click Next.

8. On the Disk/LUN Formatting screen, select whether you want to use the maximum available space or a custom amount of space from the disk. Take the default selection and click Next.

9. The Ready to Complete screen should now be up. This is a summary screen of the options you have selected for you to review one last time before adding the datastore. Click Finish.

After a few moments, the new datastore should show up on the storage screen under the Configuration tab.

Configure Network Time Protocol

You will want to configure an NTP server so that all your host and Virtual Machine clocks are in sync. Follow these steps:

1. Sign in to the vSphere client. From the home screen, select Inventory. Click the Configuration tab; under Software, click Time Configuration. This screen will show the current date and time, whether the NTP client is running, and which NTP servers are currently configured.

2. In the top right, click Properties. The Time Configuration window is the place to adjust the date and time. Or you can click Options in the lower right to configure the NTP daemon.

3. On the General tab, the service can be started, stopped, restarted, or changed to start automatically, start and stop with the host, or start and stop manually (see Figure 2.11).

Figure 2.11: Setting an NTP server

4. Click NTP Settings in the window on the left.

5. Click Add and enter the NTP server address and click OK. Select Restart NTP Service to apply changes and click OK.

6. Make sure the firewall allows for NTP traffic.

Configure Active Directory Authentication

Some environments may want to configure VMware to authenticate to Active Directory (AD) for several reasons. For example, if security roles for the company are already being managed by a team other than the

VMware administrators, then the role of VMware administrator can be granted by simply adding the administrator to the appropriate AD group. Another benefit of using AD authentication is minimizing the number of passwords required. You can log in to Virtual Center Server with your AD credentials and do not need a separate ID with its own password.

To configure Active Directory authentication, follow these steps:

1. Sign in to the vSphere client. From the home screen, select Inventory. Click the Configuration tab; under Software, click Authentication Services.

2. Click Properties in the top-right corner of the screen.

3. This should bring up the Directory Services Configuration screen. In the User Directory Service section, drop down the Select Directory Service Type list and change it from Local Authentication to Active Directory (see Figure 2.12).

Figure 2.12: Selecting the directory service type

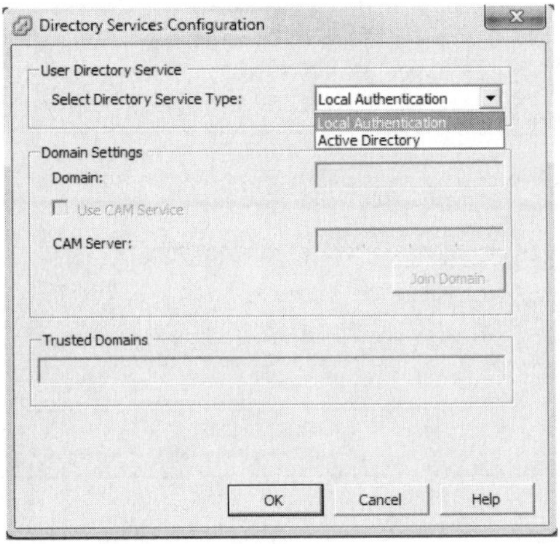

4. Once Active Directory is selected, the Domain Settings area will become active. In the Domain field, supply the fully qualified domain name of the domain you wish to join.

5. Now click Join Domain. The Join Domain window will open. Enter a username and password that has permission to join a machine to the domain and click Join Domain.

Configure the Firewall

The firewall will need to be addressed one way or another. If you have monitoring software, you will need to open a port to allow the SNMP protocol through for monitoring. Some organizations may turn off the firewall or open other ports for other software applications. To find the firewall and configure it, follow these steps:

1. Sign in to the vSphere client. From the home screen, select Inventory. Click the Configuration tab; under Software, click Security Profile.

2. Click Properties in the middle-right corner.

3. The resulting window allows you to configure ports in the firewall. Simply check or uncheck a desired service or client to allow or disallow access through the firewall. The Options button allows for fine-grained control of the highlighted service: Start, Stop, Restart, and so forth (see Figure 2.13).

Figure 2.13: ESXi firewall properties

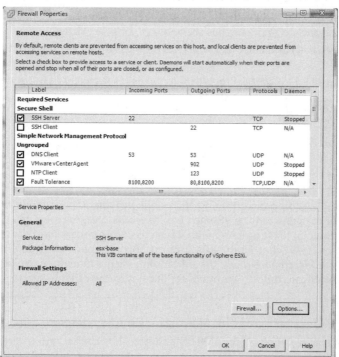

Configure Management Network

Many large organizations have a strategy of teaming their NICs and sometimes their power on key servers. In this way, an organization can bring down half of its network for routine maintenance without impacting networking or power on a server. Obviously, this is a highly desirable way to run a successful operation because it limits the amount of downtime. With VMware virtualization, and specifically High Availability (HA), you must keep a special consideration in mind as well. If the Management Network has only one physical NIC, and if something happens to that one piece of hardware and HA is enabled, vCenter will see the host as down and potentially restart the virtual machines that were on that host on another host. If the host is down, this is desirable. If only the physical NIC is down, however, this is bad, as virtual machines may be trying to run in more than one location.

To solve this issue, take the following steps to attach two or more physical NICs to the Management Network vSwitch so that networking can be achieved through redundant paths if necessary:

1. Sign in to the vSphere client. From the home screen, select Inventory. Click the Configuration tab; under Hardware, click Networking. Find the vSwitch that has the Service Console (Management Network) and click its Properties link (as shown in Figure 2.14).

Figure 2.14: Click the Properties link for the Management Network vSwitch

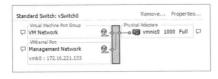

NOTE Adding or removing NICs does not affect the underlying virtual machines in the vSwitch you're working on, as long as they have at least one NIC with which to communicate and the upstream switches from NICs support port groups. If all NICs are removed from a vSwitch, the underlying virtual machines can still communicate among themselves, but not to the outside world.

---

2. Click the Network Adapters tab, click Add, and put a check mark in the box next to the VMNIC that will be the second in the team. Obviously, unclaimed adapters (as shown in Figure 2.15) are not being used by any other networking; an adapter can be used by only one vSwitch at a time.

Figure 2.15: Adding unclaimed adapters

3. Click Next. If the order of the NICs is important, adjust it here by clicking the Move Up or Move Down buttons. Click Next.

4. Review the changes and click Finish.

Now, the Management Network has two physical channels to which it can communicate with vCenter and HA (as you can see in Figure 2.16).

Figure 2.16: The Management Network has two NICs

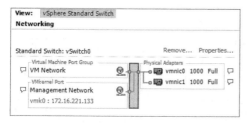

Set Up a Remote Connection to the Management Network

Before moving on to configuring the Management Network, we have to be able to get into it, either by physically standing in front of the ESXi console on the server or by remotely connecting to it. If we choose the latter, we will have to perform some initial steps. Those steps are detailed here.

Create an Account with SSH Access   To create an account with SSH access, follow these steps:

1. Sign in to the vSphere client. From the home screen, select Inventory. Click the Local Users and Groups tab. Then click the Users button at the top-left side of the Local Users and Groups window.

2. Right-click in the white space and select Add (see Figure 2.17).

Figure 2.17: Adding users

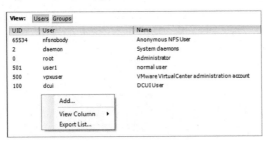

3. Fill in the login, user name, and password, and select the option Grant Shell Access To This User (as shown in Figure 2.18). Under Group Membership, use the drop-down box to assign this user to the Users group. Click Add and then OK to create the user.

Figure 2.18: Adding a user with shell access

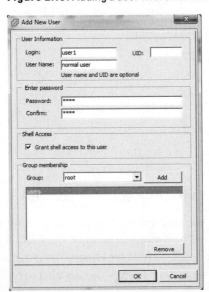

NOTE Be very aware of the syntax of the username. In VMware, usernames are case-sensitive.

Elevate Privileges to Root Access Root access to the Service Console is disabled by default. When security is important and root access is to be protected, most VMware administrators will have a secondary login to a host and then they will elevate their privileges up to root. The command su - elevates from a non-root account to the root account. While adding a user account to a host is not necessarily part of configuring the Management Network, it is still a better strategy than allowing root access.

NOTE To be granted shell access, users must also have an administrator role for an inventory object on the host. VMware defines inventory objects as folders, datacenters, clusters, resource pools, datastores, and networks. See the section in Chapter 11 on "Manage Permissions" for instructions on how to assign a role to a user.

Once the user has been assigned an administrator role on any inventory object, the user account will then have the ability to use WinSCP to transfer files to an ESXi host and to use the PuTTy SSH client to connect into the specific ESXi host. Follow these steps to get root access:

1. Open an SSH session and log in to the host with the user you granted shell access to; then issue the following command: su -

2. The console will return a password prompt. Enter the root password.

   Notice that after you entered in root's password, the $ prompt changed to #, which shows that you are logged in as root (as shown in Figure 2.19).

Figure 2.19: Elevating to root

When you're finished using root, instead of clicking the X to log out, type **exit** to drop the session back down to regular user status. This is helpful if additional non-administrator-level tasks need to be completed rather than just logging back in. Typing exit again will drop the session altogether.

3

Installing and Configuring vCenter Server

IN THIS CHAPTER, YOU WILL LEARN TO:

V Mware vCenter Server is the central management component in a vSphere environment. Without vCenter Server, ESXi hosts are simply hypervisors with the ability to run virtual machines, commonly referred to as guests. When coupled with appropriate host licensing, vCenter Server can significantly extend the capabilities of the hosts it manages. Some of the extended capabilities that vCenter Server includes are vMotion, Storage vMotion, High Availability (HA), Distributed Resource Scheduling (DRS), as well as Storage DRS (SDRS).

Keep in mind that vCenter Server does not independently contain these features. Rather, it leverages these capabilities when hosts are managed by vCenter Server and assigned licenses that include these features.

You should become familiar with vCenter Server's requirements as well as the proper installation method. A well-configured vCenter Server installation provides a solid administrative platform to manage vSphere to its fullest potential.

Prepare for Installation

One of most important components of the vSphere environment is vCenter Server. vCenter Server acts as a central management point for managing ESXi hosts, additional components (including but not limited to vCenter Update Manager, federated storage and network management, licensing, Host Auto Deployment, authentication, roles, and permissions), and web services and API exposure for partner integration.

Installing vCenter Server can be broken into three steps:

1. Ensure that your system is capable of running vCenter Server.

2. Install vCenter Server and additional components.

3. Perform basic configuration of vCenter Server and additional components as necessary.

As of this writing, vCenter Server is available only for Microsoft Windows systems. This has been a sore subject for administrators in IT shops that primarily run operating systems other than Windows. For these administrators, VMware has released a vSphere Web Client and vCenter Server Appliance, which is Linux-based. We will cover both of these in "Configure a vCenter Server Appliance," later in this chapter.

With vSphere 4.1, vCenter Server must be installed on a 64-bit Microsoft Windows platform.

To ensure that vCenter Server can accommodate the scalable performance necessary to efficiently manage ESXi hosts, VMware has provided some general requirements for the hardware, operating system, and database required to support vCenter Server.

Identify Hardware Requirements

VMware vCenter Server can be installed on a physical or virtual machine that meets the requirements listed in Table 3.1.

Building a VMware vSphere Environment

PART I

Table 3.1: Physical or Virtual Hardware Requirements for VMWare vCenter Server

Component	Requirement
Processor	Two 64-bit or a single dual-core 64-bit Intel or AMD x86–based processor with a speed of 2.0 GHz or greater. The Itanium processor is not supported. It is a best practice to use a faster processor if the vCenter Database runs on the same server.
Memory	4 GB of RAM minimum. It is a best practice to use more RAM if the database is running on the same server. The VMware vCenter Management Web services require from 512 MB to 4.4 GB of additional memory. The memory is allocated at system startup.
Database	A minimum of 2 GB of additional storage is required in addition to the storage required for the operating system installation. If the VMware vCenter Update Manager service is installed on the same system, an additional 22 GB of space is required to accommodate storage of patches. If Microsoft SQL Server 2008 R2 Express is installed as the database, 2 GB of disk space is required during the installation, with 1.5 GB reclaimed after the installation is complete.
Networking	A 100 MB network connection can be used, but a 1 GB network connection is recommended.

Meeting these requirements will ensure proper operation of vCenter Server and any additional components. When designing the environment, give additional thought to future growth or scalability of vCenter Server.

Identify Operating System Requirements for vCenter Server and vSphere Client

Because vCenter Server was developed to operate on a Windows platform, VMware supports this product on only a limited number of operating system configurations. Table 3.2 lists the operating systems for which VMware vCenter Server is supported.

Table 3.2: Operating System Requirements for vCenter Server

Operating System
Windows Server 2003 Standard, Enterprise, Datacenter, 64-bit SP2
Windows Server 2003 R2 Standard, Enterprise, Datacenter, 64-bit SP1
Windows Server 2008, Standard, Enterprise, Datacenter, 64-bit SP2
Windows Server 2008 R2, Standard, Enterprise, Datacenter, 64-bit

To manage VMware vCenter Server, you use vSphere Client to configure, manage, and monitor the environment. vSphere Client was developed using Microsoft .NET technologies and is also limited to Microsoft operating systems. Table 3.3 lists the operating systems on which vSphere Client may be installed to manage a vCenter Server.

Table 3.3: vSphere Client System Requirements

Operating System
Windows XP Pro (SP3 or greater)
Windows XP Pro (SP2 or greater, 64-bit)
Windows Server 2003 Standard, Enterprise, and Datacenter (SP2 or greater) 32-bit or 64-bit
Windows Server 2003 R2 Standard, Enterprise, and Datacenter (SP2 or greater) 32-bit or 64-bit
Windows Vista Business and Enterprise, 32-bit and 64-bit with SP2
Windows 7 Professional and Enterprise, 32-bit and 64-bit SP1
Windows Server 2008 Standard, Enterprise, and Datacenter, 32-bit and 64-bit SP2
Windows Server 2008 Standard, Enterprise, and Datacenter, 64-bit R2 SP1

There are also some best practices with regard to the domain membership of a server running vCenter Server. Following these guidelines will ensure that installation and operation run more smoothly:

- Microsoft strongly recommends that vCenter Server be joined to a Microsoft Windows domain. This will provide better security and domain capabilities to services that require it.

- If you are using Linked Mode vCenter Servers, the individual vCenter Servers may be in different domains, provided there is a two-way trust between the two domains.

In addition to vSphere Client, vSphere Web Access may be used to manage the vCenter Server installation, and it has some minimum requirements as well. The following browsers have been tested by VMware to verify proper operation of vSphere Web Access:

- Microsoft Windows Internet Explorer 7

- Microsoft Windows Internet Explorer 8

- Mozilla 1.*x* for Windows/Linux

- Mozilla Firefox 3.5

- Mozilla Firefox 3.6

Ensuring that the hardware and software requirements are met will ensure that the configuration used for vCenter Server, vSphere Client, and vSphere Web Access will provide a trouble-free installation and management platform for the vSphere environment.

Identify Database Requirements

At the heart of VMware vCenter Server and its ancillary components lie a number of databases.

Separate databases are recommended for vCenter Server and ancillary components, such as vCenter Update Manager, although it is not required for each additional component to be installed using a separate database. Installing different components on different databases can help identify problems with particular components and can result in better performance levels.

These databases do not have to be on the same machine as vCenter Server, nor do they have to reside on the same remote server. It is possible to have a vCenter instance installed on one server, with its SQL database residing on another server, and the vCenter Update Manager database on a third server. The choices are wide and depend on your operational needs. The default installation will load vCenter and required databases on the same system. The vCenter Server installation routine includes Microsoft SQL Server 2008 R2 Express Edition.

If you accept the defaults, the instance of Microsoft SQL Server 2008 R2 Express that is bundled with vCenter Server is used, and user authentication defaults to the rights of the user account performing the installation. If another supported database is used, administrative credentials are required.

NOTE If you are using any edition of Microsoft SQL Server, it is a best practice to ensure that the database service on either the local or the remote machine is also running as a domain account to aid in authentication.

The following databases are supported for vCenter Server:

- IBM DB2 9.5 Fix Pack 5 or greater and 9.7 Fix Pack 2 or greater
- Microsoft SQL Server 2008 R2 Express
- Microsoft SQL Server 2005, 32-bit and 64-bit SP3 or higher
- Microsoft SQL Server 2008, 32-bit and 64-bit SP1 or higher
- Microsoft SQL Server 2008 R2
- Oracle 10g R2
- Oracle 11g R1 11.1.0.7
- Oracle 11g R2 11.2.0.1 with patch 5

NOTE If you are planning to use Update Manager, then you will need to use either MS SQL Server or Oracle. Update Manager does not support DB2 databases. You could use DB2 for vCenter Server and MS SQL or Oracle for the VSphere Update Manager at the same time.

Identify Networking Requirements

Because vCenter is not a single standalone server, application, or isolated computing system, the pieces of the puzzle will require some form of communication between them. There are many possible configuration scenarios depending on the environment in which vCenter is being deployed.

A vCenter Server must be able to communicate with each host and each vSphere client. Furthermore, if a remote database server is utilized rather than a local instance of the database, the required TCP/IP ports for that database installation are also needed.

If an instance of vCenter Server is installed on Windows Server 2008, the installer opens the ports in the Windows Firewall during the installation. If you have any custom firewall software installed, you will need to manually make an exception to allow communication among all of the required pieces of the environment.

vCenter Server requires several ports to be open when you select a default installation. Each of these ports will be used for a different portion of the overall communications path. To enable proper communication among the components, consult a network engineer to ensure the appropriate ports are open for communication.

Table 3.4 lists ports that are required to be open.

Table 3.4: Ports required by vCenter Server

Port no.	Use
80	Redirects nonsecure requests to vCenter Server on a secure port.
389	LDAP services, Directory Services component of vCenter Server. It must be available even if vCenter Server is not part of a Linked Mode group.
443	Default port for vSphere Client communication. You can change this port, but vSphere Client and any SDK applications must use the vCenter Server name, followed by the nondefault port number.
636	vCenter Server in Linked Mode. This is the Secure Sockets Layer (SSL) port of the local vCenter Server ADAM Instance. 636 is the preferred port number, but it can be changed.
902	Multiple uses: manages and sends data to hosts, receives a heartbeat from hosts, and provides remote console access to virtual machines.
903	Remote console access from virtual machines to vSphere Client.
8080	VMware VirtualCenter Management Web Services HTTP.
8443	VMware VirtualCenter Management Web Services HTTPS for vCenter's Inventory Service.
60099	Web Service change notification.
10443	HTTPS port for the vCenter Inventory Service.
10109	Service Management port for vCenter's Inventory Service.
10111	Linked Mode Communication port for vCenter's Inventory Service.

WARNING If the default install of SQL Server was used during the install, SQL Reporting Services will be using port 80. You will have to either shut down or remove SQL Reporting Services or use a custom port for vCenter Server.

Identify Authentication Requirements

Initial authentication in vCenter Server is handled through local user accounts on the system upon which vCenter Server is installed. Authentication to manage ESXi servers is handled through vCenter Server as hosts are added to the vSphere configuration. Additionally, local accounts on each host may be created. Accounts local to ESXi hosts do not have permissions in the vCenter Server interface, even though they may have elevated privileges at the host level.

Install a Database

As previously mentioned, VMware utilizes industry-standard databases for vCenter Server. Administrators cannot easily use or access the raw data contained in the vCenter Server database. Instead, they must use vSphere Client. Components like the datacenters, clusters, resource pools, hosts, and virtual machines, along with their associated configuration and performance data, are stored in the backend database that vCenter Server is connected to. As mentioned, the default installation includes Microsoft SQL Server 2008 R2 Express Edition. The vCenter Server installer automatically creates a data source name (DSN), the database, and the database schema when using the default database software. We will examine a few alternate database installations—Microsoft SQL Server 2008 R2 (other than Express Edition) or Oracle 10g or 11g—in the following sections.

Create a vCenter Database in Microsoft SQL Server 2008 R2

The default Microsoft SQL Server 2008 R2 Express Edition installation with vCenter Server supports up to 5 hosts and 50 virtual machines. It is not considered as robust as its cousins, Microsoft SQL Server 2008

Standard and Enterprise editions, which also have enhanced feature sets.

Tables listing the differences among the various editions of Microsoft SQL Server 2008 can be found on Microsoft's website:

```
http://www.microsoft.com/sqlserver/2008/en/us/editions.aspx
```

If you have chosen to use Standard or Enterprise edition, Microsoft recommends certain configuration settings when you're creating the vCenter Server database. The database can reside on the local system or can be accessed remotely. To configure the vCenter Server database using SQL Server 2008 Standard or Enterprise edition, follow these steps:

1. If vCenter Server is part of a Windows domain, create a domain account that will be used to access the SQL Server instance.

NOTE   It is a best practice to create a dedicated domain user account, but you can also use a domain admin account.

Make sure this user has db_datawriter and db_datareader permissions on the SQL instance. Also, during initial installation and upgrades of vCenter Server, the vpxuser account must have db_owner rights on the MSDB database. This access can be revoked after an installation or upgrade.

2. Log in to the Microsoft SQL Server Management Studio with sysadmin (SA) or with a user that has sysadmin privileges, and run the following script. This script is located in the vCenter Server installation package at */vCenter-Server*/dbschema/DB_and schema_creation_scripts_MSSWL.txt.

```
use [master] go
CREATE DATABASE [VCDB] ON PRIMARY
(NAME = N'vcdb', FILENAME = N'C:\VCDB.mdf' , ↵
SIZE = 2000KB , FILEGROWTH = 10% )
LOG ON
(NAME = N'vcdb_log', FILENAME = N'C:\VCDB.ldf' , ↵
SIZE = 1000KB , FILEGROWTH = 10%)
COLLATE SQL_Latin1_General_CP1_CI_AS
go
use VCDB
```

Building a VMware
vSphere Environment

PART I

```
go
sp_addlogin @loginame=[vpxuser], @passwd=N'vpxuser!0', ↩
@defdb='VCDB', @deflanguage='us_english'
go
ALTER LOGIN [vpxuser] WITH CHECK_POLICY = OFF
go
CREATE USER [vpxuser] for LOGIN [vpxuser]
go
use MSDB
go
CREATE USER [vpxuser] for LOGIN [vpxuser]
go
```

Remember that you can change the database user, location, and database name within this script. Keep in mind that these values will need to match the DSN created to access the database.

3. Confirm that the SQL Server Agent is running.

4. To set up job scheduling and similar tasks, run the following scripts using the Microsoft SQL Server Management Studio. Run the scripts in the order listed.

```
job_schedule1_mssql.sql
job_schedule2_mssql.sql
job_schedule3_mssql.sql
job_cleanup_events_mssql
```

5. The database has now been created and is ready for a DSN to connect to the VCDB instance.

6. On the vCenter Server system, open the Windows ODBC Data Source Administrator by choosing Settings ➤ All Programs ➤ Administrative Tools ➤ Data Sources (ODBC).

7. Select the System DSN tab.

8. Click Add, select SQL Native Client, and click Finish.

9. Type an ODBC DSN name in the Name field, something like **vCenter Server**.

10. Select the server name from the Server drop-down menu and click Next. This can be the local system or a remote system.

Building a VMware
vSphere Environment

PART I

NOTE With a default installation of SQL Server, only a single instance or installation of SQL is present. If multiple SQL Server installations are present on a server, each additional installation is referred to as a named instance. The primary instance does not have a specific name, other than the server name, while named instances are typically signified as *SERVERNAME\InstanceName*.

11. Select Windows Authentication.

12. Select the database created for the vCenter Server system from the Change The Default Database To menu and click Next.

13. Click Finish.

14. A DSN that is compatible with vCenter Server is now available. When the vCenter Server installer prompts for the DSN of the database, select vCenter Server, or whatever value you entered in step 9.

Create a vCenter Database in Oracle

Not every environment uses Microsoft SQL Server. For various reasons, administrators might need to choose databases already being used in their environment. Oracle is a popular database choice, especially in environments that have a limited Microsoft footprint: It is available for many other platforms, including Linux, Solaris, and HP-UX. VMware supports several versions of Oracle, including 10*g* and 11*g*.

NOTE You don't have to have Oracle installed locally on the vCenter Server. When you're using Oracle, certain configurations are considered best practices when creating the database.

Perform these steps to create and configure the database:

1. Log on to a SQL*Plus session with the system account.

2. Run the following commands, or script, to create the database. For *datafile_path*, enter a valid path on your Oracle system:

```
CREATE SMALLFILE TABLESPACE "VPX" DATAFILE
 'datafile_path' ↵
SIZE 1G AUTOEXTEND ON NEXT 10M MAXSIZE
 UNLIMITED LOGGING EXTENT MANAGEMENT ↵
LOCAL SEGMENT SPACE MANAGEMENT AUTO;
```

3. Open a SQL*Plus window with a user that has schema owner rights on the vCenter Server database to create the database schema.

4. Locate the dbschema scripts in the vCenter Server installation package bin/dbschema directory.

5. In SQL*Plus, run the scripts in sequence on the database as shown in the following example. *path* is the directory path to the bin/ dbschema folder.

```
@path/VCDB_oracle.SQL
@path/purge_stat1_proc_oracle.sql
@path/purge_stat2_proc_oracle.sql
@path/purge_stat3_proc_oracle.sql
@path/purge_usage_stats_proc_oracle.sql
@path/stats_rollup1_proc_oracle.sql
@path/stats_rollup2_proc_oracle.sql
@path/stats_rollup3_proc_oracle.sql
@path/cleanup_events_oracle.sql
@path/delete_stats_proc_oracle.sql
```

6. Run the following scripts to set up scheduled jobs on the database. The *path* variable is the same as in step 5:

```
@path/job_schedule1_oracle.sql
@path/job_schedule2_oracle.sql
@path/job_schedule3_oracle.sql
@path/job_cleanup_events_oracle.sql
```

7. Oracle can use a local or remote Oracle instance. From the same SQL*Plus window, run the following script (where *VPXADMIN* is the user):

```
CREATE USER "VPXADMIN" PROFILE "DEFAULT" ↵
IDENTIFIED BY "oracle" DEFAULT TABLESPACE ↵
"VPX" ACCOUNT UNLOCK; ↵
grant connect to VPXADMIN; ↵
grant resource to VPXADMIN; ↵
grant create view to VPXADMIN; ↵
grant create sequence to VPXADMIN; ↵
grant create table to VPXADMIN; ↵
grant execute on dbms_lock to VPXADMIN; ↵
```

```
grant execute on dbms_job to VPXADMIN; ↵
grant unlimited tablespace to VPXADMIN;
```

8. If the Oracle database is not installed on the same system as vCenter Server, download and install the Oracle client.

9. On the vCenter Server system, open the Windows ODBC Data Source Administrator by choosing Settings ➤ Control Panel ➤ Administrative Tools ➤ Data Sources (ODBC).

NOTE   If you are using a 64-bit operating system, run the 32-bit ODBC Administrator application, which is located at `C:\Windows\SysWOW64\odbcad32.exe`.

---

10. Select the System DSN tab and click Add.

11. Select the appropriate Oracle driver for your installation and click Finish.

12. Enter the name of the DSN, such as `vCenter Server`.

13. Ensure that appropriate values appear in the TNS Names field referencing the local or remote Oracle instances. Select the appropriate TNS Service name.

14. Enter the username created in the Create User section.

15. Click OK. An Oracle database is now available for the vCenter Server installer.

Prepare and Install vCenter Server

Now that you have configured a database, you can begin installing vCenter Server.

TIP   Remember that vCenter Server includes an installation of Microsoft SQL Server 2008 R2 Express Edition, and if a database has not previously been installed, the vCenter installation will provide the ability to set up an initial database.

Installing vCenter Server consists of these steps:

1. Prepare for installation.

2. Install vCenter Server.

3. Install additional components.

4. Install vSphere Client.

5. Configure vCenter.

The steps have been segmented in this way to provide a more logical flow of how the process works. Each step is dependent on the previous task, and all the steps are detailed in the following sections.

Prepare for Installation

Before attempting to install the vCenter Server, make sure that your server meets the following criteria:

- The server meets the hardware requirements (see Table 3.1).

- The server is configured with a static IP address.

- The computer name consists of fewer than 15 characters. To conform to best practices, ensure that the computer name matches the hostname in the fully qualified domain name of the system.

- The system is joined to a domain, and not a workgroup. vCenter will be installed in a workgroup, but not all functionality is available. For example, when in a workgroup, vCenter Server will not be able to discover all domains and systems available on the network.

- A supported database is already created, unless you're using the bundled SQL Server 2008 R2 Express Edition.

- A valid DSN exists to allow vCenter Server to connect to the created database.

- The vCenter Server is able to directly access the hosts it will manage without any type of network address translation between the server and the hosts.

- The vCenter Server's fully qualified domain name is resolvable.

- The server you are installing on is not an Active Directory Domain Controller.

- The domain user account you will be installing with has the following settings on the server:

  - Is a member of the Administrators group

  - Has permission to act as part of the operating system

  - Can log on as a service

User Account for vCenter Server

During the install, the built-in system account is used by default. However, this account has more permissions and rights than vCenter Server needs. VMware recommends setting up a normal domain user, without domain administrator rights, and adding this user to the local administrator group. Once this has been set up, you can then enable Windows authentication for SQL Server for even more security. Keep in mind that for the SQL Server DSNs configured with Windows authentication, you need to use the same account as the VMware vCenter Management Webservices service and the DSN user.

Install vCenter Server

To start leveraging the capabilities and enterprise-class features of vSphere, you must obtain a copy of vCenter Server and go through the install of vCenter Server.

Obtain a Copy of vCenter Server

Because VMware does not typically ship software to its customers, to get started, you must download the vCenter Server installation media from the VMware site. The download area is located at: `http://downloads.vmware.com/`

NOTE   To download the software, you must set up an account at the VMware store, which you typically do upon purchase of VMware products.

---

vCenter Server is available in two formats:

- ISO format (DVD-ROM image file)
- ZIP format (compressed file)

Either format will install all of the components necessary, but there are differences. The ISO file may need to be burned to a DVD-ROM for the purpose of installing the software, while the ZIP file must be extracted to a location large enough to accommodate the decompressed files.

vCenter Server can be installed from a DVD-ROM, local path, mapped drive, or network share, but the software can only be installed to the local machine on a local drive.

Install vCenter Server

Once you have the installation media, follow these steps to install vCenter Server:

1. Select autorun.exe.

2. On the splash screen shown in Figure 3.1, highlight vCenter Server and then click Install to begin.

Figure 3.1: vCenter Server installer splash screen

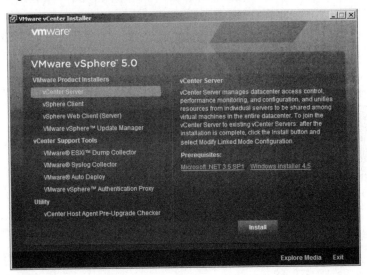

3. On the next screen, select the appropriate language for your installation and click OK.

4. The Welcome to the Installation Wizard screen appears. Click Next.

5. Click Next on the End-User Patent Agreement screen.

6. Accept the license agreement by choosing "I agree to the terms of the license agreement," and then click Next.

7. On the Customer Information screen, enter your name and organization. Below that, you have the option to enter the vCenter Server license key. If you do not enter it at this point, vCenter Server will be installed in evaluation mode, which is fully functional for 60 days. Click Next.

8. On the Database Options screen shown in Figure 3.2, select one of the following, depending on what kind of database you are using:

Figure 3.2: Database Options screen

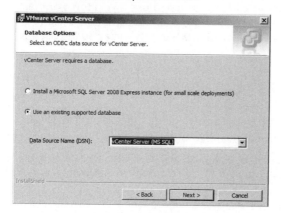

- Install A Microsoft SQL Server 2008 Express Instance
- Use An Existing Supported Database

If you choose Use An Existing Supported Database, select the database from the Data Source Name list.

9. On the next screen, if you are using SQL Server, click Next since the DSN is using Windows authentication. Otherwise, you may need to enter the database username and password.

10. Select which account will run the vCenter Server Service (see Figure 3.3). You can use the SYSTEM account or a Windows domain account. If you want to use a Windows domain account, you must be logged in to the server with this account. Fill in the password and FQDN and click Next.

Figure 3.3: vCenter Server Service screen

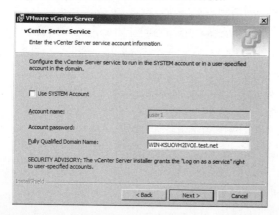

TIP It is considered a best practice to use a Windows domain account, especially if the database is utilizing SQL Server, as you can then use Windows authentication when connecting to the database.

---

11. On the next screen, accept the recommended installation path or modify it, and then click Next.

12. On the vCenter Server Linked Mode Options screen (Figure 3.4), choose to link this install to another vCenter Server or to create a standalone VMware vCenter Server instance. During an initial installation, you must create a standalone instance. Click Next.

Figure 3.4: vCenter Linked Mode Options screen

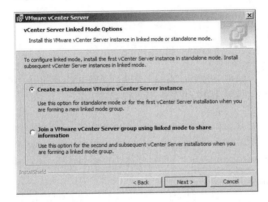

13. On the Configure Ports screen, as shown in Figure 3.5, review the default ports for vCenter Server and, if necessary, modify these ports to fit your environment. Click Next.

Figure 3.5: Configure Ports screen

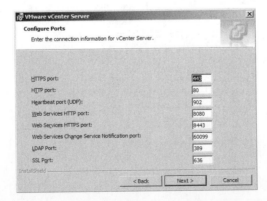

14. Review the ports used for the Inventory Service and modify these if needed. Click Next.

15. The vCenter Server JVM Memory screen (Figure 3.6) is next. Select the option that best describes your environment. Click Next.

Figure 3.6: vCenter Server JVM Memory screen

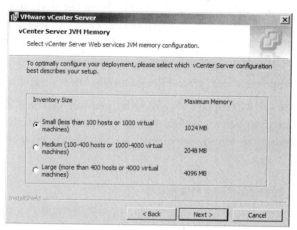

TIP JVM memory can be tuned later if needed.

---

16. The last screen has a check box that you can select which will bump up the number of the ephemeral ports that vCenter Server will use if you expect to need to power on 2,000 or more virtual machines simultaneously. Click Next to kick off the installation.

Deploy a vCenter Server Appliance

The quickest way to get vCenter Server up and running is to use the new vCenter Server Appliance. The appliance is based on a SLES 11 Linux install and is only supported on ESX/ESXi 4.0, 4.1, and ESXi 5.0. It can be downloaded from VMware and imported into an ESXi host.

NOTE vCenter Server Appliance has most of the capabilities of vCenter Server but is not quite at feature parity. For example, Link Mode is not supported with vCenter Server Appliance at this time.

To deploy a vCenter Server Appliance, follow these steps:

1. Download the vCenter Server Appliance from the VMware website. You will need the .OVF and two .VMDK files. Make sure you place all three files in the same folder on the computer on which you are running the vSphere Client.

2. From the vSphere client, go to File ➤ Deploy OVF Template.

3. The Deploy OVF Template wizard will open (see Figure 3.7). Click the Browse button and navigate to the folder where the .OVF and .VMDK files are stored. Select the .OVF file and click Open. Now click Next.

Figure 3.7: Deploy OVF Template wizard

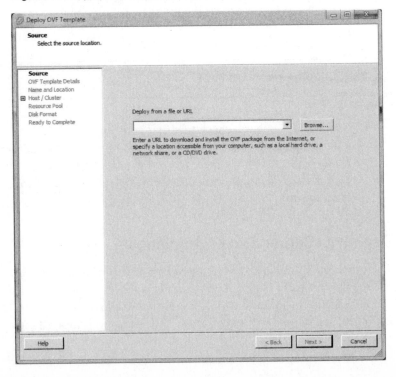

4. On the OVF Detail page, review the information and then click Next. Notice that if you wish to provision the full amount of disk space, the server will need 75 GB.

5. On the Name And Location screen, give the server a meaningful name and place it in the appropriate inventory folder. Figure 3.8 shows the server being placed in the Discovered virtual machine folder).

Figure 3.8: Placing the server in an inventory folder

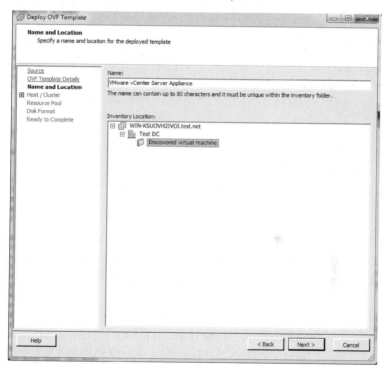

6. Next, select a host or cluster for the server. Click Next.

7. On the Disk Format screen (see Figure 3.9), choose your disk type.

Figure 3.9: Disk Format screen

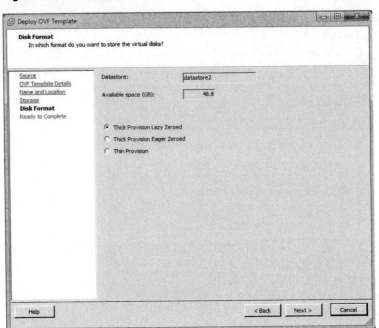

Your choices are:

- Thick Provision Lazy Zeroed: Space is allocated during the creation of the disk. Data on the physical device is not erased during creation. Data is zeroed out on first write from the virtual machine.

- Thick Provision Eager Zeroed: Space is allocated during creation. Data on the physical device is zeroed during creation. Supports clustering features such as Fault Tolerance.

- Thin Provision: The disk appears to the operating system to have the total amount of disk space but only the amount of space actually containing data is consumed on the physical disk.

8. On the Ready to Complete screen, review the summary of your selections and use the check box to specify whether you want to power the virtual machine on automatically once deployed. Click Finish.

Configure a vCenter Server Appliance

Once your vCenter Server Appliance is deployed and powered on, there are two phases of setup that have to happen: steps from the console and steps from the web browser.

Configure vCenter Server Appliance: Console Steps

There are three tasks that need to be completed from the console:

- Change the root password.
- Configure the network.
- Set the time zone.

Start by changing the root password. Follow these steps:

1. From within the vSphere Client, select your vCenter Server Appliance, right-click, and then select Open Console.

2. When you see the console (Figure 3.10), highlight Login. Hit Enter.

Figure 3.10: vCenter Server Appliance Console screen

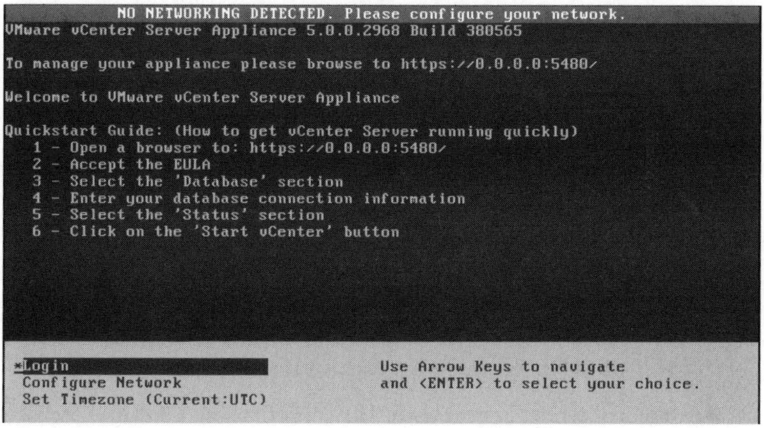

```
            NO NETWORKING DETECTED. Please configure your network.
VMware vCenter Server Appliance 5.0.0.2968 Build 380565

To manage your appliance please browse to https://0.0.0.0:5480/

Welcome to VMware vCenter Server Appliance

Quickstart Guide: (How to get vCenter Server running quickly)
    1 - Open a browser to: https://0.0.0.0:5480/
    2 - Accept the EULA
    3 - Select the 'Database' section
    4 - Enter your database connection information
    5 - Select the 'Status' section
    6 - Click on the 'Start vCenter' button




 ►Login                              Use Arrow Keys to navigate
  Configure Network                  and <ENTER> to select your choice.
  Set Timezone (Current:UTC)
```

3. Enter the default login ID (**root**) and password (**vmware**).

4. You should now have a prompt ending in #. This indicates you are logged in as the root user. Enter the command **passwd** and hit Enter.

5. Enter a new password and hit Enter. Type it in one more time to verify it and hit Enter. Depending on the password you have chosen to use, you may receive an error about the password being

based on a dictionary word as seen in Figure 3.11. The password
will still be changed.

Figure 3.11: Changing the root password

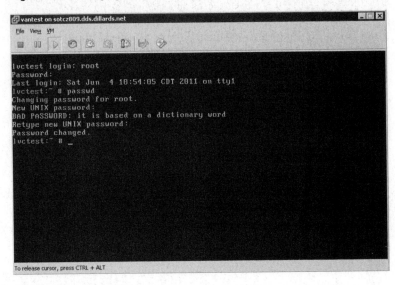

6. Type **exit** to log out.

Now it is time to specify the network settings needed to be able to
access the vCenter Server from over the network.

1. From within the vSphere Client, select the vCenter Server
Appliance, right-click, and select Open Console.

2. Click inside the console and highlight Network. Hit Enter.

3. On the Change Network Configuration screen, specify whether
you want the server to receive an IPv6 SLAAC address.

4. Specify whether you want the server to use DHCP instead of a
static address.

5. If you specified No in step 4, enter the following information as
prompted: IP address, netmask, gateway, DNS servers, hostname,
and proxy if needed.

6. Review the summary of the network settings and press Y for yes if
they are correct (see Figure 3.12).

Figure 3.12: Entering and confirming network parameters

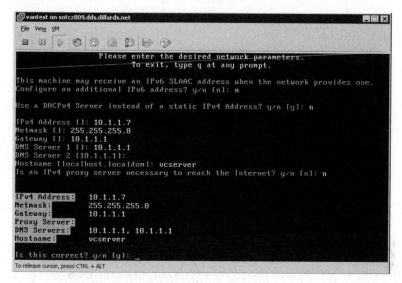

7. The main console screen (see Figure 3.10) should reappear. Test the connection by pinging the vCenter Server Appliance from a remote client.

Finally, set the time zone the server is in.

1. From within the vSphere Client, select the vCenter Server Appliance, right-click, and select Open Console.

2. Highlight Set Timezone. Hit Enter.

3. Enter numbers for the continent, country, and time zone as prompted.

4. Review the summary of your choices and enter 1 for yes if the information is correct.

Configure a vCenter Server Appliance: Browser Steps

On the main console screen of the vCenter Server Appliance, you will see the URL to enter into a client browser to access vCenter Server Web Console. From here, you will need to perform additional steps in order to get the server ready to manage your environment.

1. In your browser, enter the URL found on the vCenter Server Appliance console screen.

2. The VMware vCenter Server Appliance login screen should load (see Figure 3.13). Enter **root** as the user name and the password you entered for root when you changed it in the "Configure vCenter Server Appliance: Console Steps" section.

Figure 3.13: VMware vCenter Server Appliance Login screen

ဝ၀ၞၟ **VMware vCenter Server Appliance**

Login

User name: [   ]

Password: [   ]

[Login]

3. On the VMware vCenter Server End User License screen, click Accept EULA in the Actions section on the right hand side of the window.

4. To configure the database you wish to use, select the vCenter Server tab from along the top of the screen, and select Database.

5. In the Database Settings page, select the database type you will be using from the drop-down list (see Figure 3.14).

Figure 3.14: Database Settings screen

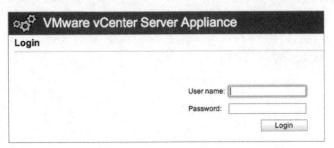

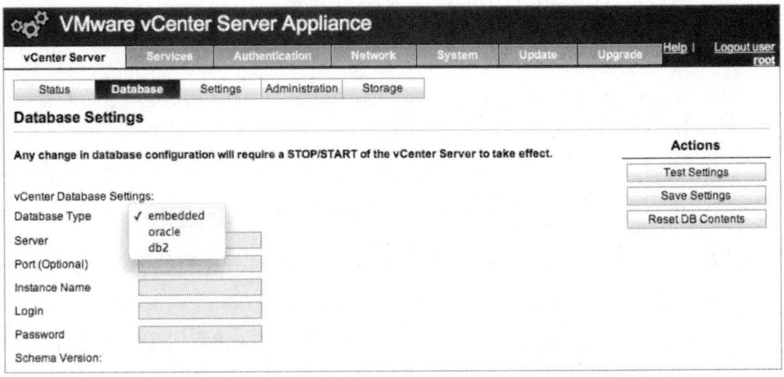

NOTE At the time of writing, Oracle is the only non-embedded databases supported for vCenter Server Appliance.

---

6. If you are not using the embedded database, enter the server and port information, instance name, login, and password for the database you will be using.

7. Test the connection by clicking Test Settings on the top-right side of the screen.

8. Once it has successfully connected, click Save Settings.

The next procedure is to set the inventory size for the vCenter Server Appliance. You need to do this in two places. Follow these steps:

1. Power off the vCenter Server Appliance.

2. Once the server is off, in the vSphere Client, right-click and select settings.

3. Under the Hardware tab, select Memory. Set the memory size based on your environment:

   - 8 GB or higher for fewer than 100 hosts and 1,000 virtual machines within the vCenter Server Appliances' inventory.

   - 12 GB or higher for between 100 and 400 hosts or between 1,000 and 4,000 virtual machines within the vCenter Server Appliances' inventory.

   - 16 GB or higher for over 400 hosts or 4,000 virtual machines within the vCenter Server Appliances' inventory.

4. Click OK to apply your memory selection.

5. Now power the vCenter Server Appliance back on and log in to the vCenter Server Web Console.

6. Click the vCenter Server tab and select Settings.

7. Select the inventory size from the drop-down list:

   - Small corresponds to the 8 GB memory settings from step 3 above.

- Medium corresponds to the 13 GB settings from step 3 above.

- Large corresponds to the 17 GB settings from step 3 above.

8. Click Save Settings.

Now, vCenter Server can be started.

1. Click the status button under the vCenter Server tab.

2. Under actions, click Start vCenter.

Once the vCenter Server Appliance has started, you can now connect using the vSphere Client just as you would connect to any other vCenter Server.

vCenter Server is now ready for you to configure. To perform these tasks, you must install vSphere Client. Additional components can be installed before or after the installation of vSphere Client. To make the process flow more evenly, let's start by installing the additional components first.

Install Additional Components

To extend the functionality of vCenter Server, additional components are included. These add-ons give vCenter Server greater functionality in the area of ESXi patching, as well as the ability to monitor and report on storage, display hardware status of ESXi hosts that are being managed by vCenter Server, and display health status of vCenter Server services.

Install vSphere Update Manager

As the vSphere environment grows, additional ESXi servers may be added. As the numbers of hosts grow, maintenance, and specifically patching, can become a burden. In the days of ESX 2.x, patches had to be copied to hosts, hosts had to be rebooted into a Linux single-user mode, and then patches were installed. Usually, it was easier to simply rebuild hosts using some type of automated scripting.

VMware released VMware Update Manager with the launch of Virtual Infrastructure 3 with the purpose of making the patching process significantly easier. In vSphere 5, this product has been rebranded as vSphere Update Manager.

NOTE With this release of vSphere Update Manager, VMware now requires 64-bit Windows; however, the database requires a 32-bit system DSN. A 32-bit system DSN for SQL Server can be created using the odbcad32.exe utility, which is installed in the SysWOW64 directory of Windows.

To take advantage of the abilities of vSphere Update Manager, follow these steps to install it:

1. Start the VMware vCenter Installer, and select vSphere Update Manager from the splash screen (shown in Figure 3.1, earlier in this chapter).

2. On the next screen, select the appropriate language setting and click OK.

3. Click Next at the Welcome Screen and Next again on the End-User Patent Agreement screen.

4. On the next screen, click "I agree to the terms of the license agreement" and click Next.

5. On the Support Information screen (see Figure 3.15), review the information about changes to vSphere Update Manager. Also, you can choose whether you want Update Manager to automatically download patches once installed. Click Next.

Figure 3.15: Support Information screen

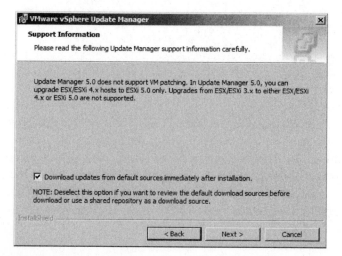

NOTE   Take note of the information stated in Figure 3.15. In previous releases of vSphere Update Manager, the ability to patch guest operating systems existed. With this release, that functionality has been removed. Also note that vSphere Update Manager supports updating an ESX/ESXi 4.x host to ESXi 5.0. Version 3.x hosts will need to be updated to 4.x host first before upgrading to 5.0, making it much more appealing to do a new install on these hosts.

6. On the vCenter Server Information screen, shown in Figure 3.16, enter the IP address or FQDN and port of the vCenter Server installation, followed by a username and password so that vSphere Update Manager can properly communicate with vCenter Server. Click Next.

Figure 3.16: Entering vCenter Server information

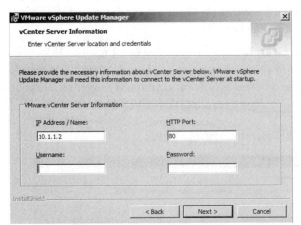

7. On the Database Options screen, select the database to be used for the vSphere Update Manager. If the default SQL Server 2008 R2 Express database was installed during the vCenter Server installation, select Install A Microsoft SQL Server 2008 R2 Instance; otherwise, select Use An Existing Supported Database and select the preconfigured DSN from the Data Source Name (DSN) drop-down menu (see Figure 3.17).

Figure 3.17: Selecting an existing database

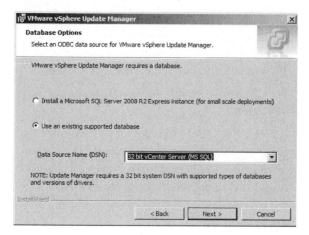

8. vSphere Update Manager requires authentication. If the DSN created uses NT Authentication, then a username and password are not required. If the database uses database authentication, then enter a username and password and then click Next.

9. On the Port Settings screen (see Figure 3.18), enter the required connection information, which tells vCenter Server, ESX, and ESXi hosts how to talk to vSphere Update Manager. Then click Next.

Figure 3.18: Entering connection information

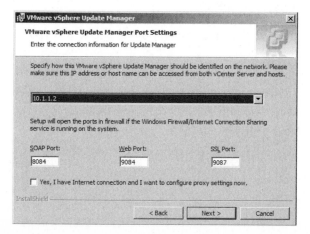

10. On the Destination Folder screen, accept the defaults or change to the directory where you want to install vSphere Update Manager and the directory to store the downloaded patches. Click Next.

11. On the Ready to Install the Program screen, click Install.

Install vSphere Web Client

The vSphere Web Client allows users to connect to a vCenter Server system to manage ESXi hosts through a web browser. This gives administrators running operating systems other than Microsoft Windows additional options to access vSphere Server. vSphere Web Client requires a 64-bit Windows operating system. The following operating systems are supported:

- Microsoft Windows Server 2003 Standard, Enterprise, and Datacenter, 64-bit SP2

- Microsoft Windows Server 2003 R2 Standard, Enterprise, and Datacenter, 64-bit SP2

- Microsoft Windows Server 2008 Standard, Enterprise, and Datacenter, 64-bit SP2

- Microsoft Windows Server 2008 R2 Standard, Enterprise, and Datacenter, 64-bit SP1

The following browsers are supported:

- Microsoft Internet Explorer 7 and 8

- Mozilla Firefox 3.5 and 3.6

Adobe Flash is required on the client computer to which you are connecting.

To install vSphere Web Client, follow these steps:

1. Start the VMware vCenter Installer, and select vSphere Web Client (Server) from the splash screen (see Figure 3.1, earlier in this chapter). Click Install.

2. On the next screen, select the appropriate language setting and click OK.

3. Click Next at the Welcome screen and Next again on the End-User Patent Agreement screen.

4. On the next screen, click "I agree to the terms of the license agreement" and click Next.

5. On the Customer Information screen, enter your name and organization. Click Next.

6. On the VMware vSphere Web Client Port Settings screen (Figure 3.19), change port settings if you need to, then click Next.

Figure 3.19: VMware vSphere Web Client Port Settings screen

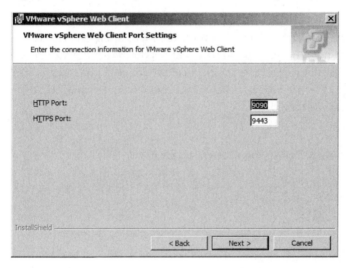

7. Accept or change the installation folder location, then click Next.

8. Click Install to start the installation.

After installation, the browser will open to the VMware vSphere Web Client Administration Tool (see Figure 3.20). At the top of the browser window, notice the red exclamation point. This message is to get you to register a vCenter Server.

Figure 3.20: Exclamation Point on vSphere Web Client

1. In the upper-right corner of the browser window, click Register vCenter Server (Figure 3.21).

Figure 3.21: Click the Register vCenter Server link.

2. The Register vCenter Server screen will open (see Figure 3.22). Fill in the FQDN of the vCenter Server in the vCenter Server URL field, enter the user name that you will use to connect to the vCenter Server system, and enter the user's password in the Password field.

Figure 3.22: Register vCenter Server screen

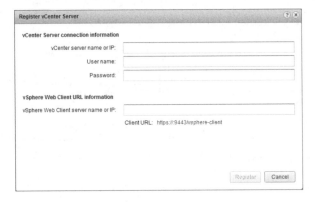

3. In the vSphere Web Client server name or IP field, enter the full qualified domain name for the vSphere Web Client.

Once the vCenter Server has been registered, you can log in from a browser using the URL below, replacing "myserver.com" with the name of the server you installed vCenter Server on. If you are familiar with vCenter Server, you should not have any problem getting around in the web client (see Figure 3.23).

```
https://myserver.com:9443/vsphere-client
```

Figure 3.23: vSphere Web Client

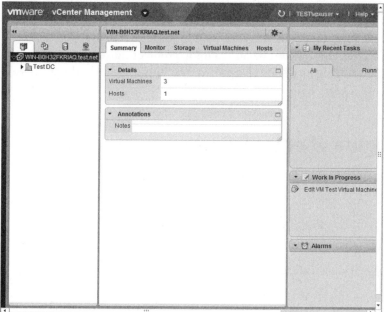

Install vSphere Client

vSphere Client is a full feature application that you install on a Windows operating system which allows the administration of a group of ESXi hosts. Follow these steps to install the vCenter Server client software:

1. Start the VMware vCenter Installer, and select vSphere Client from the splash screen shown in Figure 3.1, earlier in this chapter.

2. Select the appropriate language setting and click OK.

3. Click Next on the Welcome screen and Next again on the End-User Patent Agreement screen.

4. On the next screen, click "I agree to the terms of the license agreement" and click Next.

5. Enter the appropriate customer information on the next screen and click Next.

6. On the next screen, accept the default installation path or modify it, and click Next.

7. Click Install to start the installation.

8. On the final screen, click Finish to complete the installation.

vSphere Client is installed. Plug-ins for additional components that were installed will have to be added upon connecting to vCenter Server.

Now that vSphere Client is installed, the initial setup of the vSphere environment can begin.

Configure vCenter Server

Configuring vCenter Server includes these steps:

- Connecting to vCenter Server
- Installing plug-ins in vSphere Client
- Configuring Advanced Settings
- Creating a datacenter
- Creating clusters
- Adding hosts

Each of these steps must be accomplished to leverage the complete feature set of vSphere. For example, enterprise features such as VMware High Availability and Distributed Resource Scheduling cannot be used unless you've configured a cluster.

Connect to vCenter Server

vCenter Server operates as a Windows service on the vCenter Server system. There is no native interface in Windows to access the vCenter Server installation. This function is achieved via vSphere Client or web client.

To connect to vCenter Server:

1. Launch the VMware vSphere Client by choosing Start ➤ Programs ➤ VMware ➤ VMware vSphere Client, or by double-clicking the VMware vSphere Client on the Desktop.

2. When vSphere Client login dialog box (see Figure 3.24) opens, enter the IP address or hostname of the vCenter Server, along with a valid username and password. Alternatively, select the Use

Windows Session Credentials check box to use the context of the current user account logged in to the system.

Figure 3.24: vSphere Client login dialog box

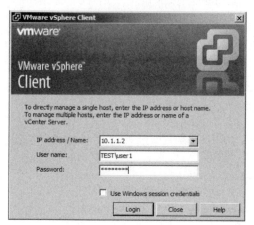

3. A Security Warning dialog box appears. This message simply states that you have not chosen to trust the certificate that the vCenter Server is configured to use. Select the option Install This Certificate And Do Not Display Any Security Warnings for "*IP/hostname.*" Then click Ignore to continue.

4. When vSphere Client loads, if you have not configured licensing for your environment, you will be presented with an Evaluation Notice, warning you about the evaluation period, and what will occur if you do not install your licenses. Click OK.

Once you're connected to vCenter Server, configuration can begin.

Install Plug-Ins in vSphere Client

Plug-ins extend the abilities of vSphere Client. VMware-provided plug-ins are installed through the Plug-ins drop-down menu in the vSphere Client interface.

The vSphere Update Manager component has a plug-in associated with it. Here's how to install it:

1. In vSphere Client, select Plug-ins ➤ Plug-in Management, as shown in Figure 3.25.

Building a VMware vSphere Environment

PART I

Figure 3.25: Select Manage Plug-ins from the Plug-ins menu.

The Plug-in Manager shown in Figure 3.26 appears. The installed plug-ins are listed, and vCenter Update Manager is listed as not installed.

Figure 3.26: Plug-in Manager

2. Click Download And Install next to vCenter Update Manager in the Status column. You'll see the progress of the download, as shown in Figure 3.27.

Figure 3.27: Installing the vCenter Update Manager plug-in

3. Choose the appropriate language and click OK. Then click Next.
4. Select I Accept The Terms In The License Agreement, and click Next.
5. On the next screen, click Install.
6. Click Finish to complete the plug-in installation.
7. When you see the security dialog box, click Ignore.
8. Click Close to close the Plug-in Manager.

Configure Advanced vCenter Server Settings

Once the basic installation of vCenter Server is complete, you can configure some additional settings to add to the overall usefulness of the installation.

These advanced settings affect the way vCenter Server behaves under normal operation. Some of these settings are configured only once, and others may need to be modified depending on how the environment is managed.

To configure vCenter Server settings, first select Administration ➤ vCenter Server Settings. The settings include the following:

License Settings   These settings are used to manage licenses for vCenter Server and ESXi hosts, as well as legacy ESX and ESXi hosts. This topic will be discussed in more detail in Chapter 4.

Statistics   These settings are used to modify the view or the statistics parameters for data collection, and provide database sizing estimations.

Runtime Settings   The Runtime settings—Unique ID, Managed IP, Name Used—distinguish this vCenter Server installation from other installations when you're using vCenter Server in Linked Mode.

Active Directory   These settings are used to set up AD timeout, query limit, validation, and validation timeout. The settings are especially important when vCenter Server is part of a large Active Directory domain environment.

Mail   These settings are used to configure a Simple Mail Transfer Protocol (SMTP) server for the purpose of sending out email alerts when alarms are triggered by issues occurring in clusters, hosts, guests, and the like.

SNMP   Use these settings to configure Simple Network Management Protocol (SNMP) to send data to external monitoring services, or to allow for the querying of information from vCenter Server by external monitoring services.

Ports   Use these settings to configure the web service ports for vCenter Server. The defaults are 80 and 443, and you should change them only if there are conflicts with other services operating on the same ports on vCenter Server.

Timeout Settings These settings are used to manage the amount of time vSphere clients should wait for a response for long and short operations. The settings can be used to tweak the timeouts when you're using vSphere Client over low-bandwidth networks.

Logging Options These settings are used to modify the logging level for vCenter Server log files. You can change the level of logging to enhance troubleshooting when there are issues in the vSphere environment.

Database The total number of connections to the database is configured here. This setting can be changed to increase or decrease the number of connections, which can increase or decrease the performance of vCenter Server.

Database Retention Policy As events occur in the vSphere environment, they are logged in the vCenter Server database. Collection of these events over time can increase the size of the database. The retention policy will allow you to purge events and tasks that are older than the number of days you configure here.

SSL Settings These settings are used to view and require SSL certificate checking between ESXi hosts when you're adding them to vCenter Server, as well as when you're using vSphere Client to connect to the console of guests.

Advanced Settings The advanced settings section allows you to change the value of a variety of settings such as the port used for the SMTP server, log file sizes, and the time to wait for a users and group query to return from Active Directory. In general, you should not change these settings unless you have a specific need to.

Create a Datacenter

To begin configuring the virtual environment, you need a datacenter. A datacenter is the logical container of clusters, ESX and ESXi hosts, resource pools, and virtual machines. Multiple datacenters are typically created when a vCenter Server instance is managing hosts and guests in multiple locations, but this is not a required configuration.

Create a datacenter using one of the following methods:

- Select File ➤ New ➤ Datacenter
- Press Ctrl+D

- Right-click on the vCenter Server name in the left panel and choose New Datacenter from the initial logon screen, as shown in Figure 3.28.

Figure 3.28: Creating a new datacenter

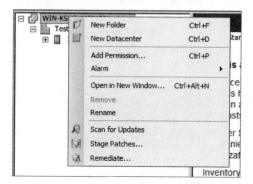

- Click Create A Datacenter on the Getting Started tab in the right panel.

The datacenter will be named New Datacenter, and the name will be highlighted, allowing you to rename the datacenter as appropriate for your environment or to coordinate with your environment's naming standards.

To change the datacenter name, simply type the new name while it is highlighted, and then press Enter.

Add a Cluster

Clusters are not a requirement in the vSphere environment, but they do provide for additional capabilities in vCenter. Clusters enable you to use features such as High Availability (HA) and Dynamic Resource Scheduling (DRS) across ESX and ESXi hosts.

To leverage these features, let's configure a datacenter:

1. Select a datacenter object, then add a cluster by using one of the following methods:

   - Select File ➢ New ➢ Add Cluster.

   - Press Ctrl+L.

   - Right-click on the datacenter and select New Cluster.

2. When the New Cluster Wizard opens, as shown in Figure 3.29, enter a name for the cluster in the Name text box.

Figure 3.29: Entering a name in the New Cluster Wizard

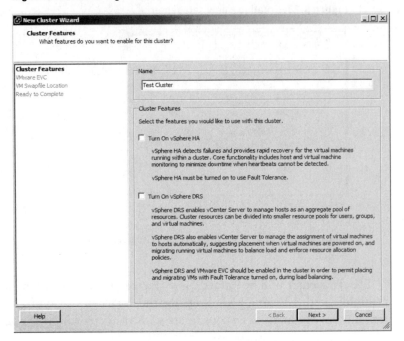

3. As cluster features are selected, the list of steps in the left panel will include additional components for configuration.

4. To enable vSphere High Availability features, select the Turn On vSphere HA check box.

5. To enable vSphere Distributed Resource Scheduling, select the Turn On vSphere DRS check box.

6. Click Next to continue.

We'll continue these steps in the next section.

Configure vSphere DRS

If you selected Turn On vSphere DRS in step 5 in the previous section, you'll see vSphere DRS options in the New Cluster Wizard, as shown in Figure 3.30. Follow these steps to configure vSphere DRS:

Figure 3.30: vSphere DRS options in the New Cluster Wizard

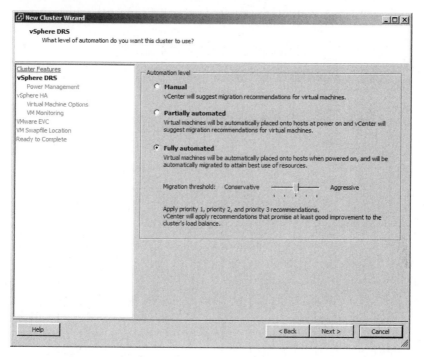

1. On the "What Level Of Automation Do You Want This Cluster To Use?" screen, the DRS feature allows vCenter to load-balance guests across hosts to make sure that there is an even load across all hosts. Select one of the radio buttons on this screen:

   Manual   Choose this option to have vCenter suggest when guests need to be migrated between hosts.

   Partially automated   Choose this option to have vCenter suggest when guests need to be migrated between hosts as well as automatically placing guests on hosts when they are powered on.

   Fully automated   Choose this option to have vCenter automatically place guests on hosts when they are powered on and automatically migrate guests to make the best use of available resources.

2. Move the Migration Threshold slider to determine whether vCenter should use aggressive or conservative decisioning for the movement of guests between hosts in the cluster.

3. Click Next after you make your choices.

4. The Power Management screen (Figure 3.31) allows vCenter to power hosts on or off as required for a cluster's workload.

Figure 3.31: Power Management options in the New Cluster Wizard

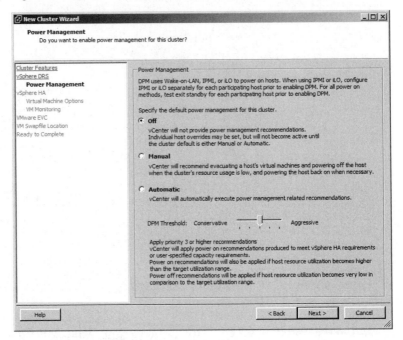

Select one of the following:

Off Choose this option to disable Power Management.

Manual Choose this option to have vCenter recommend evacuating guests from one or more hosts, and power the host off when the workload does not require the hosts. This will also automatically power hosts on when the workload requires additional host resources.

Automatic vCenter will automatically execute power recommendations. Move the DPM Threshold slider to determine whether vCenter should use aggressive or conservative decisioning for the powering on or off of hosts, depending on workload.

5. Click Next to continue.

Configure vSphere HA

If you selected Turn On vSphere HA in step 4 at the beginning of the "Add a Cluster" section, you'll see vSphere HA options in the New Cluster Wizard, as shown in Figure 3.32.

Figure 3.32: vSphere HA options in the New Cluster Wizard

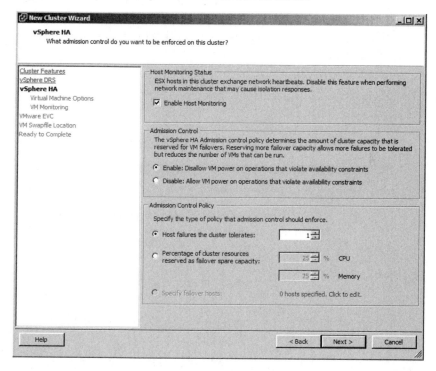

The High Availability feature lets ESX and ESXi hosts restart virtual machines when an ESX or ESXi host fails. The guests will be restarted on other hosts in the cluster.

Follow these steps to configure vSphere HA:

1. Select the Enable Host Monitoring check box to have vCenter monitor hosts through heartbeats. This option can be deselected during maintenance schedules to prevent host isolation issues, resulting in unnecessary HA failovers.

2. Select an Admission Control option. The Disable button allows guests to be powered on even if doing so would violate the available resource policy. If you click the Disable button, guests will not be powered on if they require more resources than are available.

3. Specify the type of Admission Control Policy. Select one of the available radio buttons to choose a policy based on the number of allowed host failures or the percentage of cluster resources to be reserved for HA, or to specify a specific host to fail over to. Click Next to continue.

4. Next, you'll see the Virtual Machine Options screen (Figure 3.33). Specify a VM Restart Priority for this cluster. Higher-priority guests are started first.

Figure 3.33: Virtual Machine Options in the New Cluster Wizard

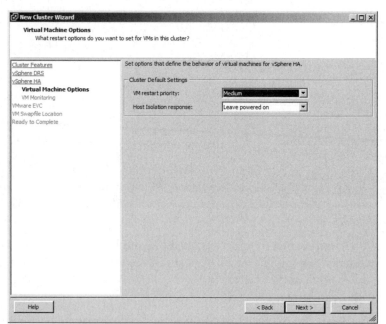

5. Select a Host Isolation Response. This option determines what a host should do with guests if it loses connectivity with vCenter and/or the default gateway. The default is Leave Powered On. The other options are Power Off and Shut Down.

Selecting Leave Powered On ensures that VMs remaining running in a HA isolation condition. This is especially important when using iSCSI or NFS-based shared storage.

NOTE The lock/split brain issue when using IP-based storage has been resolved since VSphere 4.0 Update 2. We no longer need to immediately power off hosts in an isolation condition as long as there is still IP-based storage connectivity.

Click Next to continue.

6. The VM Monitoring options (Figure 3.34) appear next. In the VM Monitoring menu, select Enabled if you want to restart guests when VMware tools heartbeats are not received in a given amount of time. Move the Monitoring Sensitivity slider to change the time threshold for monitoring the VMware tools in each guest. Click Next to continue.

Figure 3.34: VM Monitoring options in the New Cluster Wizard

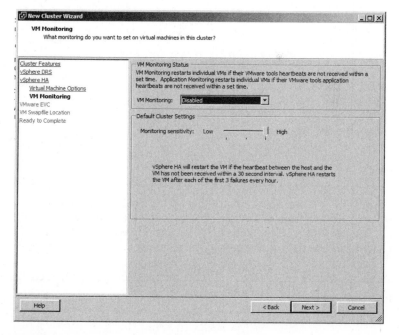

7. The VMWare EVC screen (Figure 3.35) asks if you want to enable Enhanced vMotion Compatibility (EVC) for this cluster. This feature allows you to maximize vMotion compatibility and ensures that only hosts that are compatible with those in your cluster can be added to the cluster. EVC will only present the CPU instruction set of the least capable processors to each guest. Select the appropriate radio button, then click Next to continue.

Figure 3.35: VMware EVC options in the New Cluster Wizard

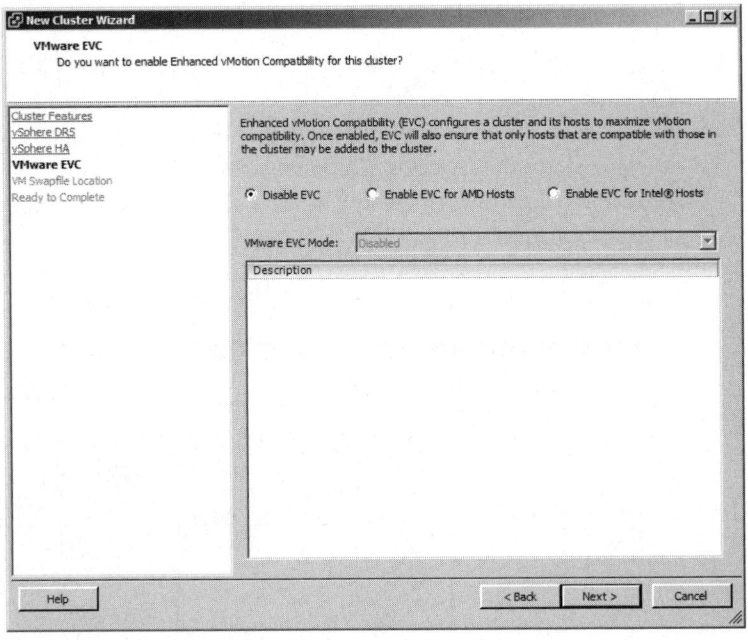

NOTE When you select either of the Enable options, a drop-down box is provided so you can select the type of hosts being used. Your selection will determine which processor instruction sets are required for a host to become part of the cluster.

8. The Swapfile Policy for Virtual Machines screen is next (Figure 3.36). Specify whether a guest's swap file is stored with the guest on shared storage, or on a dedicated datastore. Choose the desired option and click Next.

Figure 3.36: Virtual Machine Swapfile Location options in the New Cluster Wizard

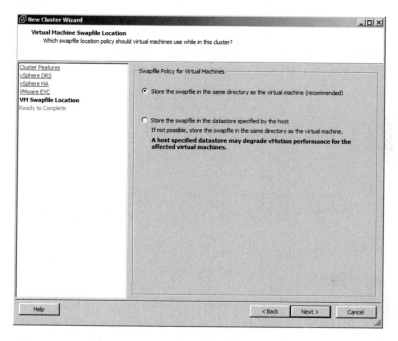

9. When you see the Ready To Complete screen (Figure 3.37), make sure the configuration settings are correct and click Finish.

Figure 3.37: Ready To Complete screen in the New Cluster Wizard

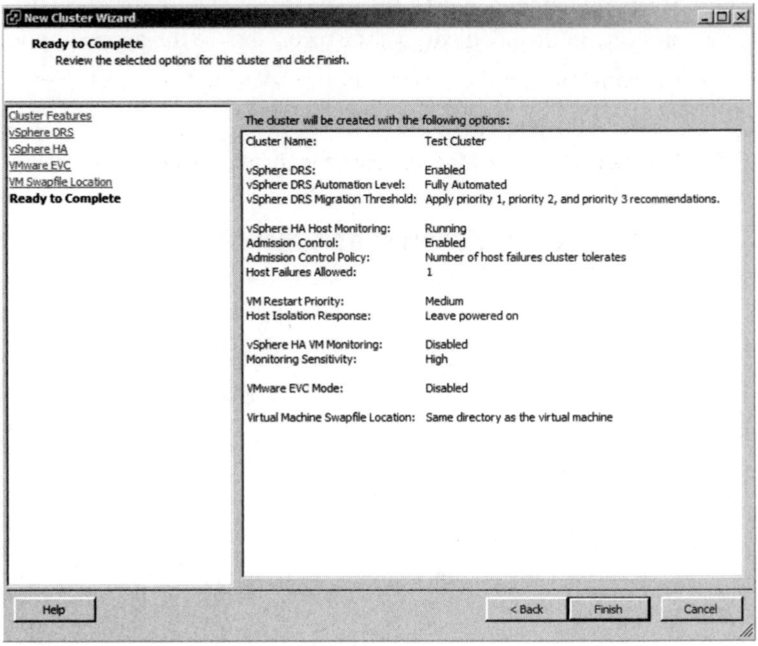

Add a Host

If vCenter Server is the central management point of vSphere, ESX and ESXi hosts are the workers of the environment. To use hosts in a managed vSphere environment, you must add them to the vCenter Server.

To add and configure a host, follow these steps:

1. Add a host using one of the following methods:

   - Select File ➢ New ➢ Add Host.

   - Press Ctrl+H.

   - Right-click on the datacenter you created, and select Add Host.

   - Click Add A Host on the Getting Started tab in the right panel when a given datacenter is selected.

   Once you complete one of these steps, the Add Host Wizard opens.

2. On the Specify Connection Settings screen, enter either the IP address or the FQDN of the ESX or ESXi host you want to add.

3. Enter **root** as the username and enter the appropriate password for the root user on the host you want to add. Then click Next.

4. Click Yes when presented with a security alert. This alert is shown because a self-generated, self-signed certificate (provided by VMware), which has not been trusted by the Windows system yet, has been installed on the host installation.

5. The Add Host Wizard will show a summary of the ESX or ESXi host you are adding and any virtual machines that may already reside on it. Click Next.

6. You will now be prompted to add a license key. If you have not installed your licenses, you can choose Evaluation Mode, as shown in Figure 3.38. Click Next when finished.

Figure 3.38: Assign License screen

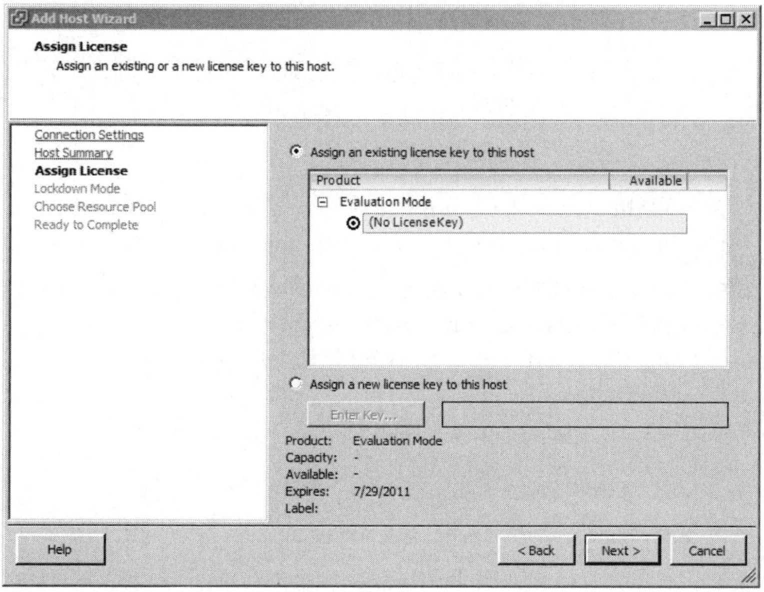

7. The Lockdown Mode screen is next. Enable this if you want only the vpxuser to have authentication permissions and to be able to perform operations against the host directly. All operations initiated by other users have to happen in vCenter Server.

8. On the Virtual Machine Location screen (shown in Figure 3.39), specify a location for the host's VMs.

Figure 3.39: Specifying a location for the host's VMs

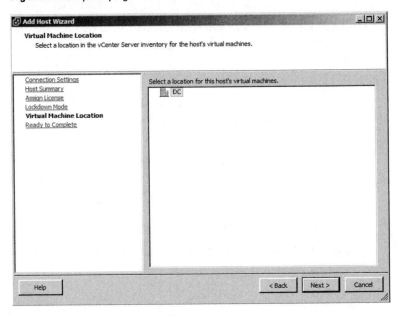

9. On the Ready To Complete screen, click Finish to add the host to the datacenter, and if you specify one, the selected cluster.

10. Now that you've added a host to the cluster, your work is not done. Clusters are only useful when the cluster contains more than one host. Add one or more additional hosts to the cluster using the same steps.

4

Understanding Licensing

IN THIS CHAPTER, YOU WILL LEARN TO:

Software has become a critical component in today's business environment. Most software vendors include a licensing mechanism to prevent users from installing more instances, or copies, of their product than they've purchased. From the vendor's perspective, the ability to limit the number of installations is vital to their revenue. If an enterprise only had to purchase a single copy of a software package simply to obtain the technology, additional purchases from a technical standpoint would not be required. The licensing model that VMware uses allows for one installation of the software for every license purchased. This chapter will discuss all the vital components of VMware licensing.

Become Familiar with VMware Licensing

How does VMware limit the number of installations a customer has in place? A manageable licensing process is necessary to enforce licensing compliance. Two methods can be used to enforce licensing: serial numbers and a licensing server.

Serial Numbers   Serial numbers are typically a complex alphanumeric code that enables software functionality and features. In some cases, serial numbers are associated with a particular email address or user's name to ensure that the serial number cannot be validated without both pieces of information.

VMware has many different products in their virtualization portfolio. Some products are targeted toward desktop use, while others are targeted at server, or enterprise, use. VMware Workstation, for instance, is a desktop-targeted application. Like many other desktop applications, VMware Workstation uses a simple serial number to unlock the product. This licensing method does not limit the number of systems the application may be installed on. The intended audience for VMware Workstation consists of systems administrators, software developers, and users who wish to use virtual appliances locally.

VMware originally licensed ESX servers using serial numbers the same way as VMware Workstation did. Additional features like virtual symmetric multiprocessing (vSMP) or vMotion required additional license keys. Unfortunately for VMware, this licensing model does not prevent unauthorized product installations.

Since the introduction of Virtual Infrastructure 3 (VI3), basic serial numbers installed on a host are designated as *host licenses*. Host licenses behave in the same fashion as workstation licenses; they can be installed many times, on separate servers. Licensing ESX in this way is not much different from licensing VMware Workstation.

VMware ESX or ESXi can still be configured with a host license today, but many of the advanced features of vSphere, such as vMotion or Distributed Resource Scheduling, inherently require vCenter control. When coupled with a vCenter installation, only the number of licensed hosts can be managed. This restricts the number of host license installations that can be used in an enterprise.

With the introduction of vSphere 5, VMware also chose to limit the amount of virtual machine memory that can be used in an environment. VMware refers to this as a vRAM entitlement. Each purchased license allows a defined set of virtual machine memory to be consumed on any host in the environment. VMware refers to this as a "pay for consumption" approach. Touted as "cloud-like" and flexible, this model allows organizations as well as public and private cloud providers to tie licensing more closely to end-user workloads rather than to physical machines.

Licensing Server Without a central licensing model, it is difficult to manage advanced features such as High Availability, Distributed Resource Scheduling, and vMotion. Advanced features are often the reason vSphere is chosen over other virtualization platforms on the market. Limiting the use of advanced features is key to VMware's business model. To this end, VMware uses a central location to manage licensing of all ESXi hosts in the environment, pool the allocated vRAM entitlement, and provide the ability to limit advanced features.

To make license management more flexible, and to enable management of advanced features, VMware uses server-based licenses in conjunction with a licensing server. Serial numbers, or a license file, are loaded into a license server. The sole purpose of this license server is to answer network requests from hosts, grant a license, and enable any advanced features licensed. A VMware host will query the license server for authorization to enable use as well as to unlock licensed features. The license server option ensures that only the number of licenses and vRAM entitlement purchased can be used. When all available licenses have been issued, no additional licenses may be granted. Similarly, when the licensed pool of vRAM is exhausted by powered-on virtual machines, any additional virtual machines that are powered on are said to be out of compliance. The sum total of vRAM entitlements for all vSphere licenses of a single

Building a VMware vSphere Environment

PART I

edition determines the total amount of virtual machine memory that can be consumed across all hosts.

NOTE VMware vCenter Essentials is the only product to impose a hard limit on consumed vRAM. vCenter Standard only provides alerts that consumed vRAM is approaching or has surpassed available pooled capacity and will continue to allow virtual machines to be powered on even after the vRAM limit has been reached.

VI3 used a separately installed Macromedia FlexLM service to provide licenses to hosts, but vSphere versions 4 and 5 use vCenter to directly issue licenses. When using vCenter 4 or 5 along with hosts of the same version, you can assign licenses distinctly to hosts, providing additional flexibility when many licenses for multiple editions are used.

Review the Versions of vSphere

To determine which version of vSphere to license, you must know which features are included with which edition. Similarly, to understand how the licensing has changed from vSphere 4 to vSphere 5, you must know which editions and features were available in vSphere 4, what is available in vSphere 5, and how the older offerings relate to the new vSphere editions. It is also important to understand the vRAM entitlement introduced with vSphere 5.

Table 4.1 presents the features available with different editions of vSphere 4.

Table 4.1: vSphere 4 editions

Features	Essentials	Essentials Plus	Standard	Advanced	Enterprise	Enterprise Plus
Cores	6	6	6	12	6	12
Virtual SMP	4-way	4-way	4-way	4-way	4-way	8-way
Host RAM	256 GB	256 GB	256 GB	256 GB	256 GB	Unlimited
Thin Virtual Disks	X	X	X	X	X	X

Features	Essentials	Essentials Plus	Standard	Advanced	Enterprise	Enterprise Plus
vCenter Agent	X	X	X	X	X	X
Update Manager	X	X	X	X	X	X
VMSafe	X	X	X	X	X	X
vStorage APIs	X	X	X	X	X	X
High Availability		X	X	X	X	X
Data Recovery		X		X	X	X
Hot Add Hardware to Guests				X	X	X
Fault Tolerance				X	X	X
vShield Zones				X	X	X
vMotion				X	X	X
Storage vMotion					X	X
DRS					X	X
vNetwork Distributed Switch						X
Host Profiles						X
Third-party multipa-thing						X

vSphere 5 consolidated the number of editions from six to five, and introduced the concept of pooled vRAM entitlements to remove physical constraints on processor cores and RAM. Each vSphere 5 CPU license entitles the purchaser to a specific amount of vRAM, or memory configured to virtual machines. Table 4.2 outlines the vSphere 5 editions and their features.

Table 4.2: vSphere 5 editions

Features	Essentials	Essentials Plus	Standard	Enterprise	Enterprise Plus
Processor Entitlement	Per 1 CPU	Per 1 CPU	Per 1 CPU	Per 1 CPU	Per 1 CPU
vRAM Entitlement	32 GB	32 GB	32 GB	64 GB	96 GB
Virtual SMP	8-way	8-way	8-way	8-way	32-way
Thin Provisioning	X	X	X	X	X
Update Manager	X	X	X	X	X
Storage APIs for Data Protection	X	X	X	X	X
High Availability		X	X	X	X
Data Recovery		X	X	X	X
vMotion		X	X	X	X
Virtual Serial Port Concentrator				X	X
Hot Add				X	X
Fault Tolerance				X	X
vShield Zones				X	X
Storage APIs for Array Integration				X	X
Storage APIs for Multipathing				X	X
Storage vMotion				X	X
DRS/DPM				X	X

Features	Essentials	Essentials Plus	Standard	Enterprise	Enterprise Plus
Distributed Switch					X
Host Profiles					X
Storage I/O Control					X
Network I/O Control					X
Auto Deploy					X
Storage DRS					X
Profile-Driven Storage					X

As you can see, with the exception of new Enterprise Plus additions, features remain largely unchanged from vSphere 4 to vSphere 5. For users who have vSphere 4, it is important to know how licensing has changed, including the move to vRAM entitlements. VMware Support and Subscription (SnS) is required for upgrading from vSphere 4 to vSphere 5. Table 4.3 lists the editions entitled to users who have a current SnS agreement.

Table 4.3: VMware edition upgrades for SnS entitlements

vSphere 4 Edition	vSphere 5 Edition	Added Features
Essentials	Essentials	8-way vSMP
Essentials Plus	Essentials Plus	8-way vSMP
		vMotion
		High Availability
Standard	Standard	8-way vSMP
		vMotion
Standard with vMotion and Storage vMotion	Enterprise	DRS/DPM

Table 4.3: VMware edition upgrades for SnS entitlements *(continued)*

vSphere 4 Edition	vSphere 5 Edition	Added Features
		Fault Tolerance
		Hot Add
		vShield Zones
Advanced	Enterprise	8-way vSMP
		DRS/DPM
		Storage vMotion
Enterprise	Enterprise	8-way vSMP
Enterprise Plus	Enterprise Plus	32-way vSMP
		Storage DRS
		Profile-Driven Storage
		Auto Deploy

As you can see in Table 4.3, there are no SnS upgrades to the Essentials, Essentials Plus, Enterprise, and Enterprise Plus editions. However, VMware has chosen to add features to all editions. These are upgrade paths that VMware has provided to give additional features to existing users, while augmenting existing vSphere 4 product offerings.

Review the Licensing Method in vSphere

VMware has always been very responsive to customer feedback. After learning that the FlexLM licensing engine in VI3 was problematic, VMware completely rewrote their own licensing management mechanism in vSphere 4. The new vCenter integrated engine vastly improved reliability and ease of use over the previous generation. The vCenter integration goes unchanged in vSphere 5.

> **NOTE** The FlexLM license server is still required if you're using vCenter 4 or vCenter 5 to manage ESX 3.x or ESX 3.5 hosts. It can be downloaded from VMware and installed separately.

When vCenter is initially installed, if no license is provided, it will operate with all features (i.e., Enterprise Plus) enabled for 60 days. If a license is provided, the features available to vCenter will be determined by those associated with the license key purchased.

When you are connected to vCenter, you can enter or install licenses for ESX 4.0, 4.1, ESXi 4.0, 4.1, and 5.0 hosts. To accomplish this, you use the licensing functions in the vSphere Client interface.

If licenses are not installed for ESX and ESXi hosts, they will operate for up to 60 days with no vRAM restrictions and all features enabled. Additional licensed features can be installed into the vCenter license service using the same method used for installing ESX and ESXi host licenses.

Manage Licenses

As mentioned earlier, the process of installing licenses in vSphere 5 is the same as that in vSphere 4, with the exception of vRAM entitlements. In both versions, adding licenses is performed through the vSphere Client that directly interfaces with vCenter.

Install Licenses

To add the license purchased for vCenter and ESX or ESXi hosts:

1. Log in to vCenter using the vSphere Client.

2. Once connected, load Licensing Administration by selecting View ➤ Administration ➤ Licensing (see Figure 4.1), or by pressing Ctrl+Shift+L.

Figure 4.1: License administration

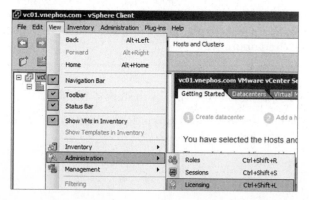

Building a VMware vSphere Environment

PART I

3. The currently installed licenses will be displayed on the licensing management tab, as shown in Figure 4.2, which shows a vCenter Server and an ESXi host in Evaluation mode.

Figure 4.2: Licensing management

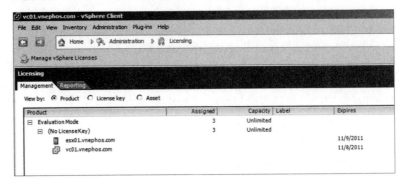

Click Manage vSphere Licenses to manage licenses in the vSphere environment.

4. The first licensing action available is Add License Keys. Enter a license key in the large window on the right. License keys are not case-sensitive and will be automatically displayed in uppercase when entered.

5. Enter a name for the license, such as vCenter Server License, to identify the type of license being added, and select Add License Keys.

TIP   Entering a descriptive name in the label field is extremely helpful, especially in medium to large environments in which license management is complex due to the large quantities and different types of licenses, and the presence of reused/recycled licenses for rolling upgrades.

---

6. Enter any additional license keys as in steps 4 and 5.

7. Review the licenses in the details window, as shown in Figure 4.3.

Figure 4.3: Review licenses added

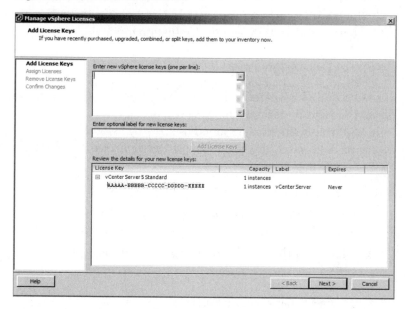

Click Next three times to get to the confirmation window. Figure 4.4 shows the licenses that have been added.

Figure 4.4: Confirmation of added licenses

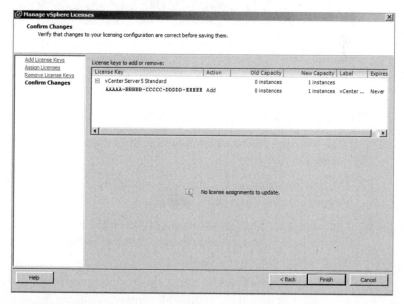

8. Click Finish to complete the license installation.

During initial installation, licenses may also be assigned to resources, including vCenter or hosts. Licenses can also be assigned after installation. That process will be detailed in the next section.

Assign Licenses

For vCenter and hosts to be able to leverage the features purchased, licenses have to be assigned to these resources.

In vSphere, features are granted to hosts by assigning licenses in Licensing Administration. To assign licenses purchased for vCenter and ESX or ESXi hosts:

1. Log in to vCenter using the vSphere Client.

2. Once connected, load Licensing Administration by selecting View ➤ Administration ➤ Licensing or by pressing Ctrl+Shift+L.

3. The currently installed licenses will be displayed in the Licensing screen, shown in Figure 4.5.

Figure 4.5: Currently installed licenses

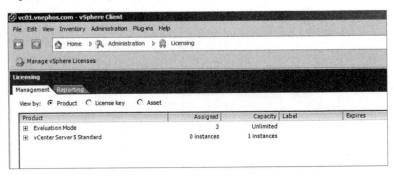

4. Click Manage vSphere Licenses to manage licenses in the vSphere environment.

5. The first licensing action available is Add License Keys. Click Next to continue to Assign Licenses.

6. The Assign Licenses window can display unlicensed assets, licensed assets, or all assets. Ensure that the Show Unlicensed Assets radio button is selected.

7. To assign licenses to ESX or ESXi hosts, select the ESX tab to display hosts that are currently unlicensed. This can be seen in

Building a VMware
vSphere Environment

PART I

Figure 4.6. To assign licenses to a vCenter Server, select the vCenter tab instead, as shown in Figure 4.7.

Figure 4.6: Assigning ESX/ESXi assets

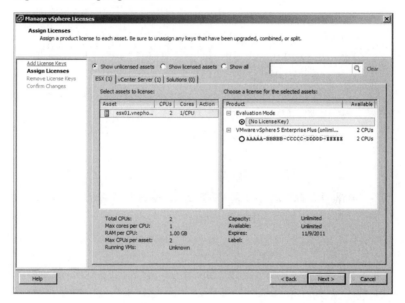

Figure 4.7: Unlicensed vCenter asset

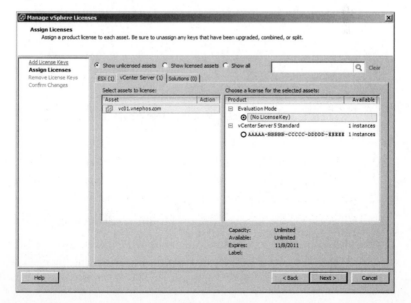

8. To assign a license to a single asset, click on a host in the Select Assets To License window. Then select a radio button next to the desired product in the Choose A License For The Selected Assets window.

9. To assign a license to multiple assets, hold the Ctrl key, and click on each host in the Select Assets To License window. Then select a radio button next to the desired product in the Choose A License For The Selected Assets window.

10. Once the licenses have been assigned to the hosts, a green circle with a check mark will be displayed to the right of the host in the Action field. You can see this in Figure 4.8 and Figure 4.9.

Figure 4.8: ESX licenses added

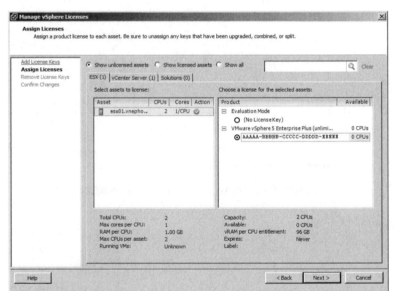

11. Select the Show Licensed Assets radio button to verify that the ESX hosts and vCenter Server or servers have been properly licensed.

12. Click Next two times to proceed to the confirmation window.

13. The confirmation window will show which licenses have been assigned to which assets, as well as which previous licenses were assigned to those assets. You can see this in Figure 4.10.

Figure 4.9: vCenter license assigned

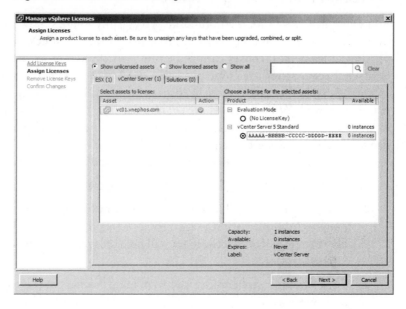

Figure 4.10: Confirming the assigned licenses

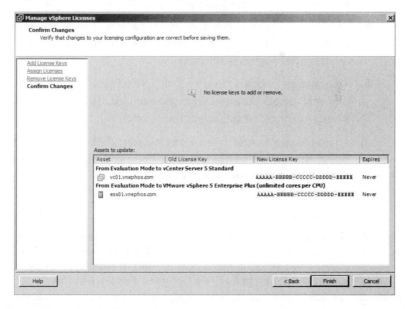

14. Click Finish to complete the license assignment process.

Unassign and Remove Licenses

Removing licenses is not a common task. Typically, there's only one time that licenses would be removed: to replace evaluation licenses with purchased licenses. Licenses cannot be removed while they are assigned to assets because they are currently being used. Assets such as hosts or vCenter Servers must have their licenses unassigned before the licenses can be removed. When licenses are *unassigned*, they are disassociated from hosts or vCenter Servers. When licenses are *removed*, they are deleted from the vSphere installation.

To unassign and remove licenses for vCenter and ESX or ESXi hosts:

1. Log in to the vCenter Server using the vSphere Client.

2. Once connected, load Licensing Administration by selecting View ➤ Administration ➤ Licensing or by pressing Ctrl+Shift+L. The currently installed licenses will be displayed in Licensing Administration.

3. Click Manage vSphere Licenses to manage licenses in the vSphere environment.

4. The first licensing action available is Add License Keys; click Next to continue to Assign Licenses.

5. The Assign Licenses window will default to displaying unlicensed assets, licensed assets, or all assets. Ensure that the Show Licensed Assets radio button is selected.

6. To unassign licenses from ESX or ESXi hosts, select the ESX tab to display hosts that are currently licensed. To unassign a license from a vCenter Server, select the vCenter tab instead.

7. To unassign a license from a single asset, click on a host in the Select Assets To License window. Then select a radio button next to No License Key in the Choose A License For The Selected Assets window.

NOTE   To unassign a license from multiple assets, hold the Ctrl key, and click on each host in the Select Assets To License window. Then select a radio button next to No License Key in the Choose A License For The Selected Assets window.

Once the licenses have been unassigned, a green circle with a check mark will be displayed to the right of the host in the Action field.

8. Select the Show Unlicensed Assets radio button to verify that the ESX or ESXi hosts and vCenter Server have had their licenses unassigned.

9. Click Next to proceed to the Remove Licenses window.

   Licenses that are not currently assigned to any assets are now available to be removed from vCenter.

10. Select the check box next to each license that is to be removed.

11. Click Next to proceed to the confirmation window.

12. Figure 4.11 shows licenses to be removed in the topmost pane. The licenses that have been unassigned from each of the assets, as well as which previous licenses were assigned to those assets, appear in the bottom pane.

Figure 4.11: Confirming that licenses have been removed

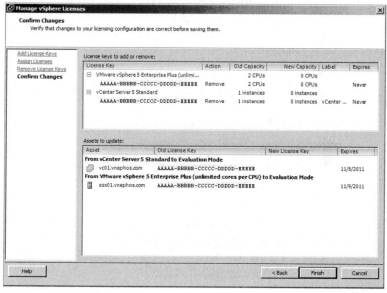

13. Click Finish to complete the license removal process.

   The process is the same for installing new production licenses and removing evaluation licenses, except that you would assign the new licenses to ESX and vCenter assets, rather than choose No License Key during the unassign process.

Change Licenses Assigned to Assets

Changing licenses assigned to assets can be accomplished in two ways:

- Through the Manage vSphere Licenses action item, as described in several earlier sections of this chapter. Depending on the number of assets in the environment, this might not be the most efficient way to perform the task.

- Through the Management tab in the Licensing component of vCenter.

To change licenses assigned to assets using the Licensing component of vCenter:

1. Log in to the vCenter Server using the vSphere Client.

2. Once connected, load Licensing Administration by selecting View ➤ Administration ➤ Licensing or by pressing Ctrl+Shift+L. The currently installed licenses will be displayed in Licensing Administration.

3. Right-click on the asset that will have its license changed, and choose Change License Key, as shown in Figure 4.12.

Figure 4.12: Selecting Change License Key

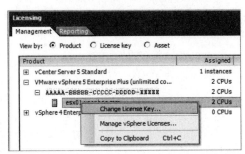

4. The Assign License dialog box will appear, as shown in Figure 4.13.

Figure 4.13: Assign License dialog box

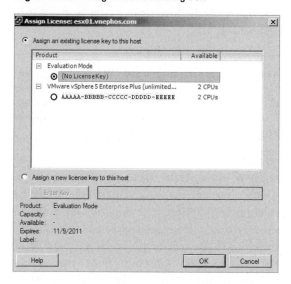

5. To assign an existing license, ensure that Assign An Existing License Key To This Host is selected, and select the radio button next to the license that is to be used.

6. To assign a new license key, select Assign A New License Key To This Host and press the Enter key. When prompted by the Add License Key dialog box, enter the new license key.

7. Click OK to complete the license reassignment or addition.

Install Licenses for Legacy Hosts

In VI3, a license server is required for the licensing of vCenter Server, ESX hosts, and ESXi hosts. This is still a requirement when using vCenter for vSphere with 3.5 ESX and ESXi hosts. This is because the previous generation of ESX does not know how to communicate with the integrated licensing of vSphere.

A typical practice when upgrading a VI3 environment is to first upgrade the vCenter Server to the highest possible revision, or build, that will accommodate the newest build of ESX or ESXi in the environment. The license server from the VI3 installation is still required to facilitate the use of ESX or ESXi 3.5 hosts.

If the license server is removed from the upgraded vCenter Server, it must be downloaded from VMware's website, because it is not included with the vSphere distribution.

TIP   It is a VMware best practice to install the license server on the same system as the vSphere vCenter Server. This is less complicated than using another system to host the licensing service, and still fulfills the requirement of only one Windows installation in the environment.

You might wonder, why not upgrade all hosts at the same time as you are upgrading the vCenter Server? Some administrators might feel more comfortable using vCenter for vSphere in production for a short time before upgrading hosts. In other situations, some hosts may not be able to be upgraded because they aren't included on the vSphere Hardware Compatibility List. Because vSphere hosts are typically more expensive than standard servers, it may not be financially feasible to replace them for a considerable time.

To manage legacy hosts in a vSphere environment:

1. Download the license server from the VMware website, or use the most recent distribution from vCenter Server for VI3 media.

2. Run the license server installation to begin.

3. When proceeding through the installation dialog boxes, choose all the defaults until you reach the Provide Licensing Info window. Enter the path to the license file obtained from the VMware License Portal, or an existing license file. Click Next, then Install, followed by Finish to complete the license server installation.

4. Log in to the vCenter Server using the vSphere Client.

5. Once connected, load vCenter Server Settings by selecting Administration ➢ vCenter Server Settings, shown in Figure 4.14.

Figure 4.14: Loading vCenter server settings

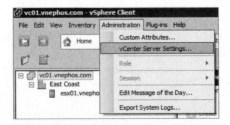

6. Select the Licensing menu from the left pane to access licensing settings.

7. In the License Server section, enter the FQDN or IP address of the system where the license server service is running. This can be the vCenter Server or another system that is running the service, as shown in Figure 4.15.

Figure 4.15: Entering the address of the license server

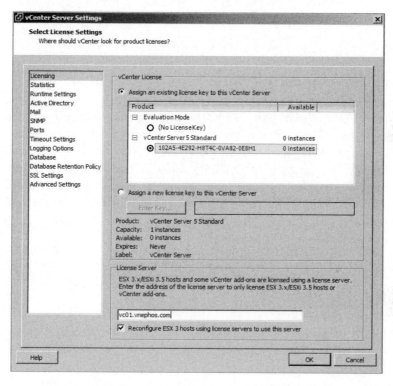

8. Ensure that the Reconfigure ESX 3 hosts using license servers to use this server check box is selected. This allows vCenter to manage the licenses that the ESX hosts are using.

9. Click OK to accept the changes.

10. To ensure the licenses are installed and recognized by vCenter, load the licensing window in vSphere by pressing Ctrl+Shift+L or selecting View ➤ Administration ➤ Licensing.

11. Figure 4.16 shows the License Server and any vSphere licenses. Click the plus (+) sign to the left of the License Server listed to view the licenses that are loaded by the license server.

Figure 4.16: Licensing Management tab

As you can see, managing licenses for legacy VI3 hosts is slightly more complicated than for ESX or ESXi version 4 and 5 hosts. There are some additional limitations when using legacy hosts. For example, you cannot manage host features from a central location. Legacy hosts have to be configured individually, through each host's configuration menu, to enable or disable features such as HA, DRS, and vMotion. Another limitation is that a vSphere 4 or 5 vCenter server can point only to a single legacy license server. This means that legacy licenses/license servers must be consolidated.

Review Installed Licenses

In any environment, it is important to know which licenses are currently in use, and whether all licenses are being leveraged appropriately. Once licenses have been installed and assigned, it is important to review them for compliance and to ensure they are assigned appropriately.

New licenses are often purchased along with new equipment. In other situations, equipment is replaced, and it is necessary to reassign licenses from older equipment to newer equipment.

VMware has provided a reporting function in the Licensing component of vCenter Server. Reporting can be viewed by Product, License Key, or Asset. This reporting function replaces the VMware Licensing Portal, which can only be accessed with Internet connectivity to VMware's website and provides only the ability to view purchased licenses. By using the reporting function in vSphere, you can easily determine which assets are using licenses.

View Licenses by Product

When you are reviewing licensing, it is good to know what products are installed in the environment. Reviewing this information is easy in the License Administration screen:

1. When connected to vCenter, load Licensing Administration by selecting View ➤ Administration ➤ Licensing or by pressing Ctrl+Shift+L.

2. The currently installed licenses will be displayed in the management tab of Licensing Administration and appear according to product.

3. By default, the listings display only the product names, the number assigned, and the total number of licenses or capacity. To get a more detailed view, click the plus (+) sign to the left of the product name. For vSphere products, the license key, the number assigned, the capacity, the label assigned to the key, and an expiration of the key, if any, will be displayed.

Figure 4.17 shows a typical view, including vCenter Server, a licensed ESXi 5 host, and unassigned ESX 4 licenses.

Figure 4.17: License view by product

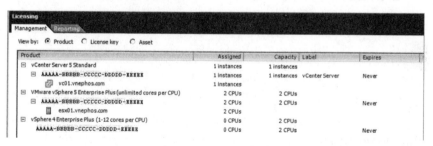

You can export this license information by clicking Export. Information organized by product will be exported to one of five different formats: comma-separated values (CSV), Microsoft Excel Workbook (XLS), Extensible Markup Language (XML), or one of two possible Hypertext Markup Language (HTML) options.

View Licenses by License Key

Viewing licensing by license key makes it easy to see which products have assets assigned. To view licenses and the products that have been assigned to those keys:

1. When connected to vCenter, load Licensing Administration by selecting View ➢ Administration ➢ Licensing or by pressing Ctrl+Shift+L.

2. The currently installed licenses will be displayed in Licensing Administration and appear according to product.

3. Click the License Key radio button to change the report to show license keys and the assets associated with them. By default, the different license keys display the license key, the product, the number assigned, the capacity, the label given, and the expiration date, if any.

4. To get a better view of which vSphere assets are using which licenses, click the plus (+) sign to the left of the product name. For vSphere products, the license key, the number assigned, the capacity, the label assigned to the key, and an expiration of the key, if any, will be displayed.

NOTE   Legacy clients will not be visible in the License Key view, because they are not licensed by a key.

Figure 4.18 shows license information with the license key as the primary reporting item. Notice that legacy clients are not visible in this report.

Figure 4.18: License view by license key

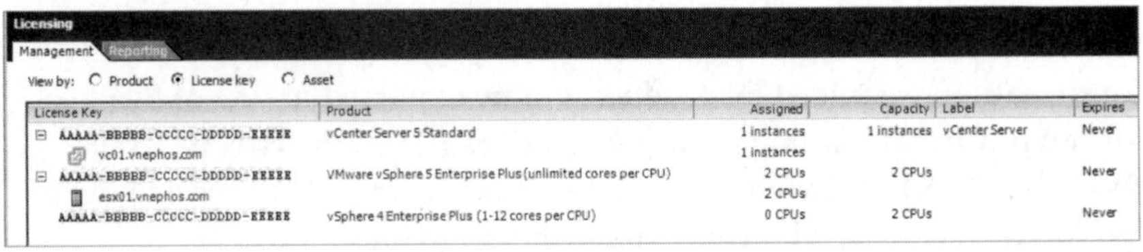

View Licenses by Asset

Viewing licensing by asset simplifies the process of determining which license is assigned to an asset. To view the Assets:

1. When connected to vCenter, load Licensing Administration by selecting View ➤ Administration ➤ Licensing or by pressing Ctrl+Shift+L.

2. The currently installed licenses will be displayed in Licensing Administration and appear according to product.

3. Click the Asset radio button to change the report to show assets.

This is the least detailed view, showing only the asset, the product assigned, the license key assigned, and the expiration date.

Figure 4.19 shows each asset in the environment and the licenses associated with each asset. This view is useful when you specifically want to know how an asset is licensed without having to drill down into the product or license keys views.

Figure 4.19: License view by asset

5

Upgrading to vSphere 5

IN THIS CHAPTER, YOU WILL LEARN TO:

This chapter provides information for existing VMware Infrastructure 4 (VI4) customers on how to upgrade to VMware vSphere 5.

Prepare for the Upgrade

Before starting the upgrade from vSphere 4 to vSphere 5, it is prudent to take the time to properly prepare. This section provides some tasks that you should complete before starting the upgrade process. Completing these tasks will help ensure that your upgrade is smooth and successful with a minimum of downtime.

Verify that the vCenter Server 5.0 hardware requirements are met.   VMware recommends a minimum of 4 GB of RAM for vCenter Server 5.0. If the database server will be running on the same system, the installed RAM should be even higher. Be sure to double-check the hardware requirements in the VMware vSphere Documentation for vCenter Server 5.0 and ensure that the system that is intended to run vCenter Server 5.0 meets those minimum requirements. It is a VMware best practice to install vCenter Server as a VM.

Verify database compatibility with vCenter Server 5.0.   vCenter Server 5.0 adds support for some databases and removes support for other databases.

If you are using one of the older databases, you must complete a database upgrade to a supported version before starting the upgrade to vCenter Server 5.0.

> **Databases Supported in vCenter Server 5.0**   Oracle 10g R2, Oracle 11g, SQL Server 2005 Express, SQL Server 2005, SQL Server 2008 and R2
>
> **Databases No Longer Supported in vCenter Server 5.0**   Oracle 9*i*, SQL Server 2000

Make a complete backup of the vCenter Server database.   Because the vCenter Server 5.0 upgrade will upgrade the database scheme, you will want to have a complete backup of the vCenter 4.*x* database before starting the upgrade.

Make a complete backup of the vCenter 4.*x* SSL certificates.   To be able to successfully "roll back" after a failed upgrade, you must have not only a copy of the database, but also a copy of the SSL certificates. Ensure that you have a complete backup of the vCenter 4.*x* SSL certificates.

Ensure that you have sufficient database permissions to upgrade the database. The upgrade to vCenter Server 5.0 modifies the database schema, and so you need elevated permissions on the database in order for this operation to succeed. Ensure that you have the proper permissions on the external database before starting the upgrade.

- On an Oracle system, the user should have the DBA role.

- On a SQL Server database, the user should have the db_owner role on both the vCenter Server database as well as the MSDB System database.

NOTE The permissions on the MSDB database are required only during the upgrade and can be removed after the upgrade is complete. It is considered a best practice to remove this permission post-upgrade.

Locate and verify the username and password used by vCenter to authenticate to external databases. You must have the login credentials, the database name, and the database server name used for the vCenter Server database. If this information is not available, the vCenter Server upgrade routine will not be able to upgrade the database.

Make sure the name of the vCenter Server computer is less than 15 characters long. vCenter Server 5.0 requires that the name of the computer be less than 15 characters. If the name is longer, you will need to shorten it. If the database server runs on the same computer, access to the database could be impacted by the name change. If you change the name of the computer, be sure to update the Open Database Connectivity (ODBC) Data Source Name (DSN) information appropriately.

Verify the upgrade path to vCenter Server 5.0. VirtualCenter 1.*x* cannot be upgraded to vCenter Server 5.0. You must perform a fresh installation of vCenter Server 5.0 instead or upgrade from 1.x to 2.5, then upgrade from 2.5.

Ensure that all ESX/ESXi host hardware is listed on the VMware Hardware Compatibility List (HCL).   Administrators should verify that all hardware in the ESX/ESXi hosts is listed on the VMware HCL for VMware vSphere 5.0. Hardware components that are not found on the HCL should be replaced with compatible components in order to ensure maximum compatibility and supportability.

NOTE   One area that might cause a problem in upgrade scenarios is 64-bit compatibility. Earlier versions of ESX/ESXi ran on 32-bit CPUs, but ESXi 5.0 requires 64-bit CPUs. Be sure to confirm that your server's CPUs are fully 64-bit-compatible.

Verify the upgrade path to ESXi 5.0.   Only environments running ESX 3.0 or later can upgrade to ESXi 5.0. Environments running ESX 2.5.5 might be able to upgrade, depending on the partition layout. ESX 2.5.5 servers with the default partition layout will not be able to upgrade to ESXi 5.0. ESX servers earlier than ESX 2.5.5 do not support an upgrade to ESXi 5.0.

After you have gone through all of the tasks listed in this section, you are ready to proceed with the upgrade of your environment from VI4 to VMware vSphere 5.

Upgrade vCenter Server

The first step in the process of upgrading your environment from vSphere 4 to vSphere 5 is upgrading vCenter Server 4.x to vCenter Server 5.0. After that step is completed, you have a variety of paths to take to get the ESX/ESXi hosts and virtual machines upgraded. You have to complete the upgrade to vCenter Server 5.0 before those options are available, because failing to upgrade vCenter Server 4.x to vCenter Server 5.0 first can result in downtime, a loss of connectivity, and the risk of potential data loss. Always be sure to upgrade vCenter Server before upgrading any other components in the VMware vSphere environment.

In most cases, you'll want to upgrade vCenter Server on the same system, as described in the next section.

It's also possible to perform an upgrade from vCenter on one system to vCenter Server 5.0 on a different system. This approach is necessary if, during the upgrade, you want to move to a 64-bit platform (vCenter

Server 5.0 supports 64-bit versions of Windows Server). This process is described in the next section.

Upgrade to vCenter Server 5.0 on the Same System

In many cases, you'll perform the upgrade from vCenter 4.*x* to vCenter Server 5.0 on the same physical system. You might consider this an in-place upgrade, because vCenter 4.*x* will be upgraded in place to vCenter Server 5.0.

Before starting the VirtualCenter 4.*x* upgrade to vCenter Server 5.0, be sure the following tasks have been completed:

- You've made a backup of the vCenter database.

- You have a backup copy of the vCenter SSL certificates.

- You have the username and password that will be used for database access.

- You have ensured that the database server software is compatible.

If these tasks have been successfully completed, you are ready to upgrade to vCenter Server 5.0.

To upgrade vCenter 4.x to vCenter Server 5.0, perform these steps:

1. Log in to the computer running vCenter Server 4.x as a user with administrative permissions.

2. Click Start ➤ Control Panel.

3. Open Administrative Tools, and then double-click Services.

4. Find the VMware vCenter Server service and stop the service.

5. Insert the VMware vCenter media into the DVD drive. Autoplay will automatically launch the VMware vCenter Installer.

6. Click the link to install vCenter Server. This launches the installer for vCenter Server.

7. When prompted, select a language for the installer and click OK.

8. At the Welcome page for the vCenter Server installer, click Next.

9. Select I Agree To The Terms In The License Agreement and click Next.

10. Enter the license key for vCenter Server. If you do not yet have the license key, you can omit the license key to allow vCenter Server to run in evaluation mode. You can license vCenter Server later using vSphere Client. Click Next to continue.

Building a VMware vSphere Environment

PART I

11. Enter the database username and password for authentication to the database specified by the existing DSN. If you are using Windows NT authentication, you can leave the username and password blank. Click Next.

NOTE If you are using Windows NT authentication, the logged-on user during the installation process should be the same user that is used to access the database.

---

12. Select Yes I Want To Upgrade My vCenter Server Database to upgrade the database schema. This step is required in order to proceed with the upgrade.

13. Select I Have Taken A Backup Of The Existing vCenter Server Database And SSL Certificates and then click Next.

14. Specify the user account under which the vCenter Server service should run. If the database is using Windows NT authentication, this account should be the same account specified earlier in the wizard and the same account that has been configured for access to the database. Click Next to continue.

15. Accept the default port numbers and click Next.

16. Click Install to start the upgrade process.

Upgrade to vCenter Server 5.0 on a Different System

In this scenario, you upgrade vCenter 4.*x* on one system to vCenter Server 5.0 on a different system.

NOTE vCenter 5.0 uses 64-bit ODBC DSNs.

To upgrade to vCenter Server 5.0 on a different system, follow these steps:

1. Copy the SSL certificates from the source system (the system running vCenter 4.*x*) to the destination system (the system that will run vCenter Server 5.0). On a Windows Server 2003 system, the SSL certificates are located in %ALLUSERSPROFILE%\Application Data\VMware\VMware VirtualCenter. On a Windows Server 2008 system, the SSL certificates are located in %ALLUSERSPROFILE%\ VMware\VMware VirtualCenter.

2. Create a 64-bit DSN that points to the existing database.

3. On the destination system, run the vCenter Server installer and follow the steps outlined in the previous section to install vCenter Server 5.0.

Regardless of the method used, after the vCenter Server upgrade, there are some postupgrade tasks that you need to perform. We'll describe these tasks next.

Install vCenter Server Appliance

New in vSphere 5.0 is the addition of the vCenter Server Appliance. VSA is an OVF which installs in about five minutes with no need for MS licensing, because it runs on SLES 11 embedded with DB2 Express. The VSA increases efficiency in your lifecycle by management because it does not require an upgrade of vCenter with each version; instead, you simply deploy a new VSA. Supported with this VSA are HA for high availability and snapshots for backup. (See Chapter 1, "Introduction to vSphere," for more information about new features.)

To install vCenter Server Appliance, follow these steps:

1. From the vSphere Client, choose File ➤ Deploy OVF Template.

2. Choose the source of the OVF File. You can enter a URL to install the package from the Internet or click the Browse button to locate the package on your computer, a network share, or a CD/DVD drive.

3. Verify the details of the Template (see Figure 5.1).

Figure 5.1: OVF Template details

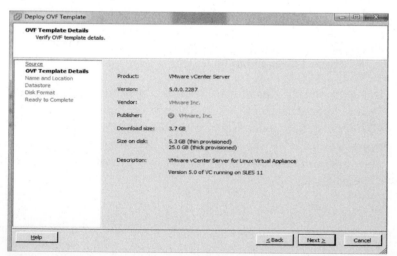

4. Choose a name for the vCenter Server.

5. Select the datastore the files will be stored on.

6. Choose the format you want to use for the virtual disks (VMDK provisioning type). You can choose Thin Provisioned Format or Thick Provisioned Format.

7. Review details and click Finish.

At this point, vCenter Server Appliance is installed and you can use it to manage the new environment. The embedded DB2 Express is supported for 5 ESXi hosts and 50 Virtual Machines; Oracle is supported as an external database for larger deployments.

Perform Postupgrade Tasks

Once the upgrade to vCenter Server 5.0 is complete, there are a number of postupgrade tasks that administrators need to perform. These tasks include upgrading additional vCenter modules like vCenter Update Manager, vCenter Converter, or Guided Consolidation; upgrading vSphere Client and plug-ins; and verifying license settings. You'll learn how to perform these tasks in the next few sections.

Upgrade Additional vCenter Modules

When you upgrade to vCenter Server 5.0, you must also upgrade the plug-ins that extend vCenter's functionality. On the VMware vCenter installation media, VMware provides installers for three vCenter Server plug-ins:

- vCenter Update Manager (VUM)
- vCenter Converter
- Guided Consolidation

If you were using a previous version of any of these plug-ins, you'll need to upgrade each of these to the version supplied on the VMware vCenter installer media. Refer to the *vSphere Upgrade Guide*, available from VMware's website at http://www.vmware.com/support/pubs, for more in-depth information on the upgrade process for each of these plug-ins.

Upgrade vSphere Client

Both ESXi and vCenter Server provide a simple web interface that makes it easy to download vSphere Client. Since at this point in the upgrade process, you've only upgraded vCenter Server and not any of the ESXi hosts, you'll only be able to use vCenter Server's web interface to download and install vSphere Client.

Building a VMware vSphere Environment

PART I

> **NOTE** It is possible to have both VMware vSphere Client and the older VMware Infrastructure Client installed on the same system at the same time. This might help ease the transition into the newer version of the software.

To download and install vSphere Client, follow these steps:

1. From the system onto which you want to install vSphere Client, open a web browser and navigate to the IP address or hostname of the vCenter Server computer.

2. Click the Download vSphere Client link.

3. Depending on the browser you use, you might be prompted to either save or run the file. If you are allowed to run the file, do so. Otherwise, save the file, and then double-click it after it has finished downloading.

4. Click the Next button on the welcome page of the VMware vSphere Client 5.0 installation wizard.

5. Click the radio button I Accept The Terms In The License Agreement and then click Next.

6. Specify a username and organization name and then click Next.

7. Configure the destination folder and then click Next.

8. Click the Install button to begin the installation.

9. Click the Finish button to complete the installation.

At this point, vSphere Client is installed and you can use it to manage the new environment. If the previous version was left installed, you can use the VI Client to manage older systems.

> **TIP** If you already have the VI Client installed to manage your VI4 environment, you can use it to log in to vCenter Server 5.0 to upgrade to vSphere Client.

Verify License Settings

In the event that you will have a mixed 3.*x*/4.*x*/5.0 environment for any length of time, you'll want to be sure that vCenter Server 5.0's license settings are correct. VMware vSphere 5 no longer needs or uses a license server, but older ESX/ESXi hosts still need a license server until they are upgraded to version 5.0. Depending on how the upgrade was handled, you might need to install a license server in order to service the older ESX/ESXi hosts.

Consider the following upgrade scenarios:

VirtualCenter with a local license server installed is upgraded to vCenter Server 5.0 on the same computer.　In this scenario, the license server for the VI3 environment was installed on the VirtualCenter Server computer before the upgrade to vCenter Server 5.0 on the same computer. The license server is preserved and remains operational after the upgrade is complete. You only need to verify that vCenter Server is using the local license server for ESX/ESXi 3.*x* hosts.

VirtualCenter with a remote license server is upgraded to vCenter Server 5.0 on the same computer.　The license server resides on a separate computer from the VirtualCenter Server computer, so it is unaffected by the upgrade to vCenter Server 5.0 and remains operational after the upgrade is complete. You just have to verify that vCenter Server 5.0 points ESX/ESXi 3.*x* hosts to the same remote license server.

VirtualCenter with a local license server installed is upgraded to vCenter Server 5.0 on a different computer.　The installation routine for vCenter Server 5.0 does not install a license server for legacy ESX/ESXi hosts, so the new computer running vCenter Server 5.0 will not have a functional legacy host license server running. If the old VirtualCenter Server computer is going to be retired, you must install a new license server into the environment and configure vCenter Server 5.0 to use that new license server for ESX/ESXi 3.*x* hosts.

VirtualCenter with a remote license server is upgraded to vCenter Server 5.0 on a different computer.　The license server is unaffected by the vCenter Server 5.0 upgrade and remains fully functional. You only need to configure vCenter Server 5.0 to use the license server for ESX/ESXi 3.*x* hosts.

To verify that vCenter Server 5.0 is using the correct license server for ESX/ESXi 3.*x* hosts, follow these steps:

1. With vSphere Client running and connected to a vCenter Server instance, select Administration ➤ vCenter Server Settings.

2. Select Licensing on the left.

3. At the bottom of the dialog box, in the License Server section, enter the correct license server host name or IP address that vCenter Server should use, as shown in Figure 5.2.

   Figure 5.2: Administrators should configure vCenter Server 5.0 to use the correct license server to provide licensing information to pre–vSphere ESX/ESXi hosts.

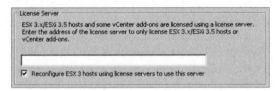

4. Click OK to save the settings and return to vSphere Client.

After completing these postupgrade tasks, vCenter Server 5.0 should be fully installed and fully operational in your environment. You're now ready to upgrade your ESX/ESXi hosts to version 5.0, as described in the next section.

Upgrade ESX/ESXi Hosts

Once you have upgraded vCenter Server to version 5.0, the process of upgrading the ESX/ESXi hosts to version 5.0 can start. You have three options for upgrading ESX/ESXi hosts:

- Use vCenter Update Manager (VUM).

- Perform a manual upgrade.

- Perform a fresh installation.

Each approach has its advantages and disadvantages. Table 5.1 compares the three approaches.

Table 5.1: Three approaches to upgrading hosts

Method	Advantages	Disadvantages
Use vCenter Update Manager.	Uses VUM and is integrated into vCenter Server. Maintains consistency.	No support for custom Service Console partitions in ESX.
Perform a manual upgrade.	Administrator has full control over the upgrade process and preserves legacy configuration information.	Custom Service Console partitions are not migrated correctly. Old mount points are preserved and additional disk space will be consumed. Lacks consistency and automation.
Perform a fresh installation.	Ensures a clean and consistent configuration of the ESXi hosts. Maintains consistency.	Some reconfiguration might be necessary after the installation unless host profiles are used.

You must evaluate which option best meets your specific needs. For organizations that already leverage vCenter Update Manager, using VUM to upgrade the ESX/ESXi hosts makes a lot of sense. Organizations that plan to use host profiles may find that using the fresh installation approach makes the most sense. Organizations that do not use VUM or host profiles might find that performing a manual upgrade makes the most sense.

The next section describes the first of these three approaches: using vCenter Update Manager to upgrade ESX/ESXi hosts.

Upgrade ESX/ESXi Using vCenter Update Manager

vCenter Update Manager not only provides the ability to patch ESX/ESXi hosts and selected guest operating systems, but also can assist in upgrading ESX/ESXi hosts to version 5.0. vCenter Update Manager will use a special type of baseline, a *host upgrade baseline*, to identify hosts that are not yet running ESXi 5.0 and specify how to upgrade the identified hosts to ESXi 5.0.

You must create the host upgrade baseline and then attach it to a container within vCenter Server, like a datacenter, folder, or cluster. After you have attached the baseline, a scan will identify those hosts that are not running ESXi 5.0, and initiating remediation will initiate the upgrade to ESXi 5.0 for the identified hosts.

NOTE   Upgrading an ESX/ESXi 3.x host to ESXi 5.0 requires an existing Virtual Machine File System (VMFS) volume. Depending on how ESX/ESXi 3.x was installed, the host might not have a VMFS volume. This would force a fresh install instead of an upgrade.

The first step, though, is creating the host upgrade baseline by performing the following steps:

1. In vSphere Client, navigate to the Update Manager Administration area by using the navigation bar or by selecting View ➤ Solutions and Applications ➤ Update Manager.

2. Click the Baselines And Groups tab. Make sure the view is set to Hosts, not VMs/VAs. Use the small buttons just below the tab bar to set the correct view.

3. Select the Upgrade Baselines tab.

4. Right-click a blank area of the Upgrade Baselines list and select New Baseline. The New Baseline Wizard starts.

5. Supply a name for the baseline and an optional description, and note that vSphere Client has automatically selected the type as Host Upgrade. Click Next to continue.

6. Select the ESX upgrade ISO and the ESXi upgrade zip files. You can use the Browse button to find the files on the vCenter Server computer or another location accessible across the network.

7. Click Next to upload the files and continue; note that the file upload might take a few minutes to complete.

8. After the file uploads and file imports are completed, click Next.

9. The next screen asks about where to place the storage for the ESX Service Console. The Service Console (referred to here as the COS, or the Console OS) resides within a virtual machine disk file (VMDK file). The upgrade baseline needs to know where to place the VMDK for the COS during the upgrade process.

10. Select Automatically Select a Datastore on the Local Host and click Next.

11. If the upgrade process fails or if the host is unable to reconnect to vCenter Server, VUM offers the option of automatically rebooting the host and "rolling back" the upgrade. You can disable that

option on the next screen by deselecting "Try to reboot the host and roll back the upgrade in case of failure." But for this exercise, leave this option selected and click Next to continue.

12. Review the summary of the options selected in the upgrade baseline. If anything is incorrect, use the Back button to go back and correct it. Otherwise, click Finish.

After you've created the host upgrade baseline, you must next attach the host upgrade baseline to one or more hosts, or to a container object like a datacenter, cluster, or folder. Let's look at attaching a baseline to a specific ESX/ESXi host. The process is much the same, if not identical, to the process for attaching a baseline to a datacenter, cluster, folder, or virtual machine.

Perform the following steps to attach the host upgrade baseline to an ESX/ESXi host:

1. Launch vSphere Client if it is not already running and connect to a vCenter Server instance.

NOTE You cannot manage, attach, or detach VUM baselines when vSphere Client is connected directly to an ESX/ESXi host using vSphere Client. You must be connected to an instance of vCenter Server.

---

2. From the menu, select View ➤ Inventory ➤ Hosts And Clusters, or press the Ctrl+Shift+H keyboard shortcut.

3. In the inventory tree on the left, select the ESX/ESXi host to which you want to attach the host upgrade baseline.

4. From the right pane, use the double-headed arrows to scroll through the list of tabs until you can see the Update Manager tab and then select it.

5. Click the Attach link in the upper-right corner; this link opens the Attach Baseline Or Group dialog box.

6. Select the host upgrade baseline that you want to attach to this ESX/ESXi host and then click Attach.

Next, you must scan the host for compliance with the attached baselines. On the Update Manager tab where you just attached the host upgrade baseline, there is a Scan link; click that link to initiate a scan. Be sure to select to scan for upgrades.

When the scan is complete, the results will show that the host is noncompliant (i.e., not running ESXi 5.0). To upgrade the host, use the Remediate button in the lower-right corner of the Update Manager tab. This launches the Remediate wizard.

To upgrade the host, follow these steps:

1. At the first screen, select the host upgrade baseline and then click Next.

2. Click the check box to accept the license terms and then click Next.

3. Review the settings specified in the host upgrade baseline. A blue hyperlink next to each setting allows you to modify the settings. To leave the settings as they were specified in the host upgrade baseline, simply click Next.

4. Specify a name, description, and a schedule for the upgrade and then click Next.

5. Review the settings and use the Back button to go back if any settings need to be changed. Click Finish when the settings are correct and you are ready to proceed with the upgrade.

vCenter Update Manager proceeds with the upgrade at the scheduled time (the default setting in the wizard is immediately). The upgrade will be an unattended upgrade, and at the end of the upgrade, the ESX/ESXi host automatically reboots. (See Figure 5.3.)

Figure 5.3: The vSphere Update Manager remediates a host for upgrade.

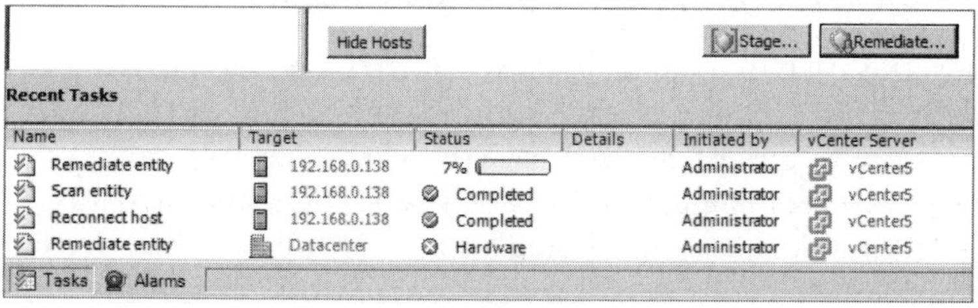

Name	Target	Status	Details	Initiated by	vCenter Server
Remediate entity	192.168.0.138	7%		Administrator	vCenter5
Scan entity	192.168.0.138	Completed		Administrator	vCenter5
Reconnect host	192.168.0.138	Completed		Administrator	vCenter5
Remediate entity	Datacenter	Hardware		Administrator	vCenter5

WARNING When you are using host upgrade baselines to upgrade your ESX hosts, custom Service Console partitions are not honored. (ESXi does not have a user-accessible Service Console, so this doesn't apply.) While the old partitions are preserved (their contents are kept intact and mounted under the /esx3-installation directory), the new Service Console will have a single partition mounted at the root directory. If you want your ESX 5.0 hosts to have a custom partition scheme after the upgrade, you won't want to use vCenter Update Manager and host upgrade baselines.

As you can see, using vCenter Update Manager creates a streamlined upgrade process. When combined with vCenter Update Manager to upgrade the VMware Tools and the virtual machine hardware, as described in the section titled "Perform Postupgrade Tasks" later in this chapter, this makes for an automated upgrade experience. Administrators who had not considered using vCenter Update Manager should reconsider based on this upgrade functionality.

For organizations that choose not to deploy vCenter Update Manager for whatever reason, their options for upgrading ESX/ESXi hosts are to upgrade with a fresh installation or to perform a manual in-place upgrade.

Perform a Manual In-Place Upgrade

A manual in-place upgrade can be performed from ESX 4.1 to ESXi 5.0 by booting from the ESXi installation CD. Most settings are preserved. Some third-party integration settings are not. For more information on upgrading using the installation CD, see Chapter 2, "Installing and Configuring ESXi."

Upgrade with a Fresh ESX/ESXi Installation

Technically, this isn't an upgrade because you aren't preserving the previous installation. However, this is a valid approach to getting your hosts running ESXi 5.0. Because the ESX/ESXi hosts are typically almost stateless—meaning that there is very little configuration data actually stored on the host—rebuilding an ESX/ESXi host with a fresh installation doesn't create a significant amount of work for you. Add in the functionality provided by host profiles, which can automate virtually all the configuration of an ESX/ESXi host, and using this approach becomes even more attractive. With host profiles, an administrator can install ESXi with a scripted installation file, join the host to vCenter Server, apply a host profile, and that's it.

NOTE   Chapter 2 provides complete information on how to install ESXi.

To upgrade your hosts with a fresh installation, the overall process would look something like this:

1. Upgrade vCenter Server to version 5.0. (You did this in the previous section of this chapter.)

2. Use vMotion to move all the virtual machines off the ESX/ESXi host.

3. Rebuild that specific host with ESXi 5.0.

4. Rejoin the host to vCenter Server.

5. Repeat steps 2 through 4 on the remaining hosts until all the hosts have been upgraded to ESXi 5.0.

After vCenter Server and all the ESX/ESXi hosts have been upgraded, you are ready to perform some important postupgrade tasks. The next section describes these tasks.

Perform Postupgrade Tasks

After vCenter Server and the ESXi hosts have been upgraded to version 5.0, there are some additional postupgrade tasks that a VMware vSphere administrator should perform.

Upgrade VMware Tools

As you probably already understand by now, the VMware Tools are an important component that should be installed in every guest operating system instance in your environment. After the ESXi hosts have been upgraded, the VMware Tools in all your guest operating system instances are now out of date and need to be updated to the latest version. This ensures that the guest operating systems are using the latest and most efficient drivers for operating in a virtualized environment.

Administrators can either upgrade VMware Tools manually, or use vCenter Update Manager. The process of manually upgrading VMware Tools is described in Chapter 9, so this section will focus on using vCenter Update Manager to upgrade VMware Tools in your guest operating system instances.

vCenter Update Manager provides a prebuilt upgrade baseline named VMware Tools Upgrade to Match Host. This baseline cannot be modified or deleted, and it works by identifying virtual machines whose VMware Tools version does not match the ESXi host upon which the virtual machine is running. You can attach this baseline to groups of virtual machines and, after performing a scan, vCenter Update Manager will identify which virtual machines are running outdated versions of the VMware Tools. You can then remediate the baseline, which will upgrade the VMware Tools in the affected virtual machines. Most Windows versions require a reboot after upgrading the VMware Tools, so be sure to plan accordingly.

Using vCenter Update Manager with the VMware Tools Upgrade to Match Host baseline is the equivalent of manually initiating an upgrade of the VMware Tools on each virtual machine independently. vCenter Update Manager helps automate the process.

Upgrade Virtual Machine Hardware

This task should only be completed after the VMware Tools have been upgraded to match the ESXi host version. Otherwise, new virtual hardware presented to the guest operating system instance inside the virtual machine may not work properly until the updated version of the VMware Tools is installed. By installing the latest version of the VMware Tools first, you ensure that any new virtual hardware presented to the guest operating system has the drivers necessary to work right away.

The process of manually upgrading the virtual machine hardware from version 4 (the version used by ESX/ESXi 3.x) or version 7 (the version used by ESX/ESXi 4.x) to version 8 (the version used by ESXi 5.0) is described in Chapter 9. You do not have to manually upgrade the virtual machine version, though; you also can use vCenter Update Manager to upgrade the virtual machine hardware version.

Like the VMware Tools, vCenter Update Manager comes with a prebuilt baseline named VM Hardware Upgrade to Match Host. When you attach this baseline, either directly or as part of a baseline group, to a number of virtual machines and then perform a scan, vCenter Update Manager will identify which virtual machines have outdated virtual machine hardware. You can then "remediate" these virtual machines. As part of the remediation, vCenter Server will shut down the virtual machines and perform a virtual machine upgrade.

NOTE   The VM Hardware Upgrade to Match Host baseline can only remediate a virtual machine with an outdated virtual machine version when the virtual machine is powered off. If the virtual machine is powered on, no upgrades will occur. As soon as the virtual machine is powered down, any pending tasks will launch and become active.

Building a VMware
vSphere Environment

PART I

PART II

Configuring Your vSphere Environment

IN THIS PART ▶

Configuring Your
vSphere Environment

PART II

6

Creating and Managing Virtual Networking

Configuring Your
vSphere Environment

PART II

Four main resources combine to provide performance, stability, and flexibility in a virtualized environment: CPU, memory, storage, and networking. This chapter focuses on the fourth component: virtual networking. Networking ensures that the infrastructure is flexible in the way IP addressing is handled, provides stability because of the physical redundancy that can be built into the infrastructure, and aids in performance by making sure that adequate bandwidth is available for servers to use. In this chapter, we are going to define the key building blocks of virtualization and demonstrate how to set them up. We will also explore best practices for setting up your environment.

Understand the Basics

In a physical infrastructure, routers and switches are separate from servers but are connected with network cables. In a virtual infrastructure, this is still the case, but there are virtual switches (vSwitches) inside a host that virtual machines connect to in order to communicate with the external world. In many cases, several network adapters connect a host with outside physical switches. Virtual switches are the core building blocks of virtual networking and combine with physical network adapters to separate—and sometimes combine—traffic to provide performance, redundancy, and isolation of networking for security purposes.

Let's start by exploring a virtualized infrastructure, starting with vSwitches. Then we will explore the network services that make up a vSwitch, learn how to physically set up redundancy on a vSwitch using NIC teaming, discover why VLANs are important to flexible networks, and learn how to view networking configurations.

Work with Virtual Switches

Virtual switches are internal to an ESXi host and allow you to network both traffic that is external to the host and traffic that never needs to leave the host (internal traffic). If virtual machines require a lot of bandwidth to communicate with one another, think about placing those VMs on the same host and sharing the same vSwitch. Internal traffic (two VMs internal to a host) has higher bandwidth capability than traffic that will hop multiple times across physical switches and network cables (outside of a host to another host or physical server). An example is when several VMs need to communicate with a database that is also on the same host and vSwitch.

You can add multiple physical network adapters to a single vSwitch to achieve additional bandwidth, balance communication routes, and provide greater redundancy that wouldn't exist with just one adapter. By default there are 128 logical ports, and there's a maximum of 4,096 usable ports on a single ESXi host.

Isolation of virtual LANs (VLANs) can be defined by adding port groups or by creating multiple vSwitches. Network labels, although not defined as a security boundary, either allow or prohibit VM portability across hosts using vMotion. Two or more hosts that have the same network will allow the use of vMotion.

Understand Network Services

A vSwitch can make two types of connections:

Virtual Machine   This connection type is the most frequently used as it is the backbone for virtual networking.

VMkernel   This connection type is used to handle host management, vMotion, Fault Tolerance, iSCSI, and NFS virtual networking.

NOTE   ESX versions prior to vSphere 5 also included a *Service Console* connection type. This connection is replaced by the *Management* VMkernel port in ESXi, which is set up by default during a host installation. All management communication from the physical world to the ESX host traversed this connection.

Use NIC Teaming

The Management VMkernel connection is a great place to employ a strategy of *NIC teaming*. This is when more than one physical network adapter is associated with a single vSwitch to form a team. This is often configured on VMkernel ports to ensure that a single physical network failure does not disrupt an entire host. Not only can a team provide a failover path in the event of hardware failure, but both NICs can share the bandwidth load that exists between the vSwitch and the physical world (uplink load-balancing).

TIP NIC teaming can also be used on other types of network services.

Configure VLANs

VLANs are one of the most important aspects of virtual networking. Use of VLANs can enhance or diminish the capabilities of the virtual infrastructure. VLANs allow for a single physical LAN segment to be broken up into different broadcast domains. This strategy is most important to larger organizations that employ many different network segments for security and performance. If, for instance, an organization has 10 different VLANs, and if an ESX host needs access to those 10 VLANs, you can accomplish this in one of two ways:

Physical connections If you want your host to have access to all 10 VLANs, you could theoretically install 10 NICs and plug 10 network cables into the host. However, in reality, this isn't always possible, and it's often not the best use of resources. Additionally, if NIC teaming is to be used for redundancy, you'll need a minimum of 20 network connections (two at a minimum for each of the 10 VLANs). Furthermore, if every host needs this same networking, soon your datacenter will be a cable management nightmare.

VLAN tagging Suppose VLAN tagging is used and each network cable is capable of carrying traffic from all network segments, each defined by a port group. In this example, fewer than 10 cables can be used. For example, you can use six network cables: two for the Management Network (which are NIC teamed), two for the vMotion VMkernel, and two for the last six VLAN segments carrying virtual machine traffic. As you can see, six cables are much easier to install and manage than a hypothetical 20 cables.

Use VLAN Tagging

VMware uses 802.1q for VLAN tagging, sometimes called *trunking*. This is a great way to set up a virtual infrastructure, as it allows for maximum flexibility with respect to networking. It is slightly more difficult to work with than regular one-for-one networking, but the added benefits that it brings far outweigh that small amount of extra work. VLAN tagging is also a godsend when network adapter ports are limited. For example, some blade servers may have a limited number. You may want to follow the VMware best practice and separate Management Network and vMotion traffic while still maintaining two physical NICs for failover and load balancing.

View Networking Configuration and Network Adapter Information

Before we start working, you need to locate where this work will be done—in other words, how and where to begin. From the vSphere Client, select the Host, select the Configuration tab, and finally select Networking.

There is also another way to view information. Next to networking information are two types of icons that, if clicked, will display summary information for the object they represent. In basic networking, the icon looks similar to a small blue dialog box. (See Figure 6.1.) In the Distributed Virtual Switch view, the icon looks like a blue circle with the letter *i* in it. (See Figure 6.2.)

Figure 6.1: View summary networking information by clicking an icon.

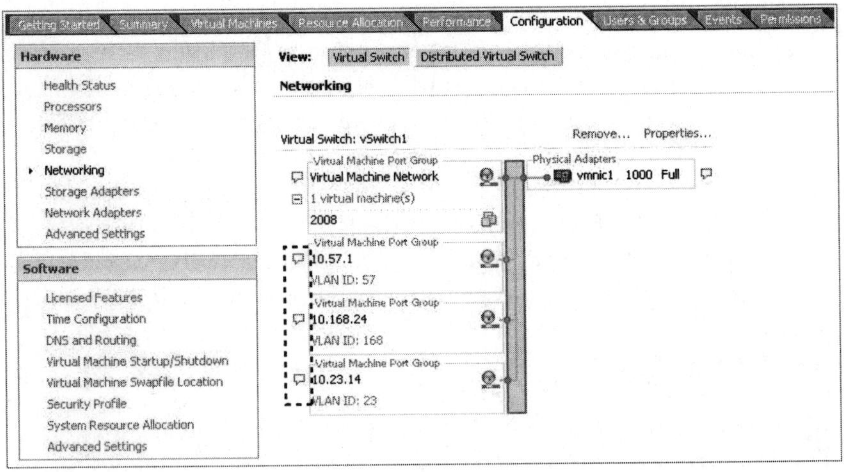

Figure 6.2: Summary information

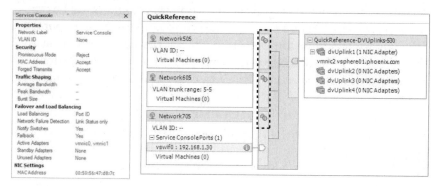

To view the network adapter information, from the vSphere Client click Host, select the Configuration tab, and then click Network Adapters (see Figure 6.3).

Figure 6.3: View networking adapter information

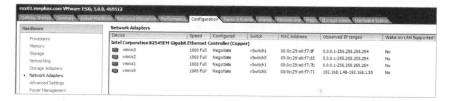

Network with vSwitches

vSphere 4 and later support networking using third party vNetwork Distributed Switches (vDS) like Cisco's Nexus 1000V and also maintain support for Standard vSwitches (vSS). vSwitches are easy to use and very functional. Let's dive into using vSwitches and set up the Management Network, assign a static IP, and create a vSwitch for virtual machine networking.

Set Up NIC Teaming on the Management Network

The Management Network is one of the most important parts of an ESXi host, and it is one of the main forms of communication with an

ESXi host. While virtual machines would continue to run and provide services without the Management Network, this would be similar to taking a cruise without a captain. Therefore, it makes sense to put extra effort into safeguarding its operation. One of the ways to accomplish this is to assign the Management Network two physical NICs; this approach ensures that if one NIC fails, communication with the host is not lost. Teaming two NICs keeps the High Availability service from assuming that the host is down, creating what is referred to as a *split brain*, and trying to restart the VMs on another host while they are still running on the disconnected host. Let's take a look at how to team a network connection by adding an adapter and possibly adjusting which adapter is the primary.

1. From the vSphere Client, select Host, click the Configuration tab, select Networking, and then click Properties (next to the vSwitch where the Management Network resides).

2. Click the Network Adapters tab, click Add, and select an available VMNIC (as shown in Figure 6.4) (if none shows, there aren't any available).

Figure 6.4: Adding unclaimed adapters

3. Click Next. You will see a screen with an option to reorder the adapters. Reordering the adapters is not relevant when using all in an Active fashion, so click Next again, and finally click Finish.

4. Click back to the Ports tab, highlight Management Network, and click Edit.

5. The Management Network Properties dialog box opens. Click the NIC Teaming tab, select the Load Balancing check box (as shown in Figure 6.5), click OK, and click Close.

Figure 6.5: Select the Load Balancing check box.

General	IP Settings	Security	Traffic Shaping	NIC Teaming	
Policy Exceptions					
Load Balancing:		☑	Route based on the originating virtual port ID	▼
Network Failover Detection:		☐	Link Status only	▼
Notify Switches:		☐	Yes	▼
Failback:		☐	Yes	▼

Assign Static IP Addresses for the Management Network

There are times when a DHCP address may have been used during multiple installations. If you need to change to static IPs, follow these steps:

1. From the vSphere Client, select the Host, click the Configuration tab, click Networking, and then select Properties (next to the vSwitch where the Management Network resides).

   The default gateway for the VMkernel can be edited in the next step or from the DNS And Routing tab.

2. Highlight the Management Network, click Edit, click the IP Settings tab, and enter your information.

Create a vSwitch for Virtual Machine Networking

During installation you'll notice an option to create virtual machine networking that is combined with the Management Network. Many administrators choose to turn off this option and/or separate virtual machine networking from the Management Network. This isolation ensures that the host is less likely to be open to attack if it is on the same network as other servers or, worse, end users.

In the following steps, we will create a vSwitch to separate the Management Network from virtual machine networking.

1. From the vSphere Client, highlight the host, click the Configuration tab, and under Hardware, choose Networking.

2. In the top-right corner, click Add Networking to open a window where you can choose a connection type. This is where you can create a VMkernel switch (used for vMotion IP storage, and host management). Regardless of the connection type, the remaining steps are similar.

3. Choose Virtual Machine and click Next to reach a screen that will allow you to either create a new vSwitch or modify an existing one. You can also choose which physical NICs to associate with the vSwitch.

4. Make sure Create A Virtual Switch is selected, choose which VMNICs to use, and click Next (see Figure 6.6).

Figure 6.6: Creating a virtual vSwitch

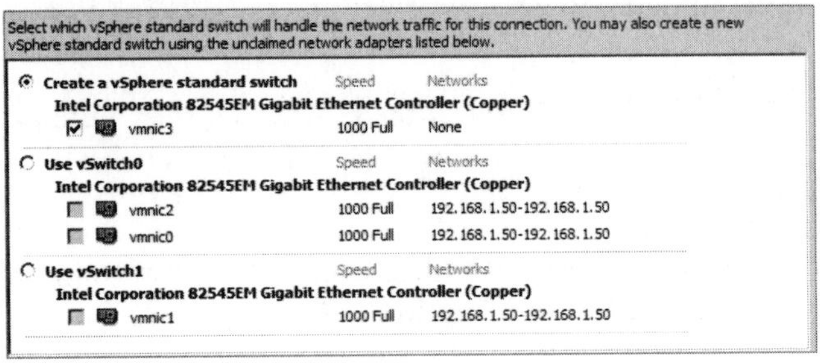

Network Labels

Network labels are nothing more than labels given to a network connection. They do not define any technical aspect of that connection, except for the ability to enable VM portability (vMotion) across hosts. For example, if one connection is called "10.57.1" and on another host that same network connection is called "10.571" (missing the second dot), then there will be errors trying to vMotion across the hosts. Therefore, a simplified networking solution (when not utilizing vNetwork Distributed Switch [DVS]) ensures that the network labels are consistent.

Another naming strategy that many organizations utilize is a label that describes the IP network or VLAN number (if trunking). This accomplishes many things. First, it is easy to identify which network a virtual machine is part of based solely on the label. Second, if virtualization is used for disaster recovery solutions, the same naming strategy can be used when recovering virtual machines on replicated LUNs, eliminating extra steps during the recovery period. IPs will not have to be looked up for each virtual machine, and/or the same labels can be utilized in a recovery destination. The virtual machine networking will work without any manual adjustment to networking.

Port Groups

Port groups are an extremely useful part of networking because they allow you to define VLANs. Imagine a virtual infrastructure that utilizes several different VLANs but does not take advantage of trunking. As described earlier, in such a setup, each host may end up needing several network adapters in order to utilize the different VLANs in the infrastructure. Or worse yet, there might be several clusters in the infrastructure where only one IP network is defined per cluster. This setup can still be useful; however, it doesn't make use of the power of the virtual infrastructure. In such a scenario, if virtual machines need to be moved to another cluster, their IP addresses must be changed. This is sometimes a challenge with applications and often requires some amount of downtime. When the hardware in a cluster is at the end of its useful life, all the virtual machines would need to be migrated. Another scenario that is challenging to negotiate with this setup is what to do if a smaller cluster has a host hardware failure and additional capacity is needed. In both situations, this setup is not as flexible as it could be.

Let's now imagine a different setup. In this example, trunking is deployed and all hosts in the infrastructure have access to the different IP networks through VLAN tagging. This means that, from a network standpoint, any virtual machine can run on any host in the infrastructure regardless of cluster boundaries. If a host fails on any cluster, its virtual machines can be migrated to another host that has excess capacity. There is no need to run a few hosts at high CPU or memory levels, because all resources in the infrastructure can be shared without networking boundaries.

With respect to port groups, enter a number between 1 and 4,094 as assigned by the network team. If 4,095 is assigned, the port group can see traffic on any VLAN. If 0 is entered, the port group can only see untagged traffic (non-VLAN).

When setting up a network label for VLAN tagging, you will need to enter a port group in the VLAN ID field (see Figure 6.7). If you are not using VLAN tagging, leave this field blank.

Figure 6.7: Network label and VLAN ID

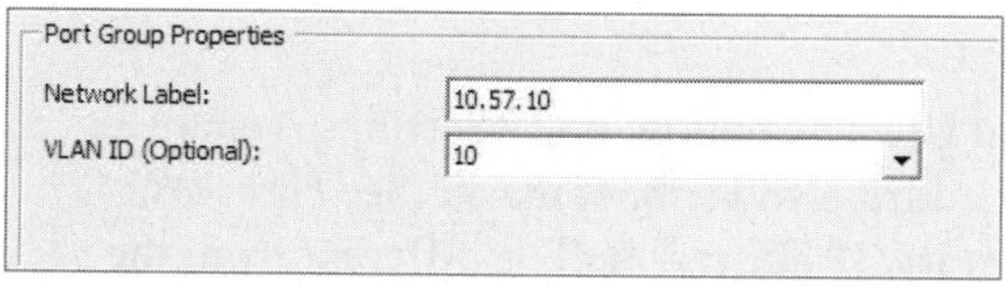

Add a VMkernel and Enable vMotion

In order to add vMotion capabilities, a VMkernel connection type must be added and configured, vMotion must be enabled, and the connection must be configured. A VMkernel connection can be added to a Management Network vSwitch or a vSwitch can be added that is separate from all other networks. Many administrators choose to add a VMkernel connection to the Management Network vSwitch and simply designate a different IP network to keep the communication distinct from other communication on the network. To do so, follow these steps:

1. From the vSphere Client, choose Host, click the Configuration tab, click Networking, and select the properties of the Management Network vSwitch.

2. Click the Add button in the bottom-left window and connection types will appear. Choose VMkernel and select Next.

3. Enter an appropriate network label. In this case, the label vMotion is simple, easy, and descriptive.

4. Select the Use This Port Group For vMotion check box (see Figure 6.8).

Figure 6.8: Enabling vMotion

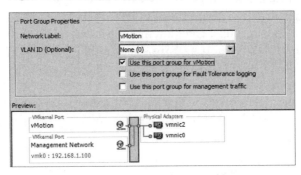

5. Click Next.

6. Make sure the option Use The Following IP Settings is enabled, then enter a static IP address and subnet mask. (See Figure 6.9) In this scenario, the static IP address will be different from the Management Network IP network.

Figure 6.9: Configuring vMotion

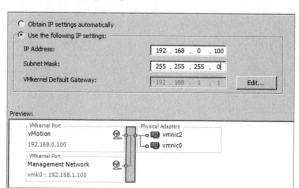

7. Click Next, click Finish, and then click Close.

Network with vSphere Distributed Switches

The old-style vSwitch had to be configured exactly the same way on each and every host it was built on, which often caused issues if one check box or label was missed on any one host.

A vSphere Distributed Switch (vDS) is a consolidated switch that spans across hosts the administrator chooses. If there is a cluster or one or more hosts that don't need that particular vDS, that vDS will not show up on those hosts. And because the vDS spans across the config-ured hosts, a virtual machine will be able to move consistently across the virtual infrastructure because the settings of that vDS are config-ured at the datacenter viewpoint. One of the great things about vSphere Distributed Switching is the ability to migrate existing vSwitches and/or connection types into a vDS and then centrally manage all networking through one interface.

The following list breaks down the vDS into easily digestible pieces:

dvUplinks   Physical NICs plug into dvUplinks. The NICs can be renamed or left to the default. When creating the vDS, choose the maximum number of NICs that any one host in the switch will have. For example, if most of the hosts will have only two pNICs (physical NICs) but one will need four pNICs, then configure the vDS with four. On some, there will be unused dvUplinks, but that is not an issue.

Port Group   A port group defines port configuration options such as teaming and failover, VLAN options, traffic shaping, and security. There may be more than one port group on any one vDS, and virtual machines may bind their vNICs (virtual NICs) to different port groups on the same vDS, depending on their needs or status in the organization.

Configure a vSphere Distributed Switch

In this section we are going to create a vDS where one did not exist before. Let's take a look at how to accomplish this:

1. From the vSphere Client, at the top-left click Home, then under Inventory click Networking (Figure 6.10). Make sure your datacenter is highlighted, right-click it, and choose New vSphere Distributed Switch (see Figure 6.11) to launch the Create vSphere Distributed Switch Wizard.

Figure 6.10: Click Networking to begin.

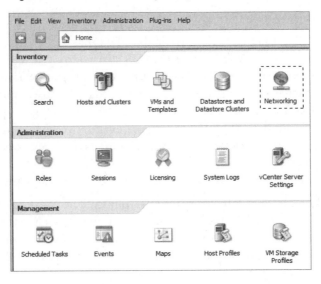

Figure 6.11: Creating a new vDS

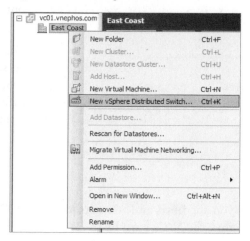

2. On the first screen (Figure 6.12), select the correct vDS version based on the lowest host version you wish to add to the vDS, and click Next. On the next screen (Figure 6.13), enter a descriptive name and specify the number of NICs in the Number of dvUplink Ports field, then click Next.

Figure 6.12: Selecting the vDS version

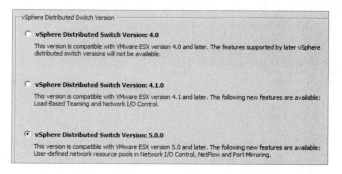

Configuring Your vSphere Environment

PART II

Figure 6.13: Naming the vDS

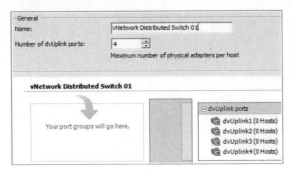

The next screen lets you add hosts and adapters to this vDS. In order to accomplish this, the NICs must be free.

TIP   Note that additional hosts and adapters may be added at a later time. Take advantage of the View Details link to learn more about the physical NICs that are being added. Click the plus sign next to your hosts to see available NICs and their details.

---

3. Click Add Now (Figure 6.14) to add the hosts and adapters; then place a check mark beside the ones you want to add and click Next.

Figure 6.14: Adding hosts and adapters to your vDS

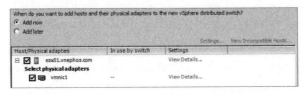

4. The next screen lets you create a default port group automatically (this is the default). If you leave this option selected, the vSphere Client will create an early-binding port group with 128 ports.

NOTE   When viewing networking on any host, you have two options: vSphere Standard Switch or vSphere Distributed Switch (vDS). If the host is not part of a vDS, no options under vSphere Distributed Switch will appear. To get an overall view of all hosts on a vDS, check the Networking section in Figure 6.10 under Inventory.

Review the setup (see Figure 6.15), and click Finish.

Figure 6.15: Reviewing the current setup

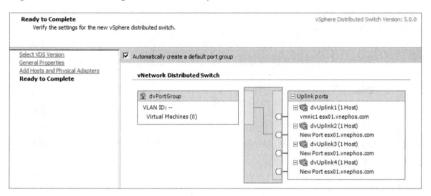

Add Hosts and Adapters to a vDS

As your infrastructure grows, you may want to add more hosts to your vDS. You may also choose to add more adapters to address performance. Let's look at this process:

1. From the vSphere Client, click Home, select Networking, highlight the vSphere Distributed Switch in question, right-click, and select Add Host.

2. On the next screen, select any additional hosts and NICs (see Figure 6.16), then click Next.

   Figure 6.16: Adding hosts and adapters to a vDS

3. Review the selection, and then click Finish.

Edit General and Advanced vDS Settings

The General settings on the vSphere Distributed Switch Settings Properties tab (see Figure 6.17) allow you to change the name and number of dvUplink ports. To access the General settings from the vSphere Client, click Home, click Networking, highlight the vDS, right-click, and select Edit Settings.

Figure 6.17: Editing General and Advanced settings

Click Advanced to access settings like MTU, Discovery Protocol, and admin contact information.

Manage Physical and Virtual Network Adapters

If you're new to the vDS, and you may find yourself wondering how to manage the moving pieces. First, we'll look at managing the physical adapters, and then we'll move on to managing the virtual adapters.

Manage Physical Network Adapters

First let's look at the process of managing physical network adapters:

1. From the vSphere Client, select Host, choose the Configuration tab, click Networking, and select the vSphere Distributed Switch view (as shown in Figure 6.18). Then choose Manage Physical Adapters.

Figure 6.18: Here you manage virtual and physical adapters.

The resulting window lets you view the adapter and remove or add an adapter.

WARNING   If you are adding a new adapter, it will remove that adapter from its current vSwitch. Be careful that the adapter being added is not currently serving virtual machines; also be aware of that adapter's ability to service the Management Network IP network. Always think through your steps when working with physical adapters, and have a backup plan on how to access the host if you lose remote connectivity.

---

2. Highlight a NIC to access the physical details on it, and then choose Click To Add NIC or Remove (see Figure 6.19).

    Figure 6.19: Reviewing the physical adapter's details

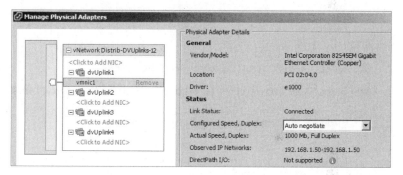

3. The Select A Physical Adapter window (see Figure 6.20) lists two types of adapters: adapters that are currently managed by other vSwitches and Unclaimed Adapters. Usually you will want to choose an unclaimed adapter. Highlight the adapter you want to add, then click OK twice.

    Figure 6.20: Choosing unclaimed physical adapters

Configuring Your vSphere Environment

PART II

Manage Virtual Network Adapters

Now we will look at managing the virtual adapters:

1. From the vSphere Client, select Host, choose the Configuration tab, click Networking, and select vSphere Distributed Switch view (as shown earlier in Figure 6.18). Then choose Manage Virtual Adapters.

   The Manage Virtual Adapters screen lets you add virtual network adapters or migrate existing network adapters from the vSwitch side.

2. In the top-left corner, click Add (as shown in Figure 6.21).

   Figure 6.21: Adding a virtual adapter

   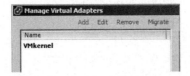

3. Select New Virtual Adapter and click Next.

4. Select VMkernel (refer to Figure 6.22), and then click Next.

   Figure 6.22: Selecting the type of virtual adapter

   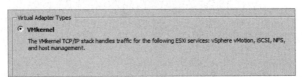

5. On the Connection Settings Screen, choose Port Group and then select the correct port. You can also use these options to enable vMotion, turn on fault tolerance logging, or create another Management Network connection (as shown in Figure 6.23).

   Figure 6.23: Specifying the port group

   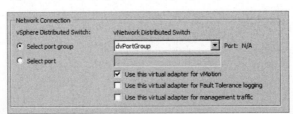

6. Make sure Use The Following IP Settings is selected, then enter the static IP settings (Figure 6.24).

Figure 6.24: Defining a static IP

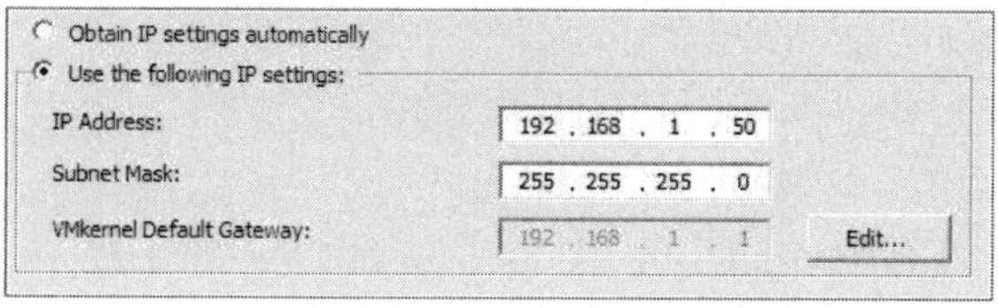

7. Review the settings, click Finish, and then click Close.

Migrate Existing Virtual Adapters into vDS

Why would you migrate existing virtual adapters into vDS? At the end of an upgrade process, you may find yourself with plenty of ESXi hosts that are all configured the same way, in the old vSwitch style, and you want to take advantage of central management. Or, you may want to get everything up and running in a format that is easier to understand and troubleshoot and, at a later time, make the move to vDS.

WARNING   Before proceeding with migration, make sure the current physical NIC associated with this vDS is capable of communicating on the same network that the Management Network is connected to. At the end of this procedure, the Management Network is going to switch to a different physical NIC. If by chance communication is lost, try unplugging the original pNIC and plugging it into the pNIC that the vDS was plugged into. Then make your changes and start over. Keep in mind that in some cases this may not be easily accomplished, or perhaps not accomplished at all.

---

1. From the vSphere Client, select Host, click the Configuration tab, select Networking, click vSphere Distributed Switch, and choose Manage Virtual Adapters.

2. In the top-left corner, click Add (in blue lettering).

3. Select Migrate Existing Virtual Adapters, as shown in Figure 6.25. Then click Next.

Figure 6.25: Migrating existing virtual adapters

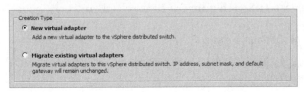

4. On the Network Connectivity screen, you'll see a list of virtual adapters to migrate. Select Management Network.

   Typically this list won't be long since it is composed only of VMkernel adapters. There is also the option of migrating another adapter from a different vDS.

5. Click Select A Port Group to reveal the drop-down arrow and then select the port group to which this virtual adapter will be assigned, as shown in Figure 6.26. Then click Next.

Figure 6.26: Selecting a Port Group

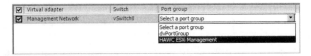

6. In the Ready To Complete screen, you will see a summary of the actions to be performed. Notice that the vmk0 (this is usually tied to the first virtual switch and it usually contains the Management Network), along with the IP address of the Management Network of that host, has been added (see Figure 6.27). Click Finish, and then click Close.

Figure 6.27: Reviewing the migration details

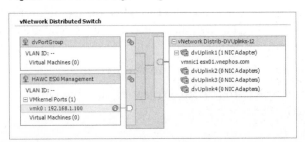

Notice that if the view in Networking is changed from vSphere Distributed Switch to vSphere Standard Switch, there is no longer an entry for the Management Network. However, as long as the port group you chose was set up correctly, communication with the host continues without interruption. Also notice that the pNIC originally associated with the Management Network on the vSwitch has not moved into the vDS.

Once everything is working, you may want to go back and move the original pNIC into this vDS for load balancing and failover of the Management Network. For details, see the section "Manage Physical Network Adapters" earlier in this chapter.

Add a dvPort Group

A dvPort group can span many hosts and is used to ensure configuration consistency for VMs and virtual ports such as vMotion. Additionally, a dvPort group defines port configuration choices for each port on a vDS by configuring how a connection is made to the physical network.

1. From the vSphere Client, select Home, select Networking, highlight the icon for vDS (in this case it is vNetwork Distributed Switch; see Figure 6.28), right-click, and select New Port Group.

Figure 6.28: Adding a dvPort group

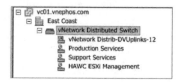

2. Enter the name, number of ports, and VLAN type (as shown in Figure 6.29), and then click Next.

Figure 6.29: Configuring VLAN trunking

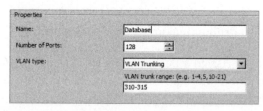

If VLAN Trunking is selected as the VLAN type, an additional option is available—VLAN Trunk Range. Enter the appropriate values for the trunked networks on the uplinked physical switch.

3. Review the settings, and then click Finish.

Edit a dvPort Group

The following steps illustrate how to edit dvPort groups:

1. From the vSphere Client, select Home, select Networking, highlight the dvPort group, right-click, and select Edit Settings.

2. In the next screen, you can modify the name, description, number of ports, and port binding (see Figure 6.30). Make your selections, and click OK.

Figure 6.30: Editing a dvPort group

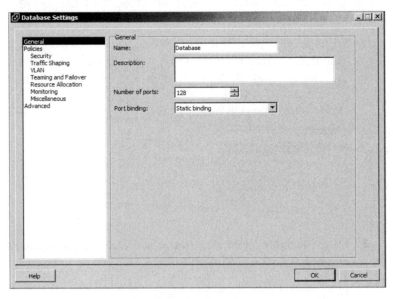

Here is a list of the port binding options and their purpose:

Static Binding   Assign a port to a virtual machine when the VM is connected to a dvPort group. This is the default binding type.

Dynamic Binding Assign a port to a virtual machine on the first power-on while in the dvPort group.

Ephemeral Choose this option when there is no port binding. This is the same binding type as the standard vSwitch.

NOTE If you're running vCenter or any of its dependent services, like a database server, as a virtual machine within your vSphere environment, you'll want to choose the Ephemeral port binding type for the dvPort Group where your VM is attached. This will avoid a "chicken & egg" scenario when the VM is rebooted and allow it to connect to the dvPort before the vCenter service starts.

Create a Private VLAN

With private VLANs, you can restrict communication between VMs even when they are on the same VLAN or network segment. Let's take a look at how to accomplish this and create a private VLAN:

1. From the vSphere Client, select Home, select Networking, highlight the DVS you want to work with, right-click, and select Edit Settings.

2. Select the Private VLAN tab; under Primary Private VLAN ID, click Enter A Private VLAN ID Here, and enter the VLAN ID number. Then click elsewhere in the window.

3. Highlight the VLAN ID just entered and it will show up under Secondary Private VLAN ID.

4. Under Secondary Private VLAN ID, enter the information in Enter A Private VLAN ID Here as before (as shown in Figure 6.31).

Figure 6.31: Creating a private VLAN

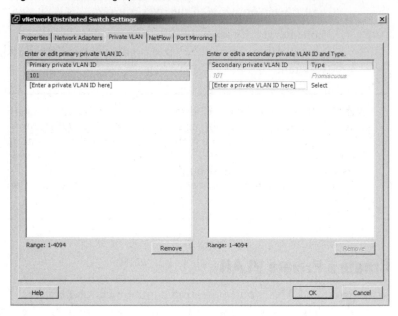

5. Highlight the secondary private VLAN you just added and select the port type. When finished, click OK.

Following are the port types available:

Promiscuous Port Communicates with all other private VLAN ports.

Isolated Port Has Layer 2 separation from other ports within the same private VLAN, with the exception of the promiscuous port.

Community Port Communicates with other community ports and transmits traffic outside the group via the designated promiscuous port.

Migrate VMs to a vDS

There are two ways to migrate virtual machines into a vDS. The virtual machines network adapter settings can be changed to reflect the new settings, or you can use a VMware migration tool to move a group of virtual machines all at one time. This tool is granular enough to allow you to pick which virtual machines to move now and which to move at a later period, or not at all. The following process demonstrates the migration tool:

1. From the vSphere Client, click Home, select Networking, highlight the vSphere Distributed Switch, right-click, and select Migrate Virtual Machine Networking.

2. From the Source Network drop-down list, choose the location of the existing virtual machines.

3. From the Destination Network drop-down list, choose the location where the virtual machines will be migrated to.

4. Click Next to view the Select Virtual Machines window.

5. Put a check mark next to the virtual machine adapters that need to be moved and click Next (see Figure 6.32).

Figure 6.32: Migrating VMs to vDS

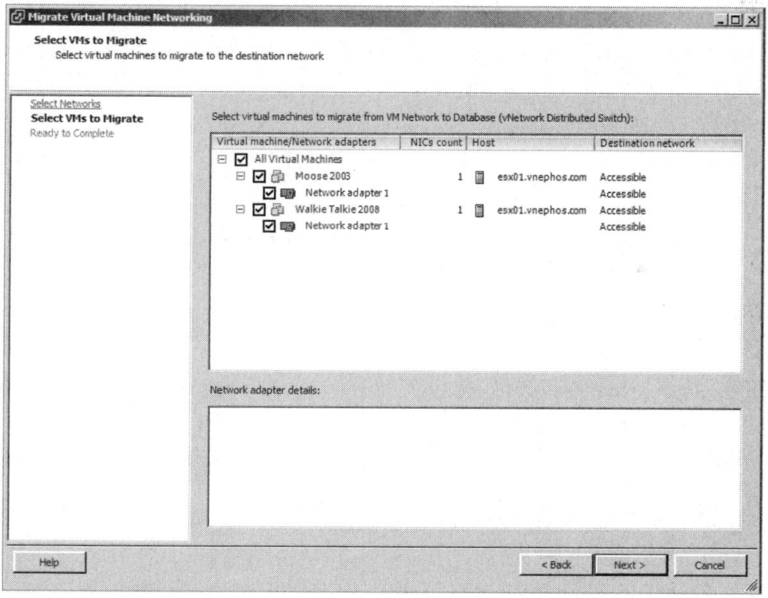

6. Review the migration summary and click Finish.

To migrate an individual virtual machine (without using the tool) into a vDS, edit the settings of the VM and simply change the network adapter settings (under Network Label) to reflect the location they will be migrated to.

Understand Advanced Networking

There are day-to-day networking activities, and then there are advanced networking topics. These are the features that help us add more functionality, help us troubleshoot, or help us grow. Take, for example, the topic of customizing MAC addresses; this is clearly networking but not something that needs to be done on a regular basis. However, it may help you provide a software-based key for some specific applications while avoiding a hardware key (think USB dongle). Let's take a look at this and other advanced networking topics.

Customize MAC Addresses

In what instances would you customize MAC addresses? There are more than a few applications out there that require some sort of license file to work, and some of them bind to the MAC address on the server. In some cases, it is possible to get a software vendor to give out a software-based license instead of a hardware-based USB key; but they will only do this for a vigilant and determined VMware administrator who won't take no for an answer. Virtual machines by default do not have static MAC addresses; therefore, if one is needed it must be assigned.

TIP Do not change the MAC address unless it is absolutely necessary. Instead, let the software do what it does best and avoid unnecessary complexity.

The allowable range for MAC addresses is from 00:50:56:00:00:00 to 00:50:56:3F:FF:FF. The last 3 bytes are configurable. Keep it simple; make the first static MAC address 00:50:56:00:00:01. Here's how:

1. From the vSphere Client, select the virtual machine and click Edit Settings.

2. On the Hardware tab, highlight the network adapter. On the right there will be a MAC address that can be changed from Automatic to Manual.

    Unfortunately, the colons will need to be typed into the interface; it isn't intelligent in this respect.

3. Enter the desired MAC address, document it (so you have it for later reference), and click OK.

Create VMkernel Ports for Software iSCSI

Some installations use Fibre Channel SAN, and others use iSCSI, which traverses Ethernet. In this section we will look at the prerequisites for using iSCSI and then show you how to set it up.

In previous versions of vSphere, binding VMkernel ports to the iSCSI Software Adapter could only be completed via the command line. In vSphere 5, VMware added this functionality to the vSphere Client GUI.

NOTE Redundancy and load balancing for the iSCSI Software Adapter are provided by multiple VMkernel ports rather than by adding multiple physical NICs to the vSwitch where the iSCSI VMkernel resides. Therefore, one of the prerequisites for Software iSCSI port binding is that an iSCSI VMkernel port must have exactly one active physical uplink and no standby uplinks.

First we are going to create new VMkernel ports, and then we will bind the iSCSI Software Adapter to them:

1. From the vSphere Client, click Host, select the Configuration tab, click Networking, select the vSwitch view, and click Add Networking.

2. Select the VMkernel, and then click Next.

3. Choose Create A vSphere Standard vSwitch.

   a. Put check marks next to the network adapters to be used with this switch and click Next.

   b. Choose an appropriate network label.

   c. Add the VLAN ID if one exists and click Next.

4. Make sure Use The Following IP Settings is selected, then enter the IP address information (see Figure 6.33). Then click Next.

Figure 6.33: iSCSI connection type

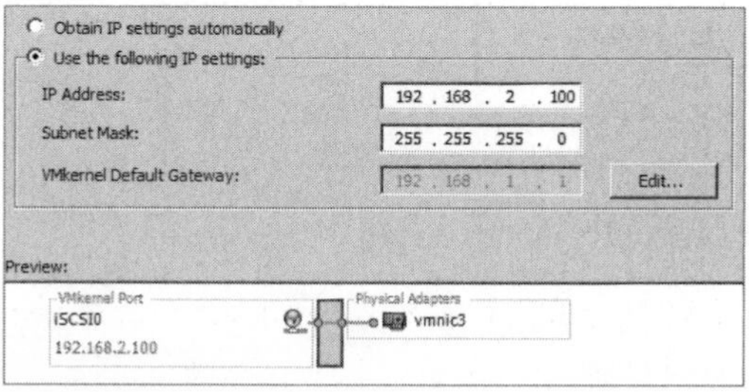

5. Finally, click Finish.

The VMkernel port has now been created. Our next step is to override the switch physical NIC failover order for the iSCSI VMkernel interface we just created:

1. From the vSphere Client, click Host, select the Configuration tab, click Networking, select the vSwitch view, and click Properties beside the vSwitch we just created.

2. Select the iSCSI VMkernel portgroup just created and click Edit.

3. On the NIC Teaming tab, select the check box labeled Override Switch Failover Order. This overrides the physical NIC failover order so that only one VMNIC is active.

4. Click the second VMNIC listed under Active Adapters.

5. Click Move Down until this VMNIC is under Unused Adapters. (See Figure 6.34)

Figure 6.34: Override physical NIC failover order

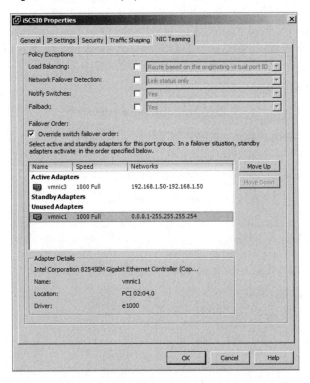

6. Finally, click OK.

Now that the first iSCSI VMkernel interface is configured to use only one physical NIC, we must create a second iSCSI VMkernel interface for redundancy and load balancing:

1. From the vSphere Client, click Host, select the Configuration tab, click Networking, select the vSwitch view, and click Add Networking.

2. Select the VMkernel, and then click Next.

3. Choose Use vSwitch (the vSwitch you created in the steps above). Choose an appropriate network label and add the VLAN ID if one exists. Then click Next.

4. Enter the IP address information, then click Next.

5. Finally, click Finish.

The second iSCSI VMkernel port has now been created. Our next step is to override the switch physical NIC failover order for the second iSCSI VMkernel interface. We'll use the opposite active and unused adapters configured for the first iSCSI VMkernel interface:

1. From the vSphere Client, click Host, select the Configuration tab, click Networking, select the vSwitch view, and click Properties beside the vSwitch we just created.

2. Select the second iSCSI VMkernel portgroup just created and click Edit.

3. On the NIC Teaming tab, select the check box labeled Override Switch Failover Order.

4. Click the second VMNIC listed under Active Adapters.

5. Click Move Down until this VMNIC is under Unused Adapters. (See Figure 6.35)

Configuring Your
vSphere Environment

PART II

Figure 6.35: Override physical NIC failover order

6. Finally, click OK.

We can now enable and bind the iSCSI Software Adapter to the VMkernel ports we just created. See Chapter 7, "Configuring and Managing Storage."

Troubleshoot Using the Command Line

Occasionally networking can be misconfigured, due to scripts not working properly, physical NICs being configured with the wrong network, or a whole host of other reasons. Being able to navigate via the command line while standing in front of the ESXi host may be the only way to get the infrastructure back in tip-top shape. Table 6.1 presents some commands that are used to accomplish just that.

NOTE If communication with an ESXi host is not possible, step up to the host console, log in to the DCUI by pressing F2, navigate to Troubleshooting Options, enable the ESXi shell, and then press Alt+F1.

Table 6.1: Handy command-line tricks

Command	Description
esxcfg-vmknic -l	Provides a list of the VMkernel network interfaces. Make sure that vmk0 is defined and that the current IP address and netmask are accurate.
esxcfg-vswitch -l	Provides a list of the current vSwitch configurations. Ensure that the uplink adapter configured for the Management Network is connected to the correct physical network.
exscfg-nics -l	Provides a list of the network adapters. Check that the uplink adapter assigned to the Management Network is up and that the speed and duplex are both accurate.
esxcfg-nics -s <speed> <nic>	Changes the speed of a network adapter.
esxcfg-nics -d <duplex> <nic>	Changes the duplex of a network adapter.
esxcfg-vmknic -a -i <new ip address> -n <new netmask> -p <portgroup name>	Adds a new VMkernel interface with the parameters specified. Note that a portgroup must be created prior to adding the VMkernel interface.
esxcfg-vmknic -d <existing portgroup name>	Removes a VMkernel interface from the specific portgroup.
esxcfg-vswitch -U <old vmnic> <Management Network vswitch>	Removes the uplink for the Management Network.
esxcfg-vswitch -L <new vmnic> <Management Network vswitch>	Changes the uplink for the Management Network.

If there are long delays when using esxcfg-* commands, DNS might be misconfigured. The esxcfg-* commands require that DNS be configured so that localhost name resolution works properly. This requires that the /etc/hosts file contain an entry for the configured IP address and the 127.0.0.1 localhost address.

Enable Cisco Discovery Protocol

Cisco Discovery Protocol (CDP) allows an ESXi host to determine which Cisco switch port is connected to a given vSwitch and will allow properties of the Cisco switch to be viewed from the vSphere Client. Obviously if Cisco hardware is not part of the organization, this procedure is not necessary or advised. This process requires logging directly into the ESXi command-line interface.

NOTE In vSphere 5, VMware added the ability to enable both CDP and LLDP (for non-Cisco branded switches) on vSphere Distributed Switches using the vSphere Client GUI. The settings can be found under the Advanced section of the Properties tab of the vDS.

After the ESXi console or SSH has been enabled using the DCUI Troubleshooting Mode, log into the host. Remember that the command line is case sensitive, and in the next step, the S in vSwitch must be uppercase and the −b must be in lowercase.

    esxcfg-vswitch -b vSwitch0

The listen mode is the default. Possible outcomes are outlined in Table 6.2.

Table 6.2: Cisco Discovery Protocol modes

Mode	Outcome
down	CDP is disabled.
listen	ESXi listens for information but doesn't return information.
advertise	ESXi sends information but doesn't gather information.
both	ESXi listens and sends information.

To switch modes, enter the following command. Note that the -B is now uppercase. If the organization does not have CDP or LLDP compatible switch hardware, change *mode* to down.

    esxcfg-vswitch -B <mode> vSwitch0

Figure 6.36 shows the available commands.

Figure 6.36: Working with Cisco Discovery Protocol

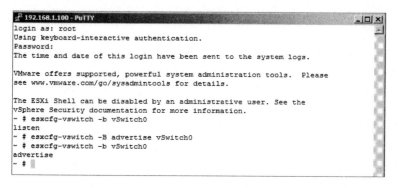

Enable IPv6

IPv6 is set to replace IPv4 because there are not enough IP addresses under the old method. You can run IPv6 in a mixed environment with IPv4. It uses a 128-bit address and all features are capable of running under this protocol. Here's how to enable IPv6:

1. From the vSphere Client, select Host. On the Configuration tab, choose Networking.

2. Choose Properties in the top-right corner of the next window.

3. Select Enable IPv6 Support On This Host and then click OK (see Figure 6.37).

Figure 6.37: Enabling IPv6

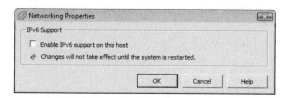

4. Reboot the host to let the changes take effect.

7

Configuring and Managing Storage

IN THIS CHAPTER, YOU WILL LEARN TO:

V Mware ESXi natively provides virtualization of CPU, memory, network, and disk resources. The first three resources have to be utilized locally on the ESXi host. Disk resources can be utilized locally or remotely.

The addition of remote storage is one of the points where VMware ESX/ESXi leaves off and vSphere takes over. Without the ability to leverage remote storage shared across two or more hosts, vSphere would be no more than a few tools to manage one or more hosts.

By using remotely shared storage attached to multiple hosts managed by vCenter Server, vSphere can leverage the combined complement of CPU, memory, network, and disk resources across a cluster.

To get started, you must become familiar with how storage works with vSphere, how to leverage it, and the steps required to use it.

Become Familiar with Storage Concepts

To best leverage the types of storage available, you must have a firm understanding of the various types of storage, and when and why they should be leveraged. For administrators designing a new vSphere implementation, this information can be crucial to choosing the appropriate storage system that meets the needs of the implementation, while also adhering to the financial constraints of the project.

Learn the Basics of Storage in vSphere

For vSphere to be able to run virtual machines, the machines must reside on storage that the host can use. The storage can reside on local disks inside the host through locally attached storage, or can be remotely presented storage. Before we go into detail about local and remote storage, it is important that you understand how the storage is used for virtual machines.

Storage for guests, templates, and ISOs is referred to as *datastores*. Datastores are logical containers that obscure the storage subsystem from the virtual machines. Block datastores are formatted with the Virtual Machine File System (VMFS) format, which is an optimized, high-performance file system. Through the use of distributed locking for the virtual disk files, multiple virtual machines can be used on a single file system by one or more VMware ESXi hosts simultaneously. This ensures that Storage Area Network (SAN) storage is safe and reliable for storing virtual machine configuration, disk, and swap files. Network Attached Storage (NAS) relies on NFS's native file system locking mechanisms, to ensure storage is safe and reliable.

Because VMFS is designed to be a clustered file system, VMFS lets multiple hosts access one or more datastores concurrently. *On-disk locking* is the process by which two or more hosts can access a shared file system without interfering with each other. This process is used to prevent more than one host from attempting to power on or operate the same virtual machine.

VMFS and NFS datastores contain virtual machine configuration files, virtual machine disk files, virtual machine swap files, directories, symbolic links, raw device mappings, and the like. VMFS on block storage maps these objects as *metadata*. The metadata is updated whenever files on the datastore are accessed or modified. This includes when guests are powered on or off, when guests are modified, and when any file attributes are modified. This metadata keeps all hosts with access to the datastore informed of the current status of any object on the datastore.

VMFS and NFS datastores can be configured through vSphere Client or through command-line options on storage systems that are recognized by the VMware ESXi host.

Table 7.1 outlines the supported maximum sizes by VMFS versions.

Table 7.1: Maximum sizes supported by VMFS versions

Version	Maximum Size
VMFS5	64 terabytes (TB) per volume
VMFS3	2 terabytes (TB) per volume

If a larger VMFS3 datastore is needed, datastores can be aggregated or extended through the use of extents, with a maximum combined size of 64 TB. Additionally, if the storage system supports the ability to grow the storage amount, datastores can be increased without having to power off any running guests on the datastore.

VMFS5 Improvements Over VMFS3

The following improvements are found in VMFS5:

- Greater than 2 TB LUN support
- Physical mode RDM supports disks larger than 2 TB
- Increased resource limits such as file descriptors
- Scalability improvements using VAAI
- Standardized on 1 block size (1 MB)
- On-line, in-place upgrades
- Can mount and unmount workflow in the vSphere Client

ESXi 5.0 supports two partition formats:

- The master boot record (MBR), which supports a maximum size of 2 TB.
- The GUID partition table (GPT), which has a maximum size of 64 TB.

With ESXi 5.0, if you create a new VMFS5 datastore, it will be formatted using GPT by default. VMFS3 continues to use the MBR format. If you are using existing VMFS3 datastores and additional space is required, consider upgrading the datastore to VMFS5.

When you are designing how storage is to be provided to vSphere hosts, keep in mind that it is difficult to determine peak-access times or optimize performance by looking at individual virtual machines. It is a best practice to run a mix of high- and low-utilization virtual machines across multiple hosts to provide an even balance of CPU and storage operations. In addition to evenly distributing the workload across datastores, remember the following guidelines:

- Only configure one VMFS datastore for each LUN presented to ESXi hosts.
- Choose a Redundant Array of Independent Disks (RAID) level that is appropriate for the type of workload the virtual machines will be running on the disk stored on the datastore. Disk RAID

levels should be configured as if the virtual disks were running on a physical system.

You need to consider whether to use a few large LUNs or many small LUNs. The key features of each method are described in the following list:

- When using a few large LUNs:

    - It's easy to create guests without having to continually provision space.

    - More space is available for snapshots and disk resizing.

    - You won't have as many datastores to manage.

- When using many smaller LUNs:

    - Space is optimized and storage is allocated on an as-needed basis, resulting in less wasted space.

    - Many RAID levels are required for different virtualized workloads.

    - You can leverage disk shares and multipathing for greater flexibility.

    - Performance tends to be better.

    - Microsoft Cluster Service requires each cluster disk resource to be in its own LUN.

Learn the Types of Supported Storage

VMware ESXi supports two basic types of storage:

Local storage is storage that is physically present in the host. This storage can either be physically housed in the host system or attached to the host using a storage controller connected to an external enclosure.

Remote storage is storage that is not physically attached to the host. It can include storage accessible to the host via a SAN or via a NAS device.

vSphere supports four disk types, as shown in Table 7.2. Keep in mind that the storage controller must be on the Hardware Compatibility List (HCL). Always refer to the current HCL reference documents at http://www.vmware.com/go/hcl.

Table 7.2: ESXi recognized disk types

Type	Installation and Booting	Virtual Machine Storage
SCSI	Yes	Yes
SATA	Yes	Yes
IDE	Yes	No
ATA	Yes	No

When you are working with local storage, the most important detail to remember is that the listed disk types are only supported if VMware ESXi supports the appropriate driver for the physical controller. For example, an Intel ICH7 SATA controller was initially supported in ESX 3.5 but is no longer supported.

To leverage the abilities of VMware High Availability, vMotion, Storage vMotion, Distributed Resource Scheduling, Distributed Power Management (DPM), and Fault Tolerance, VMware ESXi must utilize storage that is shared among several VMware ESXi hosts. For two or more hosts to share storage, that storage cannot be local to the ESXi host, but rather must be remote.

The following types of shared storage solutions are supported:

- Fibre Channel SAN
- iSCSI
- NFS

Remotely accessed storage is certified by VMware based on criteria such as the storage controller, the protocol being used to access that storage, and the backend disks in the storage system. This means that not every kind of Fibre Channel SAN, iSCSI, and NFS storage solution is supported. All three types of remote storage still have to be certified for proper support from VMware in the event of an issue. However, some storage solutions that are not on the HCL do work properly. When using the NFS protocol, storage may be supported, as long as the device providing the NFS storage is using the NFS v3 protocol.

Learn the Benefits of Remote Storage

Using ESXi with remote storage can make storage more flexible, more efficient, and more reliable if implemented properly. Additional remote storage features can include failover and load-balancing technologies. Often, a single storage system is used, providing a central location for storage management.

Implementing vSphere with remote storage offers the following benefits:

- Data is often redundant with approved remote storage systems.

- Multiple paths can be configured to access the remote storage, removing a single point of failure for storage systems.

- ESXi hosts support multiple paths to storage systems automatically and provide available paths to any guests residing on the remote storage.

- Multiple paths and redundant storage systems make guest availability less prone to host failures.

- In the event of a host failure, guests are immediately available to be recovered on other hosts in the environment that have access to the same remote storage.

- Guests can be migrated from one host to another while still running via VMware vMotion.

- Remote storage provides for the immediate recovery of guests after a host failure when used in conjunction with VMware HA (High Availability).

- Remote storage allows for the use of VMware Distributed Resource Scheduler (DRS) to load-balance guests across all hosts in a cluster.

- Remote storage allows guests uninterrupted operation when performing host maintenance—such as patching, upgrades, or host replacement—when used in conjunction with VMware vMotion and DRS.

- Leveraging remote storage also allows the use of Distributed Power Management (DPM) by consolidating workloads down to fewer hosts and shutting down the vacated hosts, facilitating lower overall power consumption.

All of these benefits of remote storage result from hosts sharing access to the remote storage in a vSphere environment coupled with the mobility of the VMware guests that reside on this remote storage. When guests are stored on shared storage, they can easily be moved from one host to another through hot or cold migrations.

Configuring Your vSphere Environment

PART II

Hot vs. Cold Migrations

A *hot migration* is simply the process of migrating a guest from one host to another while the guest is still operating. This task can be accomplished by purchasing a vSphere license that includes the VMware vMotion technology. CPU compatibility requirements between hosts are also required.

A *cold migration* refers to the task of migrating suspended or powered-off guests from one host to another. When used with shared storage, cold migrations do not have any CPU compatibility requirements as long as the guest is powered off.

Following are some of the typical operations that can be performed when using shared storage:

Zero or Minimal Guest Downtime   Zero downtime can be achieved by migrating guests from one host to another using vMotion or VMware DRS. Minimal downtime can be achieved by powering off or suspending guests, followed by migrating them to other hosts.

Guest Workload Balancing   VMware DRS allows you to manually or automatically migrate guests from one host to another to maintain an even level of host resource utilization.

Consolidated Storage   When hosts use centralized storage, all guests can be stored in the same location rather than on individual hosts. Compared to storing guests on individual hosts, consolidated storage allows for greater flexibility among hosts as well as a simplified storage architecture.

Disaster Recovery   Centralized storage provides for a central location to perform guest backups and restores. When vSphere is coupled with a storage system that incorporates replication, guests can be replicated to an alternate location for greater flexibility in recovering guests. Guests can then be restarted on hosts in the alternate location.

Simplified Storage Upgrades and Migrations   When new storage is purchased, Storage vMotion allows live migrations to be performed without interrupting end users.

Guidelines for Implementing Storage

The following guidelines apply to all three kinds of storage (Fibre Channel SAN, iSCSI SAN, and NFS):

- Choose the appropriate virtual SCSI controller for virtual machines. When creating a virtual machine, the wizard preselects the default controller based upon the operating system selected on the guest operating system page. The LSI Logic SAS and the VMware Paravirtual controllers are available only on virtual machine hardware version 7 guests or higher.

- Virtual machine volume management software cannot mirror most virtual disks. Windows dynamic disks are an exception but must be specially configured to operate properly.

The following guidelines apply to Fibre Channel SAN and iSCSI SAN storage:

- Make sure the hardware and firmware versions are compatible with vSphere ESXi hosts.

- ESXi does not support iSCSI- or Fibre Channel–connected tape devices.

- Configure only one VMFS volume for a presented LUN.

- Only configure a diagnostic partition if using a diskless (SAN boot) configuration.

- Raw device mappings should be used for raw disk access (to leverage SAN hardware snapshotting), for clustering a virtual machine with a physical machine as well as virtual-to-virtual clusters. VMware recommends all cluster data and quorum disks should be RDMs. They also can be useful for physical-to-virtual (P2V) backout plans.

- Guest-based multipathing software cannot be used to load-balance a single physical LUN.

- In Windows virtual machines on a SAN, increase the SCSI Timeout value to 60 for better tolerance of I/O delays caused by path failover or other quiesce or stun operations.

- Here are some LUN considerations:

  - LUN IDs must match across all hosts.

  - Provision LUNs to the appropriate host bus adapters (HBAs) and provision all iSCSI storage targets before attaching ESXi hosts to the SAN.

Configuring Your vSphere
Environment

PART II

- Make LUNs available to all hosts for greater flexibility using High Availability, DRS, Fault Tolerance, and vMotion.

- Remember to keep LUN IDs consistent across hosts. HBA failover is only possible if appropriate HBAs see the same LUNs.

- Ensure all systems have consistent paths to all SAN storage processors to prevent path thrashing, which can occur when vMotion or DRS is used with an active/passive SAN. (Path thrashing occurs when multiple hosts attempt to use different paths to access a datastore and cause the datastore to become unavailable.)

Configure Fibre Channel SAN Storage

Fibre Channel storage was the first supported shared storage for VMware ESX and remains a viable shared storage solution with vSphere. There are many SAN storage vendors on the market.

TIP   Before choosing any particular vendor and product offering, ensure it is on the HCL. The VMware HCL can be found here: www.vmware.com/go/hcl.

When implementing a SAN, keep the following in mind, as well as the items in "Guidelines for Implementing Storage," earlier in this chapter:

- Traditional SAN-based tools will not be visible to the virtual machines file system; only the ESXi operating system will be visible. You will have to use vSphere Client to monitor virtual machines.

- Use disk shares and Storage I/O Control (SIOC) to prioritize virtual machines sharing the same LUN.

- Here are some Fibre Channel HBA considerations:

  - When using multiple HBAs, use the same model and firmware revision for all of them.

  - A single HBA may be used for storage traffic, with a secondary HBA for failover. LUN traffic can be manually balanced across the HBAs for greater throughput on certain active/active SAN arrays. Set Path Policy to Fixed when using this configuration.

  - Set the timeout value for detecting a path failure in the HBA driver. For optimal performance, set this timeout to 30 seconds;

and for Windows guests set the standard disk timeout value within the operating system via the registry to 60 seconds.

- Configure proper HBA BIOS settings as well as queue depth if the configuration calls for something other than the default.

Fibre Channel storage can also be used for the ESXi installation. To use a Fibre Channel LUN to house the ESXi boot image, keep the following in mind:

- The HBA BIOS must be properly configured to access the SAN and presented LUNs.

- Because drivers scan the PCI bus in an ascending fashion, placing HBAs in the lowest slot number will allow drivers to detect them quickly.

- Whether using a single HBA in a non-redundant configuration, or dual HBAs in a redundant configuration, only a single path is available to hosts.

- The boot LUN having a LUN ID of 0 should be accessible only to the associated ESXi host that will be using the LUN.

- When booting from an active/passive SAN, ensure the designated storage processor's World Wide Name (WWN) is active. If the storage processor is passive, the ESXi host will fail to boot.

- Connections from the ESXi host must be made through a SAN fabric. Connecting HBAs directly to storage or through arbitrated loops is not supported.

Connect Fibre Channel Storage to an ESXi Host

In a typical configuration, Fibre Channel (FC) storage is used as a shared storage system for ESXi hosts. The vast majority of Fibre Channel storage implementations are configured in this manner. Because each Fibre Channel storage vendor has its own configuration parameters, a general installation guide cannot completely address all configuration steps for the available storage configurations available.

The basic process of connecting ESXi hosts to an FC SAN is as follows:

1. Connect FC cables from the ESXi host HBAs to the FC fabric.

2. Connect the FC cables from the storage array front-end ports to the FC fabric.

3. In the FC fabric configuration, zone the ESXi host HBAs to the front-end storage array ports using single initiator zoning.

4. Create LUNs and map them to ESXi hosts through the storage array's native presentation methods.

5. Configure multipathing as needed on the ESXi host.

ESXi hosts can now see the available LUNs when the HBAs are rescanned, as shown in Figure 7.1.

Figure 7.1: Fibre Channel devices displayed in vSphere Client

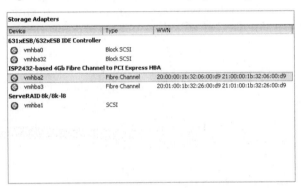

To configure and connect a specific vendor's storage system, consult VMware's Fibre Channel SAN Configuration Guide and the documentation specific to the storage system and VMware ESXi.

Manage Fibre Channel Storage on an ESXi Host

To get started with configuring FC-based datastores, the ESXi host must be aware of the LUNs that have been mapped to it. ESXi hosts will automatically scan the HBAs on initial bootup to determine which LUNs are available. If SAN storage is attached to a host after it has booted, a simple HBA rescan is required.

The time it takes to rescan the HBAs depends on the number of LUNs that are being presented to the HBAs. This does not typically take long, but it can delay the boot time of an ESXi host. The fewer LUN IDs to scan, the more quickly a host can continue with the boot process.

Modify the LUN Scanning Parameters

The VMkernel scans for LUN IDs from 0 to 255, giving a total of 256 possible LUNs for the host to recognize. Modifying the Disk.MaxLUN setting will improve the LUN discovery speed. The number of LUNs is not the only determining factor in the discovery speed, but it is a good place to start.

To change the maximum number of LUN IDs to scan, follow these steps:

1. From vSphere Client, select a host from Inventory.

2. Select the Configuration tab in the software panel and click Advanced Settings.

3. Select Disk from the list of options on the left of the Advanced Settings menu.

4. Scroll down to the Disk.MaxLUN setting.

5. Enter the largest LUN ID setting you want to scan to. For example, if LUN IDs from 0 to 30 are mapped by the SAN, enter 30 and click OK.

Sparse LUN support, enabled by default for ESXi, provides the ability to see multiple LUNs that are not sequentially numbered. For example, if you have LUN IDs of 0, 1, 3, and 6 mapped on the FC fabric, without sparse LUN support, only LUN IDs 0 and 1 would be visible to hosts in the same zone.

If LUN IDs *are* sequentially numbered, however, the discovery time can be shortened by disabling sparse LUN support. Figure 7.2 shows the setting to change to disable sparse LUN support.

Figure 7.2: Changing the sparse LUN support setting

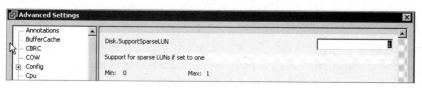

> **WARNING**   Only disable sparse LUN support if LUNs are sequentially numbered.

Take the following steps to disable Sparse LUN support:

1. From vSphere Client, select a host from Inventory.

2. Select the Configuration tab in the software panel, and click Advanced Settings.

Configuring Your vSphere Environment

PART II

3. Select Disk from the list of options on the left of the Advanced Settings menu.

4. Scroll down to Disk.SupportSparseLUN, and set the value to 0.

5. Click OK.

Rescan Storage Adapters

Rescanning the storage adapters will scan the attached storage in an attempt to discover LUNs. After rescanning the storage adapters, any storage that is available to the host's HBAs will be visible in the Details panel on the Configuration tab under Storage Adapters in the Hardware panel. To rescan storage adapters, follow these steps:

1. In vSphere Client, select a host from Inventory and click the Configuration tab.

2. In the Hardware panel, select Storage Adapters.

3. Because no datastores have been added, you only have to select Rescan All from the top-right corner of the screen.

4. To update a datastore after its configuration has been changed, select Refresh from the top-right corner of the screen.

5. If new LUNs are discovered, they will appear in the details panel. LUNs discovered after performing a rescan operation appear in the Details area of the Storage Adapters section of the vSphere Client (see Figure 7.1, earlier in this chapter).

Review and Configure Device Paths

Before attempting to create FC-based datastores, it is important to ensure that the storage paths are properly configured. SANs typically operate in an active/passive or active/active configuration.

These configurations require different path settings, depending on the configuration. It is best to follow the SAN manufacturer's recommendations when choosing the proper path configuration.

The following process will give you a better view of what paths are currently being used to communicate with attached storage:

1. From vSphere Client, select a host from Inventory.

2. Select the Configuration tab. Click Storage in the Hardware panel.

3. In the View panel, select Devices, then select the device you want to review.

4. Click Manage Paths on the right side of the Device Details panel.

5. Notice the Path Selection Policy in the top section of the Manage Paths dialog box. Figure 7.3 shows one of the three default VMware-provided path policies.

Figure 7.3: Fixed path policy

6. Depending on the type of SAN system the HBA is connected to, choose an appropriate path policy. The three default types are as follows:

> **Fixed** Uses a preferred path. If the path is unavailable, an alternate is chosen until the preferred path is available again. Active/active SANs typically use the fixed policy.
>
> **Most Recently Used (MRU)** Uses any available path. If the current path becomes unavailable, an alternative is chosen. When the original path is available again, the path is not moved back and stays on the most recently used path. Active/passive SANs typically use the MRU policy.
>
> **Round Robin** Uses an automatic pathing algorithm to determine the best path. Round robin is designed to better load-balance storage paths and I/O performance.

Additionally, any third-party path policies will be displayed if they are installed on the host. Currently, only EMC and Dell Equallogic provide the ability to use additional path policies.

7. Click Close.

Create a New FC VMFS Datastore

Follow the steps below to create a new Fibre Channel VMFS datastore:

1. From vSphere Client, select a host from Inventory.

2. Select the Configuration tab. Click Storage in the Hardware panel.

3. In the View panel, select Datastores.

4. Click Add Storage on the right side of the Datastores panel. The Add Storage wizard opens.

5. Choose Disk/LUN as the storage type and click Next. The right panel will display storage devices found after the HBAs were scanned.

6. Select a storage device and click Next.

7. Select the appropriate file system version, e.g., VMFS5, then click Next.

8. A review of the disk layout is displayed. Click Next.

9. Enter a descriptive datastore name and click Next.

10. Choose Maximum Available Space. Click Next.

Choosing Maximum Available Space will use all the available space on the LUN. It is important to remember that it is a best practice to configure only one VMFS volume, or datastore, per LUN.

11. Click Finish to complete the datastore setup process.

Configure NPIV for Virtual Machines

N-Port ID Virtualization (NPIV) is the process of allowing Fibre Channel HBAs to register multiple WWNs and use multiple addresses. It is advantageous in the situation where a WWN can be assigned to a virtual machine.

Some of the benefits of using NPIV are as follows:

- Virtual and physical systems can have SAN storage managed in the same fashion.

- NPIV prioritizes paths and provides quality of service to ensure disk bandwidth.

The limitations and requirements for NPIV to be used with guests include the following:

- The WWNs of the physical HBAs must have access to all LUNs that are to be accessed by virtual machines running on that host.

- The physical HBA used must support NPIV.

- Up to 16 WWN pairs are generated per virtual machine.

- When a guest with NPIV is cloned, the NPIV settings are not copied to the clone.

- SAN switches used must support NPIV.

- When configuring an NPIV LUN for access at the storage level, make sure that the NPIV LUN number and NPIV target ID match the physical LUN and Target ID.

- vSphere Client must be used to configure or modify virtual machines with WWNs.

- Virtual machines must be powered off when adding or modifying NPIV settings.

- Virtual machines with NPIV enabled cannot be Storage vMotioned.

To add a WWN mapping to a virtual machine, take the following steps:

1. In vSphere Client, edit the guest to which you want to assign a WWN by right-clicking the guest and choosing Edit Settings.

2. Click the Options tab and click Fibre Channel NPIV, as shown in Figure 7.4.

Figure 7.4: Fibre Channel NPIV options

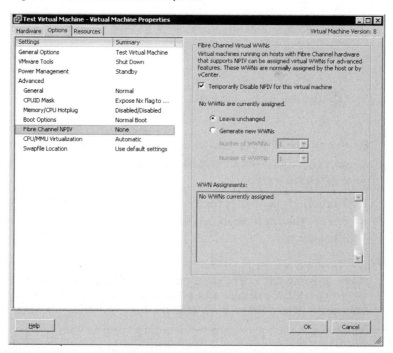

Configuring Your vSphere Environment

PART II

3. In the dialog box, select Generate New WWNs. Select the desired number of WWNN and WWPNs and click OK.

4. Click OK to close the guest configuration window.

5. Repeat steps 1 and 2 to view the WWNs that were generated, as you can see in Figure 7.5.

Figure 7.5: Generated WWNs

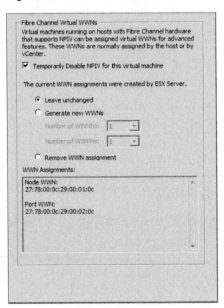

6. Record the WWNs, and give them to your SAN administrator to properly zone Raw Device Mapping (RDM) LUNs that will be used by the guest.

7. To properly configure the guest WWN within your SAN zoning, refer to the appropriate SAN documentation provided by your SAN vendor.

TIP If you want to use vMotion for a virtual machine that leverages NPIV, make sure to place the RDM file on the same datastore where the virtual machine's configuration files are.

Configure iSCSI SAN Storage

Before ESXi can work with an iSCSI SAN, you must set up your iSCSI initiators and storage. To do this, you must first observe certain basic requirements. This section discusses these requirements, provides recommendations, and then details how to provide access to the SAN by installing and setting up your hardware or software iSCSI initiators.

Become Familiar with ESXi iSCSI SAN Requirements

iSCSI storage has recently become a viable, cost-effective alternative to traditional Fibre Channel SANs.

TIP There are many iSCSI storage vendors on the market, so before choosing any particular vendor and product offering, ensure it is on the HCL. The VMware HCL can be found here: `www.vmware.com/go/hcl`.

When implementing an iSCSI SAN, keep in mind the following, as well as the items in "Guidelines for Implementing Storage," earlier in this chapter:

- The network configuration for iSCSI initiators and the iSCSI storage system should reside on a network separate from host and guest IP traffic.

- Ensure hardware iSCSI initiators are compatible with vSphere ESXi hosts.

- Ensure the iSCSI target authentication scheme is compatible with the iSCSI initiator type.

   Here are some network considerations:

   - A best practice is to provide a dedicated network for iSCSI traffic between VMware hosts and iSCSI storage systems.

   - To use software iSCSI, VMkernel networking must be configured.

   - To use hardware iSCSI, the HBA has to have network parameters configured.

   - The storage system discovery address must be pingable.

Configure Hardware iSCSI Initiators if Present

VMware ESXi supports dedicated physical iSCSI adapters installed in the ESXi host, provided they are certified and on the HCL. These physical adapters handle the iSCSI traffic in the same fashion as Fibre Channel HBAs do for Fibre Channel SANs. ESXi supports two types of hardware adapter:

Independent Hardware Adapters are capable of handling all iSCSI and network processing and management for ESXi.

Dependent Hardware Adapters depend on VMware's networking and iSCSI configuration and management interfaces.

To get started, you must configure the hardware iSCSI initiator. When doing so, ensure that network settings are correct and that iSCSI names are formatted properly.

1. Log in to either vCenter Server or an ESXi host using vSphere Client.

2. Select a host from the Inventory panel.

3. Select the Configuration tab.

4. Select Storage Adapters in the Hardware panel.

5. Configure the desired initiator by clicking Properties and then Configure.

6. Accept the default iSCSI name or enter a new name. Properly format the name to ensure compatibility with your iSCSI storage systems.

   iSCSI uses two different naming formats: iSCSI Qualified Name format (IQN) and the Enterprise Unique Identifier format (EUI). Determine which format you are using and follow that format's guidelines for the iSCSI name.

7. Enter an iSCSI alias to be used to identify the hardware iSCSI initiator.

8. Change the IP address settings to be able to utilize the iSCSI storage network.

9. Click OK.

iSCSI name changes will only be valid for new iSCSI sessions. Any existing settings will remain until iSCSI logout and re-login.

Configure Software iSCSI Initiators

VMware ESXi can use iSCSI storage without the need for physical iSCSI adapters. The VMkernel can talk directly to iSCSI targets provided the software iSCSI initiator is enabled. To use this capability, you must complete some additional networking configuration.

First, you need to enable the iSCSI initiator. Follow these steps:

1. Log in to vCenter or an ESXi host with vSphere Client.

2. Select a server from the Inventory panel.

3. Click the Configuration tab, and then click Storage Adapters in the Hardware panel.

4. Click Add in the upper-right corner.

5. Select Add Software iSCSI Adapter and click OK.

6. Select the iSCSI initiator under Storage Adapters and click Properties from within the Details pane.

7. Click Configure at the bottom right of the window.

8. Check Enabled.

9. The iSCSI name will be automatically populated. If desired, you can enter a new iSCSI name. Properly format the name to ensure compatibility with iSCSI storage systems.

10. Click OK.

A VMkernel port and one or more physical adapters are required to use iSCSI storage via the software iSCSI initiator. The number of physical adapters you want to use will dictate the network configuration:

- If only one physical adapter is used, the only networking requirement is to configure a VMkernel port mapped to the single physical adapter.

- If two or more physical adapters are used, each adapter must have a separate VMkernel port mapped to leverage iSCSI multipathing. However, there can be only one active VNIC uplink for the portgroup. All others must be "unused."

Create a VMkernel Port for Software iSCSI

A single VMkernel port can be used for communication with iSCSI targets. To configure the VMkernel port, follow these steps:

1. Log in to either the host or vCenter with vSphere Client.

2. Select the host from the Inventory panel.

3. Click the Configuration tab.

4. Click Networking.

5. Click Add Networking in the Virtual Switch view.

6. Select VMkernel and click Next.

7. Select Create A vSphere Standard Switch to create a new vSwitch, as shown in Figure 7.6.

Figure 7.6: Creating a virtual switch

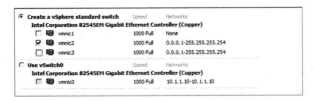

8. If using a new vSwitch, select an adapter to use for iSCSI traffic.

9. Click Next.

10. In the Port Group Properties section, enter a network label that will designate this VMkernel port, as shown in Figure 7.7.

Figure 7.7: Labeling the VMkernel port

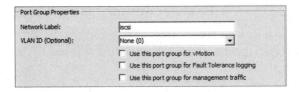

11. Click Next.

12. Specify the IP settings, as shown in Figure 7.8, and click Next.

Figure 7.8: Entering IP settings

NOTE   The network cards you are using with your iSCSI adapter must be on the same subnet (or have a layer 3 route to the iSCSI target) as your iSCSI target. Otherwise, your host will not be able to establish a session with the target.

---

13. Click Finish.

The network settings should appear similar to those in Figure 7.9.

Figure 7.9: Initial network settings

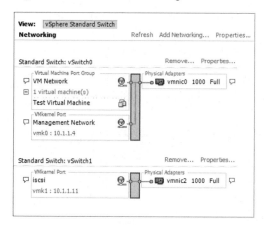

If only one physical adapter is going to be used for iSCSI traffic, configuration is complete. If more than one adapter is to be designated for iSCSI traffic, these steps may be repeated for the second adapter on a second virtual switch. Alternatively, additional VMkernel portgroups can be added on to the same vSwitch, so long as only one VMNIC is active per portgroup.

Configure Software iSCSI with Multipathing

Use this procedure if two or more network adapters are to be dedicated to iSCSI traffic and all the iSCSI network adapters are going to be connected to a single vSwitch. Each network adapter will be mapped to a single VMkernel port.

1. Log in to either the host or vCenter with vSphere Client.

2. Select the host from the Inventory panel.

3. Click the Configuration tab.

4. Click Networking.

5. Click Properties on the vSwitch being used for iSCSI.

6. Choose the Network Adapters tab, and click the add button at the bottom left to add one or more unclaimed network adapters to the vSwitch, as shown in Figure 7.10.

Figure 7.10: Add Adapter Wizard

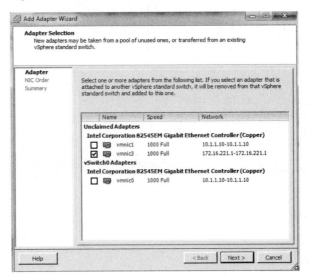

7. Click Next twice and then click Finish.

8. Ensure there is a VMkernel port for each physical adapter by viewing the Ports tab. If there are no distinct VMkernel ports for each network adapter, click Add, and follow the process described in the "Create a VMkernel Port for Software iSCSI" section earlier in this chapter.

9. At this point, all network adapters are active for all ports on the vSwitch. To map each adapter to a distinct VMkernel port:

   a. Pick a VMkernel port, and click Edit.

   b. Select the NIC Teaming tab.

   c. Select Override vSwitch Failover Order.

   d. Ensure only one network adapter is listed as active and all others (if any) are listed as Unused, as shown in Figure 7.11.

Figure 7.11: Mapping an adapter to a VMkernel port

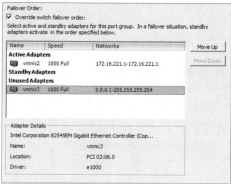

10. For each additional VMkernel port and network adapter, repeat step 1 through step 9 and choose adapters that are not assigned to other VMkernel ports. Figure 7.12 displays a configuration with two VMkernel ports using two network adapters.

Figure 7.12: Two VMkernel ports using two different network adapters

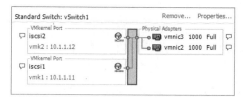

Bind iSCSI Adapters with VMkernel Adapters

Now that we have the software iSCSI adapters enabled and the VMkernel ports created, we need to bind them together. Follow these steps:

1. From within vSphere client, click the Configuration tab.

2. Within the Hardware pane on the left side, select Storage Adapters.

3. Select the iSCSI adapter from within the Storage Adapters list and click Properties in the Details pane.

4. From within the iSCSI Initiator Properties screen, select the Network Configuration tab.

5. Click Add and select one of the VMkernel adapters to bind with the iSCSI adapter (see Figure 7.13). Click OK.

Figure 7.13: Adding a VMkernel port to the software iSCSI initiator

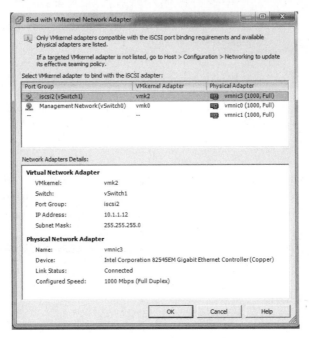

6. Repeat step 5 for any additional adapters you have.

7. Once you have added all of your adapters, click Close on the iSCSI Initiator Properties screen.

8. You should be prompted to rescan the host bus adapter. Click Yes.

Configure Jumbo Frames

Another consideration when using iSCSI storage is whether to enable jumbo frames. Jumbo frames are basically Ethernet frames that are larger than the standard 1,500 Maximum Transmission Units (MTUs). Jumbo frames can typically carry 9,000 bytes of data at a time. Therefore, they allow for bigger chunks of data to be transferred across an Ethernet network. To use jumbo frames, ensure that all devices on the network support them. vSphere supports jumbo frames up to 9,000 bytes, or 9 KB.

To configure jumbo frames on a vSwitch and VMkernel interface, follow these steps:

1. From within vSphere client, click the Configuration tab.

2. Within the Hardware pane on the left side, select Networking.

3. On the standard switch that you are using for iSCSI, click Properties.

4. On the Ports tab, select the standard switch and click Edit.

5. On the General tab in the Advanced Properties section, set the MTU size to match the largest MTU from among all NICs connected to the standard switch (see Figure 7.14). Click OK. You will need to consult the network card manufacturers' documentation to determine maximum MTU size for each card.

Figure 7.14: Configuring jumbo frames on a vSwitch

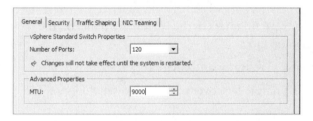

6. On the Ports tab, select a VMkernel adapter and click Edit.

7. On the General tab in the NIC settings section, set the MTU to match the value set on the standard switch in step 5 above. Click OK.

8. Repeat step 6 and step 7 for all VMkernel adapters on the standard switch, which should have jumbo frames enabled.

Configure iSCSI Targets for VMFS Datastores

Now that the iSCSI initiators have been configured, the next step is to configure ESXi to see iSCSI targets for the purpose of remote storage. iSCSI targets must be discovered by ESXi. Two methods of discovery are available:

- Dynamic Discovery (also known as SendTargets)
- Static Discovery

Each has a configuration tab in the properties of hardware and software iSCSI initiators.

Before proceeding into the configuration, it is important to know the differences between Dynamic Discovery and Static Discovery.

Whenever an initiator contacts an iSCSI device, a SendTargets request is sent to the device and asks for a list of targets on the device. When devices are seen by ESXi, they are automatically listed on the Static Discovery tab. If these targets are removed from the Static Discovery tab, the next time a SendTargets request is sent, the target may reappear. When the host is using Static Discovery, iSCSI addresses do not have to be rescanned to see storage. No SendTargets discovery request is sent to the specified iSCSI device or devices. The initiator has a list of targets it can contact and uses their IP address and target names to communicate with them.

To set up Dynamic Discovery, take the following steps:

1. Log in to vCenter or a specific host using vSphere Client.

2. Select a server from the Inventory panel.

3. Choose Storage Adapters in the Hardware panel on the Configuration tab.

4. Select an iSCSI initiator and click Properties.

5. Click the Dynamic Discovery tab, as shown in Figure 7.15.

Figure 7.15: Dynamic Discovery tab

6. Click Add to add a new iSCSI device that will initiate the SendTargets communication, as shown in Figure 7.16.

Figure 7.16: Initiating the SendTargets communication

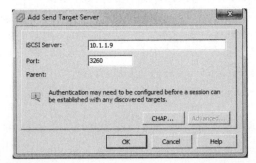

7. In the Add Send Targets Server dialog box, enter the IP address or iSCSI name of the iSCSI device and click OK.

Once successful communication has occurred between the initiator and the iSCSI device, the iSCSI server address will be displayed on the Dynamic Discovery tab, as shown in Figure 7.17.

Figure 7.17: iSCSI Server address is listed.

Additionally, any iSCSI storage targets discovered will appear in the Static Discovery tab. This is shown in Figure 7.18.

Figure 7.18: Discovered iSCSI targets are listed in the Static Discovery tab.

TIP   If an address, iSCSI name, or port is added incorrectly, the connection will fail. To modify the entry, it must be deleted and re-added properly, as Dynamic Discovery targets cannot be modified. To remove a Dynamic Discovery server, select it and click Remove.

With iSCSI initiators, in addition to the Dynamic Discovery method, you can also use Static Discovery, where you manually enter the IP addresses and the iSCSI names of the targets to be contacted. To set up Static Discovery, follow this procedure:

1. Log in to vCenter or a specific host using vSphere Client.

2. Select a server from the Inventory panel.

3. Choose Storage Adapters from the Hardware panel on the Configuration tab.

4. Select an iSCSI initiator and click Properties.

5. Click the Static Discovery tab.

6. Click Add to add a new iSCSI target. Enter the IP address or DNS name in conjunction with the target device name, as shown in Figure 7.19.

Figure 7.19: Add Static Target Server

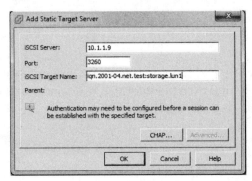

7. Click OK to add the Static target.

8. To remove a target, select the target and click Remove.

Static Discovery targets behave similarly to Dynamic Discovery targets in that they cannot be edited. If changes are required, the Static target will have to be removed and a new target added.

Configure CHAP Authentication

Unlike the Fibre Channel protocol, the iSCSI protocol does not limit physical devices to physical ports. With iSCSI operating over standard Ethernet, any device could potentially communicate with any other device on the same network. To address the situation where data is not protected between devices, the iSCSI protocol supports authentication. VMware ESXi supports Challenge Handshake Authentication Protocol (CHAP) for the purpose of securing iSCSI communications. CHAP authentication primarily uses a private value, known as a *CHAP secret*, to secure connections between iSCSI devices. This whole process can be simply described as password authentication. The hosts and the iSCSI targets must know the CHAP secret, or password, to be able to communicate with each other.

CHAP uses a three-way handshake algorithm to verify the identity of your host and, if applicable, of the iSCSI target when the host and target establish a connection. The verification is based on a predefined private value, or CHAP secret, that the initiator and target share.

When VMware ESX 3.0 was released, CHAP authentication could only be accomplished at the adapter level. This proved problematic if many different iSCSI devices were available to be used and they did not share a common CHAP secret. This remains true in VMware ESXi 5.0 with hardware-independent iSCSI initiators.

Using the software or dependent iSCSI initiator, however, VMware ESXi 5.0 not only supports CHAP authentication at the adapter level, but also at the level of each individual target. This addition provides VMware administrators with greater flexibility to communicate with many iSCSI targets that have one or more CHAP secret values. Table 7.3 displays the CHAP authentication levels supported by hardware and software iSCSI initiators.

Configuring Your vSphere Environment

PART II

Table 7.3: Adapter- and target-level CHAP authentication

Initiator Type	Adapter-Level CHAP	Target-Level CHAP
Independent	Yes	No
Dependent	Yes	Yes
Software	Yes	Yes

VMware ESXi 5.0 provides some additional levels of security and flexibility when hosts use iSCSI targets. With CHAP authentication, the authorization is only from the host to the iSCSI target. Mutual CHAP authentication has been added in vSphere to provide for two-way authentication between hosts and iSCSI targets. Not only does the host have to authenticate against the iSCSI target, but the iSCSI target has to authenticate with the host for data to flow between them. This provides for a more secure solution than simple one-way CHAP.

Additionally, CHAP authentication can be configured with some variable security levels that alter the behavior of authentication in securing data communications. Table 7.4 displays the different CHAP security levels.

Table 7.4: CHAP security levels

CHAP Security Level	Behavior	Supported Initiators
Do Not Use CHAP	CHAP authentication is not used. This disables authentication.	Software, Dependent Hardware, Independent Hardware
Do Not Use CHAP Unless Required By The Target	The host prefers not to use CHAP but will use CHAP authentication as an alternative.	Software, Dependant Hardware
Use CHAP Unless Prohibited By The Target	The host prefers CHAP authentication but will use connections that do not have CHAP enabled.	Software, Dependent Hardware, Independent Hardware
Use CHAP	CHAP authentication is required. There will be no successful connections without CHAP authentication.	Software, Dependent Hardware

When you configure CHAP settings, ensure that the iSCSI targets being used have the appropriate settings. Additionally, when you configure iSCSI targets, it is important to remember that the CHAP name and CHAP secret values are different for hardware and software iSCSI initiators:

Software iSCSI   CHAP name has a 511-character limit and the CHAP secret has a 255-character limit.

Hardware iSCSI   CHAP name has a 255-character limit and the CHAP secret has a 100-character limit.

When you are configuring CHAP authentication on iSCSI targets, plan accordingly to be able to accommodate software iSCSI initiators, hardware iSCSI initiators, or a combination of both.

NOTE   Keep in mind that all discovery addresses or static targets inherit the CHAP parameters that are set up at the initiator level.

To configure CHAP authentication for iSCSI targets, begin with these steps:

1. Log in to vCenter or an ESXi host using vSphere Client.

2. Select a server from the Inventory panel.

3. Click Storage Adapters in the Hardware panel of the Configuration tab.

4. To configure a desired iSCSI initiator, select the initiator and click Properties.

5. On the General tab, click CHAP.

6. To configure one-way CHAP, do the following under CHAP:

   a. For software iSCSI initiators, in the CHAP (Target Authenticates Host) section, select any of the options other than Do Not Use CHAP. If you want to configure Mutual CHAP, select Use CHAP.

   b. Specify the CHAP name. Make sure that the name you specify matches the name configured on the storage side.

   ▪ To set the CHAP name to the iSCSI adapter name, simply select Use Initiator Name.

   ▪ To set the CHAP name to anything other than the iSCSI adapter name, deselect Use Initiator Name and enter a name in the Name field.

   c. Enter a one-way CHAP secret to be used as part of authentication. Be sure to use the same secret that you enter on the storage side.

Figure 7.20 shows a one-way CHAP configuration in the CHAP Credentials window.

Figure 7.20: One-way CHAP configuration

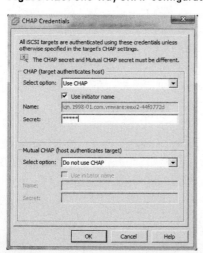

7. To configure Mutual CHAP, first configure one-way CHAP by following the directions in step 6. Be sure to select Use CHAP as an option for one-way CHAP. Then specify the following in the Mutual CHAP (Host Authenticates Target) section:

   a. Select Use CHAP.

   b. Specify the name or choose Use Initiator Name.

   c. Enter the secret. Make sure to use different secrets for the one-way CHAP and Mutual CHAP.

Figure 7.21 shows a Mutual CHAP configuration in the CHAP Credentials window.

Figure 7.21: Mutual CHAP configuration

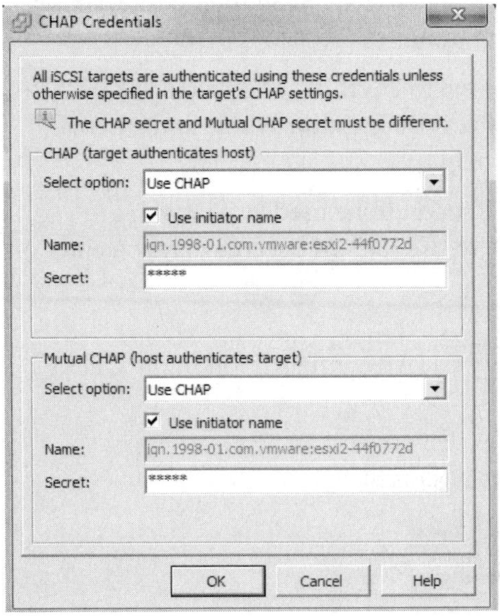

8. Click OK.

9. Rescan the adapter.

When CHAP and Mutual CHAP parameters are modified, they are only valid for new iSCSI connections. Any persistent connections will use the previous iSCSI credentials until you log out and log in again.

Set Up Per-Discovery and Per-Target CHAP Credentials

For software and dependent hardware iSCSI, you can configure different CHAP credentials for each discovery address or static target:

1. Log in to vCenter or an ESXi host using vSphere Client.

2. Select a server from the Inventory panel.

3. Click Storage Adapters in the Hardware panel of the Configuration tab.

4. Select the software iSCSI initiator and click Properties.

5. Select the Dynamic Discovery tab to configure authentication at the iSCSI storage system level.

6. From the list of available targets, select a target and click Settings, and then click CHAP. Figure 7.22 displays the CHAP Credentials screen with the default settings inherited from the software iSCSI initiator.

Figure 7.22: CHAP Credentials screen

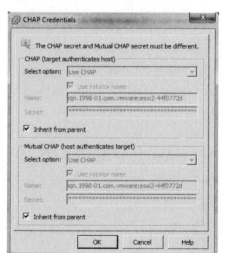

7. To configure one-way CHAP authentication, do the following in the section CHAP (Target Authenticates Host):

    a. Deselect Inherit From Parent.

    b. Select any of the options other than Do Not Use CHAP. If you want to configure Mutual CHAP, select Use CHAP.

    c. Specify the name or choose Use Initiator Name.

    d. Enter the CHAP secret for authentication. This must match the secret value on the storage side.

8. Mutual CHAP is configured only after CHAP is configured in the previous step. Specify the following under Mutual CHAP:

    a. Deselect Inherit From Parent.

    b. Select Use CHAP.

    c. Enter the Mutual CHAP name.

    d. Enter a Mutual CHAP secret. This secret value cannot be the same as the CHAP secret.

9. Click OK.

Static Discovery targets can also be configured with independent CHAP and Mutual CHAP values by performing the following steps:

1. Click the Static Discovery tab, select an iSCSI target, and click Settings.

2. Click CHAP.

3. Perform steps 6 through 9 in the preceding list for each Static Discovery target that will be using CHAP or Mutual CHAP authentication.

4. Rescan the adapter.

If any CHAP or Mutual CHAP values change, they will be used for new iSCSI sessions. For existing sessions, new settings will not be used until you log out and log in again.

Create a New iSCSI VMFS Datastore

To add an iSCSI datastore, take the following steps:

1. From vSphere Client, choose a host from Inventory.

2. Select the Configuration tab, and then select Storage in the Hardware panel.

3. In the View panel, select Datastores.

4. Click Add Storage from the right side of the Datastores panel. The Add Storage wizard will open.

5. Choose Disk/LUN as the storage type and click Next. The right panel will display storage devices found after the HBAs were scanned.

6. Select a storage device and click Next. A review of the disk layout is displayed.

7. Click Next.

8. Enter a descriptive datastore name and click Next.

9. Choose Maximum Available Space. Click Next.

   Choosing Maximum Available Space will use all of the available space on the LUN. It is a best practice to configure only one VMFS volume, or datastore, per LUN.

10. Click Next.

11. Click Finish to complete the datastore setup process.

Configure NFS Storage

The Network File System (NFS) protocol is another remote storage option supported by vSphere. As with iSCSI, NFS storage is accessed via an Ethernet network. Keep in mind that NFS storage is actually not a VMFS datastore, but rather a remotely mounted NFS export. Storage multipathing is not available with NFS storage. However, you do have the option of providing multiple VMNICs for the purposes of resiliency and portgroup load balancing.

Configure NFS Storage with ESXI

NFS-based storage has been around for approximately 25 years and several different versions have been released over that time. vSphere currently supports version 3, or NFSv3. Any device that provides storage using NFSv3 should work with vSphere, but to be certain, ensure the device is on the HCL. The VMware HCL can be found here: `http://www.vmware.com/go/hcl`.

When implementing NFS storage, keep in mind the following:

- Make sure the hardware and firmware versions are compatible with vSphere ESXi hosts.

- Storage vendor documentation should be consulted for additional NFS device configuration and host configurations.

- Eight NFS datastores are supported by default.

- A maximum of 256 NFS datastores can be mounted to an ESXi host.

- As with iSCSI storage, it is best to have a dedicated and secure Ethernet network for NFS storage, separate from host and guest IP traffic.

- In Windows virtual machines, increase the SCSI Timeout value parameter for better tolerance of I/O delays caused by path failover.

- ESXi does not restrict the size of the NFS datastore. The maximum size is determined by the NFS server.

- The use of non-ASCII characters is supported if the NFS server also includes international support.

Create a VMkernel Port to Connect to NFS Storage

For our example, the procedure for creating a VMkernel port to connect to NFS storage is identical to the steps for creating one for software iSCSI. For the step-by-step instructions, please refer to the earlier section "Create a VMkernel Port for Software iSCSI."

NOTE   There are different steps for configuring VMkernel portgroup load balancing for NFS if Ethernet cross-stack/802.3ad link aggregation is supported on the upstream switches. This procedure is beyond the scope this book.

Another configuration option to consider enabling when using NFS storage is jumbo frames. Jumbo frames also are covered in detail in the section "Create a VMkernel Port for Software iSCSI."

The default installation of vSphere supports a maximum of eight NFS datastores. You can use up to 256 NFS datastores if you modify the NFS.MaxVolumes parameter before attaching the first NFS datastore if needed. To change the maximum number of NFS volumes, follow this procedure:

1. Log in to either the host or vCenter with vSphere Client.

2. Select the host from the Inventory panel.

3. Click the Configuration tab.

4. Click Advanced Settings within the Software pane.

5. Click NFS in the left panel of Advanced Settings.

6. Scroll until the NFS.MaxVolumes setting is visible. (See Figure 7.23.)

Figure 7.23: NFS.MaxVolumes setting

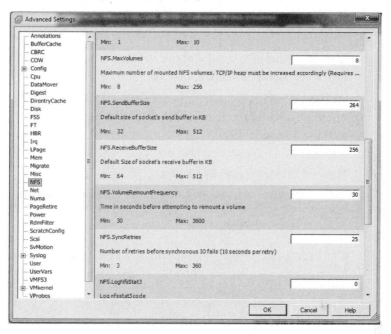

7. Change the NFS.MaxVolumes setting to the number you want.

8. Click OK.

9. Reboot the ESXi host.

Attach a NFS Mount as a Datastore

NFS datastores are different from both FC and iSCSI VMFS volumes. The file system that the ESXi host uses is not a VMFS formatted file system. Also, there is no way to configure the amount of space that the host sees from vSphere Client without setting up an option like quotas on the NFS server. The space available to the host is configured on the NFS device. Follow these steps to add an NFS mount as a datastore:

1. From vSphere Client, choose a host from Inventory.

2. Select the Configuration tab, and then select Storage from the Hardware panel.

3. In the View panel, select Datastores.

4. Click Add Storage on the right side of the Datastores panel.

5. The Add Storage wizard will open. Choose Network File System as the storage type and click Next.

6. As shown in Figure 7.24, in the Server text box, enter the fully qualified domain name (FQDN) or IP address of the NFS storage device.

Figure 7.24: Mounting an NFS export

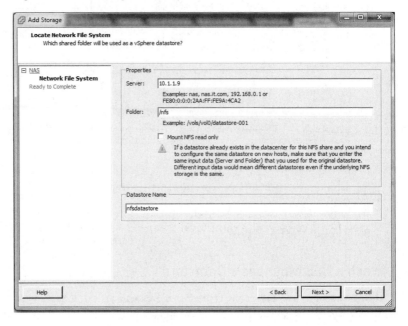

7. In the Folder text box, enter the name of the NFS export.

8. In the Datastore Name text box, enter the name of the datastore.

9. Click Next. A review of the NFS mount configuration is displayed.

10. Click Finish to complete the datastore setup process.

Script for Adding and Removing NFS Datastores

An alternative to working through the steps outlined in the "Attach a NFS Mount as a Datastore" section is to log in to the ESXi console and run an esxcfg-nas command similar to the example:

```
esxcfg-nas -a -o 10.1.1.9 -s /nfs nfs-datastore
```

The parameters in the example command work as follows:

- −a adds a new NFS filesystem.

- −o sets the host name or IP address.

- −s sets the name of the share on the remote server.

If you are adding multiple NFS datastores, you can write a script to mount them all at once. You would then run this script across all hosts that need the NFS datastores. This is an easy way to ensure the datastore names are consistent across all hosts.

```
#!/bin/bash
esxcfg-nas -a -o 10.1.1.9 -s /nfs1 nfs-datastore1
esxcfg-nas -a -o 10.1.1.9 -s /nfs2 nfs-datastore2
esxcfg-nas -a -o 10.1.1.9 -s /nfs3 nfs-datastore3
```

To remove an NFS mount using the esxcfg-nas command, use the −d option, like this:

```
esxcfg-nas -d nfs-datastore
```

NOTE   It is important to note that the -d option does not delete the data on the remote NFS server. You are simply removing the NFS datastore from the ESXi host. By contrast, when you delete a VMFS datastore, the data will be lost.

Configuring Your vSphere Environment

PART II

8

High Availability and Business Continuity

IN THIS CHAPTER, YOU WILL LEARN TO:

Configuring Your vSphere Environment

PART II

nformation technology (IT) professionals in organizations of all sizes and types seek to minimize downtime, planned or unplanned. Downtime means lost productivity, and lost productivity means lost money. In some organizations, the amount of money lost due to downtime can be quite significant. VMware vSphere provides a number of features that help reduce or eliminate downtime, both planned and unplanned.

Minimize Planned Downtime

There are a variety of reasons why planned downtime might be necessary. Perhaps you, as a system administrator, need to perform hardware maintenance on a physical server. Perhaps a storage array needs to be upgraded or replaced. In either case, VMware vSphere offers two key features that help you minimize the amount of planned downtime that is required in many instances. In this section, we'll review both features: vMotion (live migration of virtual machines) and Storage vMotion (live migration of virtual machine storage).

Configure and Use vMotion

vMotion is the live migration of running virtual machines from one physical ESXi host to a second physical ESXi host, without any downtime or without any interruption in service. Generally, you can use vMotion to move virtual machines without your end users even knowing that a live migration occurred. This enables you to easily change the location of running virtual machines on the fly in response to changing business needs. If you need to take a physical ESXi host down in the middle of the day for emergency hardware maintenance, you can use vMotion to move all the virtual machines on that host to another host and then take the first ESXi host down for maintenance. When the maintenance is complete, you can use vMotion to bring the virtual machines back to the original host again. All of this occurs without any downtime or interruption of service to the applications running within the virtual machines.

NOTE vMotion is a core component of VMware vSphere and is leveraged in a number of different ways. VMware Distributed Resource Scheduler (DRS) uses vMotion as the mechanism to balance workload distribution across a cluster of ESXi hosts. Maintenance mode uses vMotion to vacate an ESXi host so that the host can be taken offline for maintenance. vSphere Fault Tolerance (FT), discussed later in this chapter, uses a form of vMotion to create the secondary VM.

Configure an ESXi Host for vMotion

vMotion has several prerequisites that the ESXi hosts must meet before you can use it to migrate a running virtual machine:

- The source and destination ESXi hosts must use the same processor family (Intel or AMD) and generation (Xeon 55*xx*, AMD 83*xx*). Migrations between different versions of the same processor family—for example, between a Xeon 55*xx* and a Xeon 54*xx*—are possible only when using Enhanced vMotion Compatibility (EVC).

- The source and destination ESXi hosts must have identically configured virtual machine port groups and/or must participate in the same vSphere Distributed Switch.

- The ESXi hosts must be managed by the same vCenter Server instance.

- The source and destination ESXi hosts must have Gigabit Ethernet or better connectivity within the same Layer 2 broadcast domain.

- Licensing.

Once all the other requirements have been met, the final step in configuring vMotion on an ESXi host is to create one or more VMkernel ports and enable them for vMotion. These VMkernel ports must have Gigabit Ethernet or better connectivity to the physical network.

The procedure for creating a VMkernel port differs depending on whether you are using a vSphere Standard Switch or a vSphere Distributed Switch.

To create a VMkernel port on a vSphere Standard Switch and enable it for vMotion, use these steps:

1. Select the ESXi host on which you want to create the VMkernel port and click the Configuration tab.

2. Click the Networking link.

3. Select the Virtual Switch button to view the vSphere Standard Switch configuration for the selected ESXi host.

4. Click the Add Networking link. This opens the Add Network wizard.

5. Select the VMkernel radio button, and then click Next.

6. Select whether to create a new virtual switch or use an existing virtual switch, as appropriate for your environment. If you are creating a new virtual switch, you must also select the network interface cards (NICs) that will serve as uplinks for the new virtual switch. Click Next when you are ready to proceed.

7. Supply a name for the VMkernel port and a VLAN ID, if necessary.

8. Select the check box Use This Port Group For vMotion, and then click Next.

9. If you want to use Dynamic Host Configuration Protocol (DHCP), select Obtain IP Settings Automatically. Otherwise, select Use The Following IP Settings and then enter the IP address, subnet mask, and VMkernel default gateway. Click Next when you are finished.

10. Review the configuration and, if it is correct, click the Finish button to exit the wizard. Otherwise, use the Back button to go back and make the necessary changes.

To create a VMkernel port on a vSphere Distributed Switch and enable it for vMotion, follow these steps:

1. Select the ESXi host on which you want to create the VMkernel port, and then click the Configuration tab. Note that this host must already be a member of the vSphere Distributed Switch.

2. Click the Networking link.

3. Select the Distributed Virtual Switch button to view the vSphere Distributed Switch configuration for the selected ESXi host.

4. Click the Manage Virtual Adapters link.

5. In the Manage Virtual Adapters dialog box, click Add link. This opens the Add Virtual Adapter wizard.

6. Select the New Virtual Adapter radio button, and then click Next.

7. Select the VMkernel radio button and click Next.

8. With the Select Port Group radio button selected, choose an existing port group to host the new VMkernel port. If you don't already have a port group for the VMkernel port, you must cancel this process, create the port group, and then restart these steps.

9. Be sure to select the Use This Virtual Adapter For vMotion check box.

10. Once you've selected a port group and selected the Use This Virtual Adapter For vMotion check box, click Next.

11. If you want to use Dynamic Host Configuration Protocol (DHCP), select the Obtain IP Settings Automatically radio button. Otherwise, select the Use The Following IP Settings radio button and then enter the IP address, subnet mask, and VMkernel default gateway. Click Next when you are finished.

12. Review the configuration and, if it is correct, click the Finish button to finish the wizard. Otherwise, use the Back button to go back and make the necessary changes.

After you've created the VMkernel port and enabled it for vMotion on at least two hosts, you are ready to migrate a running virtual machine, assuming you've ensured that the ESXi hosts meet the other requirements listed earlier.

Use vMotion to Migrate a Virtual Machine

In the same way that the ESXi hosts have requirements in order to use vMotion, virtual machines must also meet certain requirements in order for vMotion to work. The requirements for a running virtual machine to migrate using vMotion are as follows:

- The virtual machine must reside on shared storage that is accessible to both the source and destination ESXi hosts. This includes the virtual machine's disk, configuration, log, and nonvolatile random access memory (NVRAM) files.

- The virtual machine must not be connected to any device physically available to only one ESXi host, such as a floppy drive, CD/DVD drive, serial port, parallel port, or raw disk storage. This includes a Raw Device Mapping (RDM) storage LUN zoned to only one host.

NOTE RDMs can operate in virtual mode or in physical mode. Physical mode RDMs allow the use of SAN management agents inside a VM and LUNs up to 64 TB in size, but limit VM snapshot capability. For more detailed information, consult the VMware vSphere documentation.

Configuring Your vSphere Environment

PART II

- The virtual machine must not be connected to an internal-only virtual switch (that is, a virtual switch without any connectivity to the physical network).

- The virtual machine must not have its CPU affinity set to a specific CPU.

Once you have verified that a virtual machine meets these requirements, you are ready to actually migrate a virtual machine using vMotion. To do so, perform these steps:

1. Right-click the virtual machine you wish to migrate and from the context menu, select Migrate. This starts the Migrate Virtual Machine wizard.

2. Select the Change Host radio button, and then click Next.

3. Select the destination host or cluster to which this virtual machine should be migrated. If vCenter detects an incompatibility, the details will be displayed in the lower portion of the Migrate Virtual Machine wizard and the Next button will be grayed out, as shown in Figure 8.1. You will need to correct the reported compatibility issues before you can proceed. If no compatibility issues are listed, click Next to continue.

Figure 8.1: The Migrate Virtual Machine wizard won't allow a vMotion operation to continue if compatibility issues are detected.

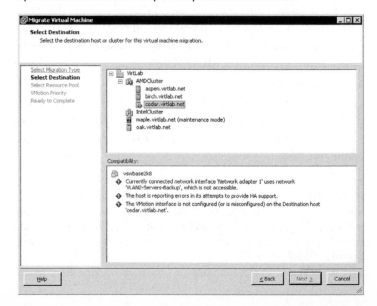

4. If multiple resource pools exist on the destination ESXi host or cluster, you must select the desired destination resource pool, and then click Next. This option will not appear if the destination host or cluster does not have more than one resource pool.

5. Select Reserve CPU For Optimal vMotion Performance (Recommended) to set aside guaranteed CPU resources for the live migration. Otherwise, as the text indicates on the Migrate Virtual Machine wizard, the duration of the vMotion operation might be extended. Click Next.

6. Review the settings and, if everything is correct, click Finish. Otherwise, click the Back button to go back and change the settings as needed.

vSphere Client's Tasks pane will show the progress of the vMotion migration. If the migration fails, you will need to troubleshoot the failure.

Troubleshooting vMotion

Some common configurations problems that users see with vMotion are as follows:

- The ESXi hosts do not have a VMkernel NIC enabled for vMotion. You'll need to create a VMkernel NIC and enable it for vMotion, as explained in the section titled "Configure an ESXi Host for vMotion" earlier in this chapter.

- The virtual machine has a virtual device backed by a physical resource (like a CD/DVD or floppy drive, serial port, or parallel port). All such devices must be marked as Disconnected in the virtual machine's settings. More information on how to correct this situation is provided in Chapter 9.

- The CPUs on the source and destination host are not compatible. It may be possible to resolve this issue using Enhanced vMotion Compatibility (EVC); otherwise, there is no supported workaround. EVC is described in more detail in Chapter 1.

- The source and destination ESXi hosts do not have matching port groups or do not participate in the same vSphere Distributed Switch. Ensure that network settings are consistent on both hosts or that both hosts participate in the same vSphere Distributed Switch.

Configuring Your vSphere Environment

PART II

Migrate Virtual Disks with Storage vMotion

Similar in nature to vMotion, Storage vMotion is a technology that allows you to migrate the storage of a running virtual machine from one storage location to a second storage location with no downtime. This gives you a powerful tool for balancing storage workloads, migrating to new storage solutions, or responding to changing storage requirements.

Unlike vMotion, Storage vMotion does not require any specific configuration on each ESXi host, other than connectivity to the source and destination datastores. Also unlike vMotion, you can use Storage vMotion with VMs on local storage. Because the ESXi host must have connectivity to both the source and destination datastores, you can't perform a local-to-local migration of storage using Storage vMotion, but you can perform local-to-shared or shared-to-local storage migrations.

To migrate a running virtual machine using Storage vMotion, follow these steps:

1. Right-click the running virtual machine whose storage you want to relocate and select Migrate.

2. In the Migrate Virtual Machine wizard, select Change Datastore and click Next.

3. If there are multiple resource pools on the ESXi host, select the destination resource pool. If you want the resource pool to remain unchanged, select the same resource pool in which the VM is currently located. Click Next.

4. Select the destination datastore. If vCenter detects a compatibility error, that error will be displayed at the bottom of the dialog box. You will need to cancel the wizard, correct the error, and then restart the process. Click Next to continue.

5. Select the Same Format As Source radio button to preserve the format of the virtual machine's virtual disk files. Otherwise, select Thin Provisioned Format or Thick Format as appropriate. Click Next.

6. Review the configuration and, if everything is correct, click Finish. Otherwise, use the Back button to go back and make the necessary changes.

The Tasks pane of vSphere Client displays the progress of the Storage vMotion operation. Depending on the size of the disks being migrated, the process may be lengthy. There is no downtime during the actual disk migration process, although virtual machine performance may be negatively impacted.

The most common problem with Storage vMotion involves VM snapshots. In vSphere versions prior to vSphere 5, a VM may not have an active snapshot in order for you to migrate the storage using Storage vMotion. All snapshots must be committed and removed before Storage vMotion can migrate the storage. If the snapshots cannot be committed, you have the option of using vCenter Converter Standalone, as outlined in Chapter 10, to perform a virtual-to-virtual migration to commit the snapshots.

Protect Against Host Failure

Downtime isn't always planned, and a key part of ensuring high availability and business continuity is protecting against unplanned downtime as well. The two primary causes of unplanned downtime are host failure (when an ESXi host fails for some reason) and VM failure (when the guest operating system within a virtual machine fails for some reason). In this section, we'll discuss how to protect against host failure; in the next section, you'll learn how to guard against VM failure.

VMware vSphere provides two features that are intended to help you protect against the failure of an ESXi host:

- vSphere High Availability (HA) uses a heartbeat to detect the failure of an ESXi host and restarts virtual machines when it detects a host failure.

- vSphere Fault Tolerance (FT) uses VMware's vLockstep technology to keep two virtual machines mirrored in real time. If the host where the primary VM is running fails, the secondary VM takes over almost instantaneously.

NOTE   vSphere FT requires vSphere HA to be enabled before it can be enabled.

Set Up vSphere High Availability

vSphere High Availability (HA) provides functionality to automatically restart virtual machines in the event of a physical host failure. vSphere HA accomplishes this through the use of an agent that runs on each ESXi host; this agent communicates with the agent on other hosts within a

Configuring Your vSphere Environment

PART II

vSphere HA-enabled cluster. When the agent detects that a host has failed, the VMs on that host are automatically restarted on an available host in the cluster. As the vSphere administrator, you have the ability to configure key parameters such as failover capacity and VM restart priority.

Because vSphere HA requires communication between the ESXi hosts, it is sensitive to network failures. You should ensure that the management interfaces on your ESXi hosts have adequate network redundancy. vCenter Server will warn you if an ESXi host does not have management network redundancy, as you can see in Figure 8.2.

Figure 8.2: vCenter will warn you if ESXi hosts do not have sufficient management network redundancy.

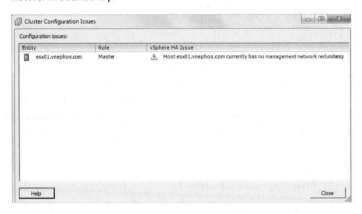

NOTE   vSphere HA running on ESX/ESXi hosts prior to vSphere 5 is very sensitive to name resolution issues. Be sure that domain name system (DNS) name resolution is working correctly on all ESX/ESXi hosts in the cluster. Each ESX/ESXi host should be able to resolve both the short name and the fully qualified domain name (FQDN) for all the other ESX/ESXi hosts in the cluster.

Enabling vSphere HA on a Cluster

After you've verified the prerequisites and you're ready to enable vSphere HA on an existing cluster of ESXi hosts, follow these steps:

1. Right-click the cluster and select Edit Settings.

2. Select the Turn On vSphere HA check box.

3. Click OK to apply the settings.

When you click OK, vCenter will start configuring the HA agent on each ESXi host. The Tasks pane in vSphere Client will show you the progress of configuring vSphere HA on each host in the cluster.

After vSphere HA has been enabled on a cluster, there are additional settings you can adjust, including admission control and admission control policy. These are discussed next.

Configuring vSphere HA Failover and Capacity Settings

For the most part, vSphere HA is self-configuring. When you enable vSphere HA as described previously, vCenter configures each of the hosts, and the hosts will begin sending and receiving heartbeats. There are a couple of settings, however, that you might need to adjust for your specific environment. Figure 8.3 shows the settings dialog box for a vSphere HA–enabled cluster.

Figure 8.3: Admission Control and Admission Control Policy are two additional settings you might need to configure for vSphere HA.

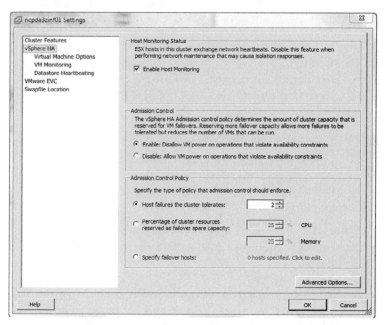

As you can see in Figure 8.3, Admission Control has two possible settings:

Enable: Disallow VM Power On Operations That Violate Availability Constraints   With this setting, vCenter will prevent the user from powering on more VMs than the vSphere HA–enabled cluster can handle based on the configured failover capacity. This ensures that the cluster is always capable of handling the VMs running on the hosts in the cluster, even during times of degraded capacity.

Disable: Allow VM Power On Operations That Violate Availability Constraints   When Admission Control is set to Allow VM Power On Operations That Violate Availability Constraints, vCenter will not prevent the user from starting more VMs than the cluster can handle based on the configured failover capacity. In times of degraded capacity due to one or more ESXi host failures, some VMs might not have enough resources to run.

The Admission Control setting is affected by the Admission Control Policy, which controls the failover capacity for the vSphere HA–enabled cluster. There are three possible ways to specify failover capacity for the cluster, as you can see in Figure 8.3:

Host Failures The Cluster Tolerates   This option allows you to specify the number of ESXi host failures the cluster should be able to handle. For example, in a cluster of four ESXi hosts, setting this value to 2 means that the cluster should plan for a maximum of 50 percent capacity on the cluster.

Percentage Of Cluster Resources Reserved As Failover Spare Capacity   This option allows you to specify a percentage of overall capacity that should be reserved. In a cluster of four ESXi hosts, setting this value to 25 percent is roughly analogous to setting the host failures setting to 1.

Specify Failover Hosts   This option allows you to specify particular hosts that should be used as failover in the event of an ESXi host failure.

You might need to adjust these settings based on your environment. For example, if you have a four-node cluster and you want to be sure that you do not run more virtual machines than could be handled if one of those nodes failed, you would set Admission Control to Disallow VM Power On Operations That Violate Availability Constraints. In the Admission Control Policy settings, you would specify Host Failures The Cluster Tolerates as 1.

Setting VM Restart Priority and Isolation Response

vSphere HA also provides you with the option of configuring the VM restart priority. This value can be set on a cluster-wide basis, as well as on a per-VM basis. Together, this allows you to grant a higher priority to more important workloads and force less important workloads to use a lower priority when restarting. Figure 8.4 shows the user interface for setting both the cluster-wide VM restart priority as well as the per-VM restart priority.

Figure 8.4: You can configure VM restart priority on a cluster-wide basis as well as on a per-VM basis.

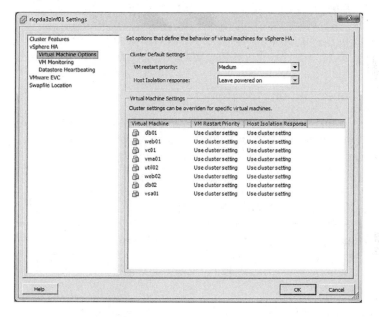

In addition to VM restart priority, you can also set the host isolation response on a cluster-wide basis as well as on a per-VM basis. The *host isolation response* is what happens when an ESXi host in a vSphere HA–enabled cluster loses connectivity to all the rest of the hosts in the cluster. In this instance, the ESXi host must determine the answer to this question: Am I isolated from the network, or did the rest of the cluster go offline?

The answer to this question is determined by attempting to get a response to a ping to the default isolation address or by attempting to update a datastore heartbeating file on a shared storage volume. The default isolation address is, by default, set the same as the default gateway for the ESXi host's management interfaces. Additionally, vSphere

HA automatically chooses two datastores shared across the cluster for heartbeating. If the ESXi host receives a response from the isolation address or can continue to access the heartbeating datastores, then it knows that it is not isolated from the network and that the rest of the cluster must be offline. If the ESXi host does not receive a ping response and cannot access the heartbeating datastores, it will determine that it is isolated and then trigger the isolation response. The default isolation response is to leave virtual machines powered on. This is so that other hosts in the cluster can't start up the virtual machines. You may want to change the isolation response either for the entire cluster or on a per-VM basis. This is accomplished in the same way as the VM restart priority, as shown in Figure 8.4.

So far we've described the majority of the configuration that you might need to perform for vSphere HA. However, in some instances, you may need to set advanced options. We'll explore these options next.

Setting Advanced Options for vSphere HA

In many cases, most users will never need to bother with the Advanced Options button (shown earlier, in Figure 8.3). However, in some cases, you might have a need to set a specific value here. Table 8.1 describes a few of the most commonly used values.

Table 8.1: Commonly used vSphere HA Advanced Options

Advanced Option	Value	Description
das.usedefaultisolationaddress	True or False.	Instructs ESXi whether to use the default isolation address (the default gateway for the management interfaces).
das.isolationaddress[x]	Value is an IP address. [x] is a unique optional value from 1 to 10.	Specifies the IP address(es) that an ESXi host should use to determine if it is isolated.
das.failuredetectiontime	Value is time in milliseconds.	If a host has received no heartbeats from another host, it waits this amount of time before declaring that host as failed.
das.failuredetectioninterval	Value is time in milliseconds.	Specifies the heartbeat interval among ESXi hosts in a vSphere HA–enabled cluster.

After setting any of these values, you must right-click on the ESXi hosts in the cluster and select Reconfigure For HA for the new setting to take effect.

Troubleshooting vSphere HA

Prior to vSphere 5, the most common problem with vSphere HA revolved around name resolution. Misconfigured DNS settings, such as different domain names within the cluster, caused vSphere HA to fail to configure correctly. After many complaints regarding this issue and others, VMware completely rewrote vSphere HA in vSphere 5 and DNS is no longer a dependency. However, if you're running older versions of ESX/ESXi, it is imperative that you ensure that every host is able to resolve the short and FQDN name of every other host in the cluster in addition to the vCenter Server before you attempt to enable vSphere HA.

Some other common problems with vSphere HA include the following:

- The management interface's default gateway does not respond to ping requests. In this case, vSphere HA won't function correctly because hosts will not be able to determine whether they are isolated. Use the das.usedefaultisolationaddress and das.isolationaddress advanced settings to specify a different isolation address.

- The network architecture during a failure may cause isolation response events. In some cases, convergence after a network failure may exceed the default interval that ESXi hosts use to determine host failures. You can increase the default intervals and failure detection times as described in the section "Setting Advanced Options for vSphere HA," earlier in this chapter.

Set Up vSphere Fault Tolerance

Another feature within VMware vSphere used to provide High Availability is vSphere Fault Tolerance. vSphere FT utilizes VMware's vLockstep technology to keep two virtual machines—a primary VM and a secondary VM—in perfect synchrony with each other. These mirrored VMs run on two different physical hosts. If either of these physical hosts fails, the virtual machine will continue running on the other host, ensuring a seamless failover with no downtime in the event of a host failure.

Configuring Your vSphere Environment

PART II

Because vSphere FT builds on top of vSphere HA, the two features work together to protect the VM workload in all different host failure scenarios. Consider these three examples:

- In the event of the failure of the ESXi host on which the primary (protected) VM is running, the secondary VM becomes the new primary and takes over seamlessly. vSphere FT creates a new secondary VM on another ESXi host.

- In the event of the failure of the ESXi host on which the secondary VM is running, the primary VM continues running without any interruption. vSphere FT creates a new secondary VM on another ESXi host.

- In the event both of the ESXi hosts involved fail, vSphere HA will restart the primary VM on a new ESXi host. vSphere FT will then create a new secondary VM on another ESXi host.

Examining vSphere FT Requirements

vSphere FT has some configuration requirements that you must satisfy before you can enable it on a specific virtual machine. Requirements to support vSphere FT exist at the cluster, host, and virtual machine levels:

- vSphere HA must be enabled on the cluster. Host monitoring should also be enabled for the cluster.

- Host certificate checking must be enabled on all hosts that you will use for vSphere FT. Host certificate checking is enabled by default.

- All hosts must have a vMotion and a Fault Tolerance Logging NIC configured.

- At least two hosts must have CPUs from the same compatible CPU group. Maximum flexibility is possible when all the hosts in the cluster have compatible CPUs.

- All hosts must run the same ESXi version and patch level.

- All hosts must have access to virtual machine networks and datastores.

ESXi hosts have the following requirements to use vSphere FT:

- Hosts must have a CPU that supports vSphere FT.

NOTE VMware Knowledge Base article 1008027, "Processors and Guest Operating Systems that Support VMware Fault Tolerance," available from VMware's website at http://kb.vmware.com/kb/1008027, contains information on the CPU types supported by vSphere FT.

- The ESXi host must have Hardware Virtualization enabled in the BIOS. Some hardware manufacturers ship servers with Hardware Virtualization disabled.

- The hardware vendor should certify the host as FT-capable. You can refer to the VMware Hardware Compatibility List (HCL) for hardware compatibility information. The list is available at: www.vmware.com/resources/compatibility/search.php.

- As mentioned earlier, each ESXi host must have both a vMotion and a Fault Tolerance Logging NIC configured.

Finally, vSphere FT has the following requirements for virtual machines that are to be protected:

- Virtual machines must be stored on shared storage.

- Virtual machines cannot use physical mode RDMs. Virtual mode RDMs are acceptable.

- Virtual machine disk (VMDK) files must be Thick Provisioned with the Cluster Features option enabled.

- Virtual machines must not have a snapshot. Snapshots must be committed before you can enable vSphere FT.

- Virtual machines must have only a single virtual CPU (vCPU). VMs with multiple vCPUs cannot have vSphere FT enabled.

- Virtual machines cannot have CD/DVD or floppy drives that are backed by a physical device.

- Virtual machines cannot be configured to use paravirtualization.

- Virtual machines cannot have USB or sound devices.

- Virtual machines cannot use N-Port ID Virtualization (NPIV); this topic is discussed in Chapter 7.

- Virtual machines cannot use NIC passthrough.

- Virtual machines cannot use the paravirtualized SCSI (PVSCSI) device. Chapter 9 provides more information on paravirtualized devices.

Configuring Your vSphere Environment

PART II

In addition, vSphere FT will disable certain other features once it is active. Extended Page Tables/Rapid Virtualization Indexing (EPT/RVI) and device hot-plugging are disabled or turned off after vSphere FT is enabled for a virtual machine.

Configuring an ESXi Host for vSphere FT

Assuming that you have enabled vSphere HA, the first step in configuring vSphere FT is configuring a Fault Tolerance Logging NIC. As with a vMotion NIC, the procedure for configuring a Fault Tolerance Logging NIC depends on whether you are using a vSphere Standard Switch or a vSphere Distributed Switch.

Perform these steps to configure a Fault Tolerance Logging NIC with a vSphere Standard Switch:

1. Select an ESXi host in the cluster and click the Configuration tab.

2. Click the Networking link.

3. Select the Virtual Switch button to view the vSphere Standard Switch configuration for the selected ESXi host.

4. Click the Add Networking link. This opens the Add Network wizard.

5. Select the VMkernel radio button, and then click Next.

6. Select the radio button to either create a new virtual switch or use an existing virtual switch, as appropriate for your environment. If you are creating a new virtual switch, you must also select the NICs that will serve as uplinks for the new virtual switch. Click Next when you are ready to proceed.

7. Supply a name for the VMkernel port and a VLAN ID, if necessary.

8. Select the Use This Port Group For Fault Tolerance Logging check box, and then click Next.

9. If you want to use Dynamic Host Configuration Protocol (DHCP), select the Obtain IP Settings Automatically radio button. Otherwise, select the Use The Following IP Settings radio button and then enter the IP address, subnet mask, and VMkernel default gateway. Click Next when you are finished.

10. Review the configuration and, if it is correct, click the Finish button to exit the wizard. Otherwise, use the Back button to go back and make the necessary changes.

To create a VMkernel port on a vSphere Distributed Switch and enable it for Fault Tolerance Logging, follow these steps:

1. Select the ESXi host on which you want to create the VMkernel port, and then click the Configuration tab. Note that this host must already be a member of the vSphere Distributed Switch.

2. Click the Networking link.

3. Select the Distributed Virtual Switch button to view the vSphere Distributed Switch configuration for the selected ESXi host.

4. Click the Manage Virtual Adapters link.

5. In the Manage Virtual Adapters dialog box, click the Add link. This opens the Add Virtual Adapter wizard.

6. Select the New Virtual Adapter radio button, and then click Next.

7. Select the VMkernel radio button and click Next.

8. With the Select Port Group radio button selected, choose an existing port group to host the new VMkernel port. If you don't already have a port group for the VMkernel port, you must cancel this process, create the port group, and then restart these steps.

9. Be sure to select the Use This Virtual Adapter For Fault Tolerance Logging check box.

10. Once you've selected a port group and selected the Use This Virtual Adapter For Fault Tolerance Logging check box, click Next.

11. If you want to use Dynamic Host Configuration Protocol (DHCP), select the Obtain IP Settings Automatically radio button. Otherwise, select the Use The Following IP Settings radio button and then enter the IP address, subnet mask, and VMkernel default gateway. Click Next when you are finished.

12. Review the configuration and, if it is correct, click the Finish button to finish the wizard. Otherwise, use the Back button to go back and make the necessary changes.

After you have ensured that all the requirements are met, you are ready to enable vSphere FT for a virtual machine.

Enabling vSphere FT for a Virtual Machine

vSphere FT is enabled on a per–virtual machine basis. This provides you with flexibility in choosing which virtual machines should be protected using vSphere FT, and it allows you to mix protected and unprotected VMs within the same cluster and on the same ESXi hosts.

Configuring Your vSphere Environment

Perform the following steps to enable vSphere FT for a specific virtual machine:

1. Many guest operating systems must be powered off in order to enable vSphere FT. VMware KB article 1008027, referenced earlier in this chapter, provides information on which guest operating systems must be powered off on which hardware platforms in order to enable vSphere FT. If necessary, power down the virtual machine by right-clicking on a virtual machine and selecting Power ➢ Shut Down Guest.

2. Right-click the virtual machine and select Fault Tolerance ➢ Turn On Fault Tolerance.

3. In the Turn On Fault Tolerance dialog box, click Yes to confirm the operation. The dialog box informs you that the VM disk may need to be converted and that a memory reservation will be put into place as part of the process of enabling vSphere FT.

vCenter Server will create the secondary VM on a second ESXi host and then synchronize it with the primary VM. You can use the Fault Tolerance area of the VM summary screen, shown in Figure 8.5, to check on the status of a VM's protection.

Figure 8.5: The Fault Tolerance area of the VM's Summary tab in vCenter provides additional information on the status of a VM's protection.

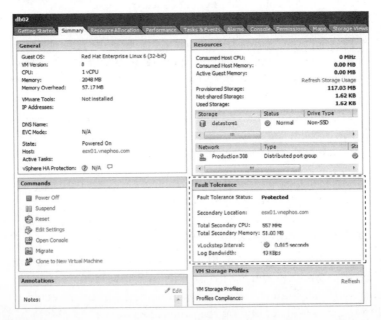

In the event you need to disable vSphere FT, follow these steps:

1. Right-click the virtual machine that currently has vSphere FT enabled and select Fault Tolerance ➤ Turn Off Fault Tolerance.

2. Click Yes in the Turn Off Fault Tolerance dialog box to confirm the operation.

vCenter Server will unregister and destroy the secondary VM and disable vSphere FT for the selected VM. Note that the memory reservation set by vSphere FT remains, and if the disks were converted to Thick Provisioned that conversion is not reversed.

Troubleshooting vSphere FT

The most common problems with vSphere FT relate to incorrect configuration of either the ESXi hosts or the virtual machines. Here are some common configuration problems:

- The host's CPU is not supported for vSphere FT.

- Hardware virtualization extensions are not enabled in the server's BIOS.

- The virtual machine is using a physical mode RDM or a virtual device backed by a physical resource (like a CD/DVD or floppy drive).

- The virtual machine is using NPIV.

- The virtual machine has an active snapshot.

- The virtual machine is using the paravirtualized SCSI (PVSCSI) device. PVSCSI devices are not supported with vSphere FT.

Guard Against VM Failure

In addition to ESXi host failure, the failure of the guest operating system within a virtual machine is another source of unplanned downtime. vSphere can monitor virtual machines for failure, and restart them if it detects a failure; this feature is called *VM Monitoring*.

VM Monitoring is an extension of vSphere HA and requires vSphere HA to be enabled. Using the heartbeats from the VMware Tools or a third-party monitoring tool via the vSphere HA API, VM Monitoring will watch the status of virtual machines and applications. VM Monitoring also watches the I/Os from virtual machines. When the heartbeats and the I/Os stop—presumably due to a failure of the guest operating system or application within the VM—VM Monitoring will restart the VM automatically.

You can control the sensitivity of VM Monitoring as well as enable or disable VM Monitoring or VM and Application Monitoring on a per-VM basis within a cluster.

To enable VM Monitoring or VM and Application Monitoring, follow these steps:

1. Right-click the vSphere HA–enabled cluster and select Edit Settings.

2. From the list on the left, select VM Monitoring.

3. Choose VM Monitoring or VM and Application Monitoring from the VM Monitoring drop-down box.

Now you can customize the sensitivity to the heartbeats from the virtual machines using the settings in the Default Cluster Settings area of the dialog box. Table 8.2 summarizes the predefined sensitivity settings.

Table 8.2: VM Monitoring predefined sensitivity settings

Slider Bar Setting	Predefined Values	Action
Low	2-minute interval to receive a VM heartbeat	Restarts the VM a maximum of 3 times every 7 days
Medium	60-second interval to receive a VM heartbeat	Restarts the VM a maximum of 3 times every 24 hours
High	30-second interval to receive a VM heartbeat	Restarts the VM a maximum of 3 times every hour

If these predefined settings aren't sufficient, enable the Custom check box and you can set the Failure Interval, Minimum Uptime, Maximum Per-VM Resets, and Maximum Resets Time Window settings directly, as shown in Figure 8.6.

Figure 8.6: You can set custom values for VM Monitoring to meet the needs of your environments.

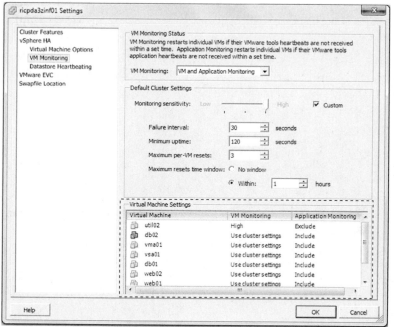

As mentioned earlier, you can customize, even disable, VM Monitoring on a per-VM basis within the cluster. In the Virtual Machine Settings area of the dialog box—refer to Figure 8.6—you can select one of the predefined values (Low, Medium, High), specify a custom value, or even disable VM Monitoring or Application Monitoring entirely for that VM. This allows you a great deal of control over which VMs should be monitored. In addition, it allows you to disable monitoring for VMs that do not have the VMware Tools installed. Keep in mind that installing the VMware Tools is always recommended, however.

9

Managing Virtual Machines

IN THIS CHAPTER, YOU WILL LEARN TO:

M anaging virtual machines is where most VMware vSphere administrators will spend their time. vSphere 5 provides a full set of virtual machine management features to help you with these tasks.

Create Virtual Machines

Creating virtual machines is an essential and fundamental task for any vSphere administrator. It's important for you to understand the various ways of creating virtual machines, why each method is useful, and when to use each method. Fortunately, the very nature of virtualization with VMware vSphere—namely the ability to quickly and easily create or modify virtual machines—means that making a mistake when creating a virtual machine is usually not a big deal.

vSphere Web Client

New to vSphere 5 is the vSphere Web Client, which allows administrators to connect to vCenter Server through a web browser. This tool offers a connection option other than Windows and a lower bandwidth connection. While conceptually the same as the vSphere Client, the location and the steps to get to things are slightly different. If you are familiar with the vSphere Client, it will not take long to find your way around the web client.

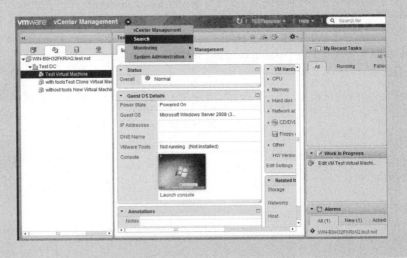

Some features of vSphere Web Client worth noting include:

- Summary panels can be arranged to suit your preference.
- Advanced search option allows you to save searches.
- Wizards and workflows can be minimized and resumed.

For a vSphere administrator just getting started with VMware vSphere, the first step will generally be to create a new virtual machine from scratch. That process is described in the next section.

Create a New Virtual Machine

To streamline the creation of a new virtual machine, vCenter Server provides a wizard to walk you through the process. To invoke this wizard, right-click on a datacenter, cluster, host, or resource pool and select New Virtual Machine. This will invoke the Provision New Virtual Machine wizard.

> **NOTE** From within the vSphere Web Client the New Virtual Machine wizard is called the Provision Virtual Machine Wizard. To open it, right-click within a datacenter, cluster, host, or resource pool, select Inventory, and then select Create Virtual Machine.

To create a new virtual machine after invoking the Provision Virtual Machine wizard, follow these steps:

1. At the first screen in the Provision Virtual Machine wizard, select Custom in order to see all the configuration options for a new virtual machine. Click Next.

2. Specify a name for the new virtual machine and select a location for the virtual machine in the inventory. The Inventory Location box shows the contents of the VMs And Templates inventory view within vCenter Server. Click Next.

3. Depending on the object selected when the wizard was invoked, the next screen prompts you to select a location where the virtual machine will run.

- If you right-clicked in a datacenter to invoke the wizard, select a host or cluster on which to run this virtual machine.

- If you right-clicked in a cluster to invoke the wizard and that cluster is configured for manual automation with VMware Distributed Resource Scheduler (DRS), the wizard prompts you to select a specific host within the cluster. This is also true when you right-click in a resource pool hosted in a cluster set for manual automation.

TIP For clusters whose DRS automation level is set to Fully Automated, the user does not have to select a host on which to run the virtual machine. The placement of the virtual machine onto a host in the cluster happens automatically, This is called *intelligent placement*.

- If the cluster has multiple resource pools, you are prompted to select the resource pool in which the virtual machine should reside. This is also true for parent resource pools with multiple child pools.

Once you have selected the appropriate location for the new virtual machine, click Next.

4. Select the datastore where the virtual machine's virtual machine disk (VMDK) files should reside. After you have selected the desired datastore, click Next.

5. If the VMware environment also includes hosts running earlier versions of ESX/ESXi, select Virtual Machine Version 7. Otherwise, select Version 8. Click Next to continue.

6. Use the radio buttons to select the correct guest operating system family, and then use the drop-down list to select the specific version of that guest operating system. For example, if the guest will run 64-bit Windows Server 2008, select the Microsoft Windows radio button and choose Windows Server 2008 (64-Bit) from the drop-down list. Click Next to continue.

7. Choose the number of virtual sockets and virtual cores this virtual machine should have. Click Next to continue.

TIP Don't overprovision virtual machines. Assign only the resources that the virtual machine will need. It's easy to go back later and assign additional vCPUs or memory, should the applications within the virtual machine need them.

---

8. Select the amount of memory to be assigned to the virtual machine. Note that the slider bar provides some reference points, such as the minimum recommended amount, the default recommended amount, and the maximum recommended amount. After selecting the amount of memory to assign to the VM, click Next.

9. Choose how many virtual network interface cards (NICs) to assign to the virtual machine. For each NIC, select the appropriate adapter type, as shown in Figure 9.1. The E1000 adapter is the default for many guest operating systems and is supported by drivers supplied with many guest operating systems. Click Next to continue.

Figure 9.1: Each virtual network interface card must have a specific adapter type selected. The E1000 adapter type is compatible out of the box for many guest operating systems.

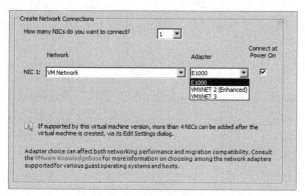

10. Select the appropriate SCSI controller for the guest operating system. Newer guest operating systems will support the LSI Logic SAS controller. Otherwise, select the LSI Logic Parallel controller. Click Next to continue.

VMWare Paravirtual Controller

The VMware Paravirtual controller is supported on the following guest operating systems:

- Windows Server 2008 R2 (64-bit)
- Windows Server 2008 (32-bit and 64-bit)
- Windows Server 2003 (32-bit and 64-bit)
- Windows XP (32-bit and 64-bit)
- Windows Vista (32-bit and 64-bit)
- Windows 7 (32-bit and 64-bit)

Red Hat Linux 5 (32-bit and 64-bit) does not support boot disks using a PVSCSI controller.

11. Select Create A New Virtual Disk, and then click Next.

12. Specify a size for the new virtual disk; then specify whether the disk should be one of the following disk types:

    - Thick Provision Lazy Zeroed: Space is allocated during the creation of the disk. Data on the physical device is not erased during creation. Data is zeroed out on first write from the virtual machine.

    - Thick Provision Eager Zeroed: Space is allocated during creation. Data on the physical device is zeroed during creation. Supports clustering features such as Fault Tolerance.

    - Thin Provision: The disk appears to the operating system to have the total amount of disk space but only the amount of space actually containing data is consumed on the physical disk.

13. If the virtual disk should be stored in a different datastore than the virtual machine configuration files, select Specify A Datastore and choose the datastore where the virtual disk should be located. Otherwise, the default selection of Store With The Virtual Machine is fine. Click Next to proceed.

14. You can change the SCSI ID of the virtual disk in the Virtual Device Node section, but this is rarely changed during virtual machine creation. The default is SCSI 0:0.

15. You can also select to make the virtual disk an independent disk, which precludes the use of virtual machine snapshots. If a disk is configured to be an independent disk, you must select Persistent or Nonpersistent, which controls how changes to the virtual disk are managed. Click Next to continue.

16. Review the configuration listed. If everything is correct, click Finish to complete the creation of the new virtual machine. Otherwise, use the Back button to go back through the wizard and change settings where necessary.

The new virtual machine will appear in vSphere Client in the appropriate location. In the Hosts And Clusters inventory view, the virtual machine will appear in the cluster, host, or resource pool where it will run. In the VMs And Templates inventory view, it will appear in the datacenter or folder where it is stored.

Creating new virtual machines from scratch is fine, but what if you need to create a new virtual machine that is the same as an existing virtual machine? In this instance, you have the option of using vCenter Server's cloning functionality, as described in the next section.

Clone an Existing Virtual Machine

vCenter Server offers you the ability to create new virtual machines by cloning existing virtual machines. This makes it very easy to quickly create a number of virtual machines whose configuration is exactly the same. vCenter Server clones not only the virtual machine configuration, but also its virtual hard disks. This makes the clone truly an exact copy of the original.

In many cases, though, you won't want exact copies of the original. Consider a virtual machine that already has an instance of Windows Server 2008 installed. Cloning that virtual machine to create an exact copy would also create an exact copy of the guest operating system, which would then create problems with duplicate IP addresses and duplicate network names. To work around this issue, vCenter Server lets you customize the cloned virtual machine and the guest operating system inside the cloned virtual machine.

Configuring Your vSphere Environment

PART II

> **NOTE** Customizing the cloned virtual machine or the guest OS inside the cloned virtual machine isn't absolutely required. What if you wanted to use vCenter Server's cloning functionality to create a backup of a virtual machine? In that case, customization would defeat the purpose of using cloning.

Note that in order to customize virtual machines with a legacy Windows-based guest operating system, you have to copy Sysprep files onto the vCenter Server. (Sysprep is installed by default on Windows Server 2008.)

To clone an existing virtual machine, follow these steps:

1. In vSphere Client, navigate to either Hosts And Clusters inventory view or VMs And Templates inventory view.

2. Right-click the virtual machine that should serve as the original for the clone, and select Clone from the context menu. This launches the Clone Virtual Machine wizard.

> **NOTE** From within the vSphere Web Client the Clone Virtual Machine wizard has been consolidated into the Provision Virtual Machine wizard. To open it, right-click on a virtual machine and select Clone.

3. Specify a name for the cloned virtual machine and select a location in the inventory for the virtual machine to be placed. Click Next to continue.

4. Select the host or cluster on which the virtual machine should run. Click Next.

5. If you selected a cluster that either does not have VMware DRS enabled or has VMware DRS configured for manual automation, the wizard prompts you to select a specific host within the cluster. Select a host and click Next.

6. If multiple resource pools are available on the selected cluster or host, choose the correct resource pool and click Next.

7. Select the datastore where the virtual machine should be stored.

TIP   If the cloned virtual machine's virtual disk files should be stored separately from the virtual machine configuration files, use the Advanced button to specify different locations.

---

8. Select the format—Same Format As Source, Thick Provision Lazy Zeroed, Thick Provision Eager Zeroed, Thin Provision—for the cloned virtual machine's virtual disks. Click Next to continue.

9. If you want to leave the cloned virtual machine exactly the same as the original, select Do Not Customize. Otherwise, select Customize Using The Customization Wizard and click Next. If you have previously created a customization specification, select Customize Using An Existing Customization Specification.

NOTE   Steps 10 through 20 assume you are cloning a virtual machine with a Windows-based guest operating system. The steps are different for other guest operating systems.

---

10. Provide a name and organization, and then click Next.

11. Select Use The Virtual Machine Name and click Next.

12. Supply the product key for the Windows guest OS and select the correct server license mode. Click Next to continue.

13. Enter and confirm the password for the Administrator account, and then click Next.

14. Select a time zone and click Next.

15. If there are commands you want to run during the Sysprep process, enter them here. Otherwise, just click Next.

16. Specify the network settings. It's generally best to select Typical Settings. Click Next to continue.

17. Specify whether the cloned virtual machine should join a workgroup or a domain, and supply credentials if joining a domain. Click Next.

18. Leave Generate A New Security ID (SID) selected and click Next.

19. If you would like to save the answers supplied so far in vSphere Client Windows Guest Customization wizard, supply a name and

Configuring Your vSphere Environment

PART II

a description, and then click Next. Otherwise, uncheck Save This Customization Specification For Later Use.

20. Click Finish to complete the guest customization (not the cloning process).

21. Review the settings. If everything looks correct, click Finish to start the cloning process. Otherwise, use the Back button to go back and change settings as necessary.

vCenter Server will clone the virtual machine. You can track the progress of the cloning operation via the Tasks pane of vSphere Client. If you select Power On This Virtual Machine After Creation on the final screen of the Clone Virtual Machine wizard, vCenter Server will automatically power on the cloned VM and perform the customization. Otherwise, the customization will occur the first time the VM is powered on.

TIP Cloning virtual machines is most powerful and most useful when you clone virtual machines that already have the guest operating system installed. Use cloning and customization specifications to provide quick and easy cloning of virtual machines and entire guest operating systems.

In addition to cloning existing virtual machines, vCenter Server can deploy virtual machines by cloning them from a special object known as a *template*.

Deploy a Virtual Machine from a Template

vCenter Server can not only clone existing virtual machines but also create new virtual machines by cloning a template. The next section, "Create a Template," provides more information on exactly what templates are and how they are created and managed. Once you have created a template, you can deploy new virtual machines based on that template easily and quickly in much the same fashion as cloning virtual machines. All the same benefits apply—the new virtual machine deployed from a template has the same hardware configuration, the same data on the virtual disks, the same identity, and so forth assuming no guest customization or Sysprep was performed during the deployment. vCenter Server can perform customization on the guest operating system just as when you clone existing virtual machines. Aside from the fact that this involves a template, the process is identical.

To deploy a virtual machine from a template, simply right-click the template and select Deploy Virtual Machine From This Template. This launches the Deploy Template wizard. The Deploy Template wizard follows the same steps outlined in the earlier section "Clone an Existing Virtual Machine," so refer back to those steps for more detailed information.

NOTE   Templates are only visible in the VMs And Templates inventory view and from within the datastores view.

Using templates instead of existing virtual machines to deploy new virtual machines does have some advantages, as discussed in the next section.

Create a Template

Since vCenter Server offers you the ability to clone virtual machines, why would you need a template? As with virtual machines, you can clone templates to create new virtual machines. Unlike virtual machines, templates cannot be powered on, and the configuration of a template cannot be modified. If you want to ensure that the base configuration being cloned is not modified or tampered with, marking the base virtual machine as a template will achieve that goal.

There are two ways to create a template:

- Convert an existing virtual machine to a template.

- Clone an existing virtual machine to a template.

Both of these operations are visible on the context menu of an existing virtual machine. While they accomplish the same task—creating a template—the process these two operations follow is very different, each with its own advantages and disadvantages. Converting an existing virtual machine to a template is the fastest, so that's the approach discussed first.

Convert an Existing Virtual Machine to a Template and Back Again

To convert an existing virtual machine to a template, you only need to right-click a virtual machine and select Template ➤ Convert To

Template. Figure 9.2 shows the option to convert a virtual machine to a template. That's all there is to it—just select the menu option, and the selected virtual machine will be marked as a template.

Figure 9.2: Converting a virtual machine to a template

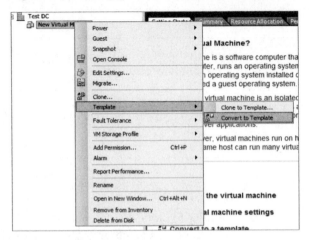

NOTE   To access the Clone option from within the vSphere Web Client, right click the virtual machine within the Inventory option.

While it is marked as a template, the virtual machine's configuration cannot be modified, and the virtual machine cannot be powered on. Otherwise, the virtual machine's virtual disks are left intact and unchanged.

Because the virtual machine and its disks are left unchanged, you can also convert from a template back to a virtual machine. This is extremely useful because it allows you to convert a template to a VM, make configuration changes or install patches, and then convert it back to a template again.

To convert a template back into a virtual machine, follow these steps:

1. In the vSphere Client, navigate to the VMs And Templates inventory view.

2. Right-click the template that should be converted back to a virtual machine and select Convert To Virtual Machine. This opens the Convert Template To Virtual Machine wizard.

3. Select a host or cluster to run the virtual machine and click Next.

4. If the cluster does not have VMware DRS enabled or VMware DRS configured for manual automation, select a specific host within the cluster and select Next.

5. If the cluster has multiple resource pools, select a resource pool and click Next.

6. Review the settings. If everything is correct, click Finish. Otherwise, use the Back button to go back and change settings as needed.

NOTE You cannot use the vSphere Web Client to convert a template to a virtual machine.

When you convert a template back into a virtual machine, the template will disappear from the VMs And Templates view. The virtual machine will appear in both the VMs and Templates view as well as the Hosts And Clusters, the datastore, and network views.

In the event—for whatever reason—you do not want to convert an existing virtual machine into a template, vCenter Server can also clone a VM into a template. This functionality is discussed in the next section.

Clone an Existing Virtual Machine to a Template

There may be situations in which you don't want to convert a virtual machine into a template. In these cases, you can still take advantage of the benefits of templates by simply cloning the virtual machine to a new template. Thus, the existing virtual machine is left intact and untouched, but you gain the benefit of an unchangeable template for deploying new virtual machines.

To clone an existing virtual machine into a template, follow these steps:

1. In vSphere Client, navigate to either the Hosts And Clusters inventory view or the VMs And Templates inventory view.

2. Right-click the virtual machine that should be cloned to a template and select Template ➢ Clone To Template. This starts the Clone Virtual Machine To Template wizard.

3. Specify a name for the new template and select a location in the inventory. Keep in mind that the inventory view shown is the VMs And Templates inventory view.

4. Select a host or cluster on which to store this template, and then click Next.

5. If you selected a cluster that does not have VMware DRS enabled or has VMware DRS enabled but configured for manual automation, select a specific host within the cluster and select Next.

6. Select a datastore in which to store the template's files.

7. Choose a disk format—Same Format As Source, Thick Provision Lazy Zeroed, Thick Provision Eager Zeroed, or Thin Provision— and click Next.

8. Review the settings. If everything is correct, click Finish to start the cloning process; otherwise, use the Back button to go back and change settings as necessary.

NOTE You cannot use the vSphere Web Client to clone a virtual machine directly to a template. You would need to clone the virtual machine, then convert the clone to a template.

---

vCenter Server will clone the selected virtual machine into a new template according to the settings specified in the Clone Virtual Machine To Template wizard. Note that there is no option for customizing the template. That's because the guest OS customization will take place when new virtual machines are deployed from this template. There is no need to perform customization when creating a template.

Along with creating templates to use for deploying new virtual machines, you have a number of other methods for creating virtual machines. This variety gives you a great deal of flexibility to use the method best suited for the need at hand.

Of course, creating virtual machines isn't the sum of what you need to do when it comes to virtual machines. Many times you have to modify virtual machines after they've been created. The next section covers modifying virtual machines.

Modify Virtual Machines

There are many reasons why an existing virtual machine might need to be modified:

-   The application or applications within the virtual machine need more memory than was initially allocated to the virtual machine.

- You have to attach a virtual CD-ROM device to the virtual machine to install software or software updates.

- The virtual machine needs to be attached to a different network segment.

The procedure for many of these tasks is similar. Aside from two specific instances, which are described in the next section, making any of these changes requires you to open the Virtual Machine Properties dialog box by right-clicking the virtual machine and selecting Edit Settings. Figure 9.3 shows the properties dialog box for a virtual machine.

Figure 9.3: The Virtual Machine Properties dialog box is the central point for modifying virtual machines.

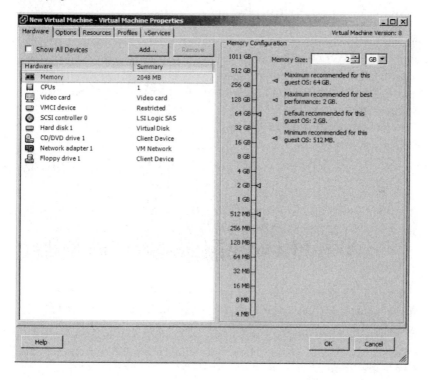

Reconfigure the Hardware of a Virtual Machine

Reconfiguring a virtual machine's hardware is a fairly broad task that could involve changing the amount of memory assigned to a VM; connecting or disconnecting a floppy drive, CD/DVD drive, or network card; or changing the disk controller type. This section describes how to perform three very common tasks:

- Attach or detach a CD/DVD drive
- Connect or disconnect a network interface card
- Change the network to which a network interface card connects

While it's not possible to describe all the various configuration tasks that you can perform on a virtual machine, these three examples provide an idea of how to reconfigure the hardware for a virtual machine. Most, if not all, of the other configuration tasks are performed in much the same manner.

Attach or Detach a CD/DVD Drive

Working with virtual CD/DVD drives on virtual machines is an extremely common task. You will often need to gain access to a CD/DVD in order to install software or add components to the guest operating system. But where, exactly, is the CD/DVD drive for a virtual machine? That's a good question!

You have three options for getting access to a CD/DVD drive in a virtual machine:

- Map the CD/DVD drive in the virtual machine to the ESXi host's CD/DVD drive and use a CD/DVD in the physical drive.
- Map the CD/DVD drive in the virtual machine to an ISO file that is an image of the physical CD/DVD.
- Map the CD/DVD drive in the virtual machine to the CD/DVD drive on the client system running vSphere Client.

TIP Using ISO files provides the most flexibility and the greatest performance, but it does require creating an ISO file from the physical CD/DVD in some cases. It is handy to create an ISO library that is on a shared datastore. Place common software and operating system ISOs on this datastore for easy access from all your ESXi hosts.

In all three situations, the process is the same. To mount a CD/DVD into a virtual machine, follow these steps:

1. Right-click the virtual machine into which the CD/DVD should be mounted and select Edit Settings.

> **NOTE**   From the vSphere Web Client, right-click the virtual
> machine and select Configuration ➤ Edit Settings.

2. Make sure the Hardware tab is selected.

3. From the list of hardware on the left, select CD/DVD Drive 1.

4. The next step depends on what method is used to map the CD/
   DVD into the virtual machine:

   - To map the CD/DVD to the physical CD/DVD in the system
     running vSphere Client, select the Client Device radio button.
     Note that the Connected and Connect At Power On options
     under Device Status will be disabled.

   - To map the CD/DVD to the physical CD/DVD in the ESXi
     host, select the Host Device radio button and then choose
     the correct host device from the drop-down list. Generally,
     /dev/scd0 is a valid option. If the VM is running, check the
     Connected check box to immediately connect the CD/DVD
     drive. Otherwise, select Connect At Power On to have the CD/
     DVD drive connected when the VM powers on the next time.

   - To map the CD/DVD to an ISO image, select Datastore ISO
     File and then use the Browse button to navigate to an ISO
     image stored on a reachable datastore. To connect the CD/
     DVD drive immediately, select Connected; otherwise, select
     Connect At Power On to have the CD/DVD drive connected
     when the VM is next powered on.

5. Click OK to save the changes and return to vSphere Client.

VMware also provides a handy toolbar button to help streamline this
task, as shown in Figure 9.4. This toolbar button provides easy access to
the same options outlined previously.

Figure 9.4: This toolbar button provides quick access to connect or disconnect a
CD/DVD drive.

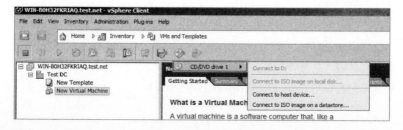

Configuring Your vSphere
Environment

PART II

If you need to simply connect or disconnect a CD/DVD, just open the Virtual Machine Properties dialog box, select the CD/DVD drive, and then simply select the Connected check box. This toggles the connection state of the CD/DVD drive.

To boot a virtual machine from a CD/DVD, configure the drive as described previously and select Connect At Power On. The CD/DVD drive in the virtual machine will be connected when the VM is powered on and the VM will—if the CD/DVD is bootable—boot from the CD/DVD drive.

TIP   Best practices state that vSphere administrators should not leave CD/DVD drives connected in virtual machines. Remember to disconnect CD/DVD drives in virtual machines when they are not being used.

Connect or Disconnect a Network Interface Card

Connecting or disconnecting the virtual network interface card (NIC) in a virtual machine is analogous to inserting or removing the network cable from the back of a physical system. When the virtual NIC is connected, it's as if the virtual network cable is plugged in. When the virtual NIC is disconnected, the virtual network cable is unplugged.

To connect or disconnect a virtual NIC, follow these steps:

1. Open the Virtual Machine Properties dialog box by right-clicking a virtual machine and selecting Edit Settings.

NOTE   From the vSphere Web Client, right-click the virtual machine and select Configuration ➤ Edit Settings.

---

2. Select the Hardware tab.

3. From the list of hardware on the left, select the desired network interface card.

4. Select the Connected check box to toggle the value.

5. To ensure that the NIC starts up as connected, make sure the Connect At Power On option is checked.

6. Click OK to return to vSphere Client.

If a virtual machine has multiple virtual network interface cards, each of the virtual network interface cards can be independently connected or disconnected. Just as a physical network cable can be pulled out of the back of a physical computer at any time, you can connect or disconnect a virtual NIC at any time, whether the virtual machine is powered on or powered off.

Change the Network to Which a Network Interface Card Connects

In addition to connecting or disconnecting the virtual NIC, you may also need to change the network to which the virtual NIC connects. This process is similar to connecting or disconnecting the virtual NIC.

To change the network to which a virtual NIC connects, follow these steps:

1. Right-click the virtual machine whose virtual NIC should be changed and select Edit Settings.

NOTE   From the vSphere Web Client, right-click the virtual machine and select Configuration ➤ Edit Settings.

---

2. Select the Hardware tab, and then select the virtual NIC from the list of hardware on the left.

3. From the Network Label drop-down list, select the desired network to which this virtual NIC should connect.

4. Click OK to save the changes and return to vSphere Client.

Although this changes the connection for that virtual NIC, you must still perform any necessary reconfiguration within the guest operating system. The reconfiguration within the guest operating system would include things like changing the assigned IP address, subnet mask, and default gateway.

The creation and configuration of the virtual networks to which the NICs connect is described in more detail in Chapter 6, "Creating and Managing Virtual Networking."

Add Hardware to a Virtual Machine

There may be instances where in addition to reconfiguring a virtual machine, you have to add hardware. Perhaps the applications running within the virtual machine need more memory, or perhaps the guest operating system is consistently using all the CPU cycles being given to it. Maybe more disk space is needed. In any case, you can quickly and easily add hardware to the virtual machine to address the need.

Only certain types of hardware can be added while a virtual machine is running. These include USB controllers, network adapters, virtual hard disks, some SCSI devices, memory, and CPU (with hardware version 8). To add other types of hardware, you must first shut down the virtual machine.

NOTE VMware vSphere supports features called *hot add* and *hot plug*, where hardware can be added while the guest operating system in a virtual machine is running. This feature is supported for Windows Server 2003 Enterprise Editions (hot add memory only) and Windows Server 2008 (hot add memory only for standard editions). The feature must be enabled before you can use it. Ironically, the virtual machine must be powered off in order to enable hot add.

Adding hardware to a virtual machine is generally similar regardless of the type of virtual hardware being added. The next few sections describe how to add a network adapter, a virtual disk, memory, or an additional CPU to a virtual machine.

Add a Network Adapter to a Virtual Machine

Network adapters, referred to as Ethernet adapters in the vSphere Client user interface, can be added to a virtual machine when the virtual machine is running or powered off.

To add a network adapter to a virtual machine, follow these steps:

1. Right-click the virtual machine and select Edit Settings. This opens the Virtual Machine Properties dialog box.

NOTE From the vSphere Web Client, right-click the virtual machine and select Configuration ➤ Edit Settings.

---

2. Click Add. This opens the Add Hardware wizard.

3. Select Ethernet Adapter, and then click Next.

4. Under Adapter Type, select the type of network adapter to add to the virtual machine.

5. Under Network Connection, select Named Network With Specified Label. Use the drop-down to select the correct port group or distributed virtual port group.

6. Under Device Status, leave Connect At Power On selected. Click Next.

7. Review the settings. If everything is correct, click Finish. Otherwise, use the Back button to go back and change settings as needed.

8. In the Virtual Machine Properties dialog box, the new network adapter will be listed with a status of Adding. Click OK to commit the changes and return to vSphere Client.

Once the task in the Tasks pane completes, you must take steps in the guest operating system to recognize the new hardware (if the virtual machine is running). In Windows, for example, you should open Device Manager and scan for new hardware. This gives you the opportunity to configure the new hardware appropriately.

Add a Virtual Hard Disk to a Virtual Machine

Virtual disks can usually be added to a virtual machine when the virtual machine is powered off or powered on. However, you cannot add a new virtual disk to a new SCSI controller while the VM is running.

To add a virtual hard disk to a virtual machine, perform these steps:

1. Right-click the virtual machine and select Edit Settings. This opens the Virtual Machine Properties dialog box.

NOTE From the vSphere Web Client, right-click the virtual machine and select Configuration ➢ Edit Settings.

---

2. Click Add. This opens the Add Hardware wizard.

3. Select Hard Disk, and then click Next.

4. Select Create A New Virtual Disk, and then click Next.

TIP Administrators who simply need to add an existing virtual disk to a virtual machine can select the Use An Existing Virtual Disk option.

---

5. Under Capacity, specify a size for the new virtual disk.

6. Under Disk Provisioning, select options to use thin provisioning or to support Fault Tolerance. These options are mutually exclusive.

7. Under Location, leave the default option of Store With The Virtual Machine selected. Click Next.

8. Leave the Virtual Device Node at the default setting, unless you need the new virtual disk to have a separate SCSI controller. If a separate SCSI controller is needed, set the Virtual Device Node to SCSI (1:0).

9. Under Mode, select whether the disk will be an independent disk and, if it is an independent disk, whether it will be a persistent disk or a nonpersistent disk. Click Next.

10. Click Finish if the settings are correct. Otherwise, go back using the Back button and change settings as needed.

11. The new virtual disk (and new SCSI controller, if one is being added) will be listed in the Virtual Machine Properties dialog box with a status of Adding. Click OK to commit the changes and return to vSphere Client.

As with adding a new network adapter, you must perform some additional configuration within the guest operating system after vSphere Client has completed the addition of the new virtual disk. In Windows, for example, you must run the Disk Management console and select Action ➤ Rescan Disks. The new virtual disk should then appear and can be formatted as desired.

Add Memory to a Virtual Machine

Memory can only be added to a virtual machine when the virtual machine is powered off (although recall from the earlier note in the "Add Hardware to a Virtual Machine" section that there is limited support for hot-adding memory in specific configurations).

TIP If you previously specified a Memory Limit on the Resources tab, be sure to adjust that limit or the benefits of the additional memory won't be realized.

To add memory to a virtual machine, perform these steps:

1. Ensure that the virtual machine to which memory will be added is powered off. Shut down the virtual machine first, if necessary.

2. Right-click the virtual machine and select Edit Settings.

NOTE   From the vSphere Web Client, right-click the virtual machine and select Configuration ➤ Edit Settings.

---

3. From the list of hardware on the left, select Memory.

4. Use the slider bar or the Memory Size box to specify the new memory setting for the virtual machine.

5. Click OK to commit the changes and return to vSphere Client.

Generally, the guest operating system will recognize the additional memory when the virtual machine is booted after making this change.

Add a CPU to a Virtual Machine

You need to power off a virtual machine in order to add a virtual CPU (vCPU).

To add a vCPU to a virtual machine follow these steps:

1. Power off the virtual machine if it is not already powered off.

2. Right-click the virtual machine and select Edit Settings.

NOTE   From the vSphere Web Client, right-click the virtual machine and select Configuration ➤ Edit Settings.

---

3. From the list of hardware on the left, select CPUs.

4. Chose the desired number of virtual sockets from the Number Of Virtual Sockets drop-down box. Then select the desired number of cores per socket from the Number Of Cores Per Socket drop-down box.

5. Click OK to save the changes and return to vSphere Client.

Depending on the guest operating system in the virtual machine, additional work might or might not be required in order to take

Configuring Your vSphere Environment

advantage of the additional vCPU. Refer to the documentation for the particular guest operating system to know for sure.

Remove Hardware from a Virtual Machine

In general, the virtual machine needs to be powered off in order to remove hardware from the virtual machine. There are some exceptions, like network adapters and virtual disks, but otherwise the virtual machine should be powered off.

Once a virtual machine is powered off, opening the Virtual Machine Properties dialog box—by right-clicking on the virtual machine and selecting Edit Settings—allows you to remove hardware using the Remove button at the top of the window. Clearly, removing some types of virtual hardware will have a significant impact; if you remove the only virtual disk for a virtual machine, for example, it won't be able to boot.

There are few intricacies to removing some types of hardware:

- You can't remove SCSI controllers directly. Instead, you must remove all the virtual disks or SCSI devices attached to those controllers, and vSphere will remove the controllers automatically.

- You can't "remove" memory. Instead, you need to lower the amount of memory assigned to the virtual machine using the slider. The same goes for vCPUs.

- The video card cannot be removed.

Aside from these exceptions, removing hardware is usually as straightforward as selecting the hardware item and clicking the Remove button. The item will be marked in strikethrough text with a status of Removed. Once you click OK to commit the changes, the hardware will be removed from the virtual machine.

Manage Virtual Machine Hardware Versions

As VMware's virtualization products have evolved, so too have the capabilities of the virtual machines running on them. With the release of VMware vSphere 5, VMware adds support for version 8 of the virtual machine hardware in their server virtualization product suite.

As discussed in the section "Create Virtual Machines," earlier in this chapter, vCenter Server prompts you to select either version 8 or version 7. In most cases, you won't need to worry too much about virtual machine hardware versions. There are really only three instances in which the virtual machine hardware version becomes important:

- After an upgrade
- When maintaining a mixed environment
- When you are importing and exporting virtual machines to or from other VMware virtualization platforms

In these situations, the two tasks that you need to know how to perform are determining the virtual machine hardware version and upgrading the virtual machine hardware. These tasks are described in the following sections.

Determine the Virtual Machine Hardware Version

vCenter Server provides an easy and straightforward way of determining the current virtual machine hardware version.

To view the current hardware version for a virtual machine, simply right-click the virtual machine and select Edit Settings. In the upper-right corner of the dialog box the current hardware version is displayed, as shown in Figure 9.5. Alternatively the hardware version is listed as VM Version on the summary tab of the virtual machine within the General section.

Figure 9.5: Virtual machine hardware version on the Summary tab.

TIP   The hardware version is also found in the virtual machine's configuration (VMX) file as the `virtualHW.version` directive.

Configuring Your vSphere Environment

PART II

Why is knowing the hardware version of a virtual machine important? Some features of VMware vSphere are not supported with older virtual machine versions. These features correspond to the physical hardware on the ESXi host where the virtual machine is created. The virtual machine features include the number of virtual PCI slots available, the maximum number of CPUs, maximum amount of memory supported, and BIOS. Virtual machine hardware versions older than 8 can run on ESXi 5.0 but may be limited on functionality. You may need to keep an earlier version of virtual machine hardware if you need to migrate the virtual machine to an ESX/ESXi 4.x host, or want to add a disk to virtual machine that was created with an earlier version of ESX/ESXi.

Table 9.1 describes what you can do with different virtual machine hardware versions and hosts.

Table 9.1 Compatible virtual machine hardware versions and hosts

Hosts	Version 8	Version 7	Version 4	vCenter Server
ESXi 5.0	Create, edit, run	Create, edit, run	Edit, run	5.0
ESX/ESXi 4.0	Not supported	Create, edit, run	Create, edit, run	4.x
/ESXi Server 3.x	Not supported	Not supported	Create, edit, run	2.x and later

NOTE   You can also power on version 3 hardware on an ESXi 5.0 host and upgrade it to version 8.

If a virtual machine has not been created as, or upgraded to, Virtual Machine version 8, that virtual machine cannot take advantage of these new features. Fortunately, there is a virtual machine hardware upgrade process that allows you to convert older hardware versions to version 8 VMs, and that process is described in the next section.

Upgrade Virtual Machine Hardware

If you need to use a new feature of VMware vSphere that requires Virtual Machine version 8, you can upgrade the virtual machine to the new version.

The virtual machine version cannot be upgraded when the virtual machine is powered on.

WARNING   Before upgrading the virtual machine hardware, you should install the latest version of the VMware Tools, as described later in this chapter in the section "Install or Upgrade the VMware Tools."

To upgrade a virtual machine to version 8, follow these steps:

1. Shut down the virtual machine.

2. Right-click the virtual machine and select Upgrade Virtual Hardware.

NOTE   From within the vSphere Web Client, right-click the virtual machine and choose Configuration ➤ Upgrade Virtual Hardware.

---

3. Click Yes in the Confirm Virtual Machine Upgrade dialog box.

Upon next boot, the guest operating system in the virtual machine might detect new hardware as a result of the virtual machine version upgrade, and in some cases might indicate that a reboot is necessary. Once such reboots have been completed, the virtual machine is ready to take advantage of VMware vSphere–specific features, like VMware Fault Tolerance.

NOTE   Hardware upgrades and VMtools upgrades can be automated by using vSphere Update Manager.

Perform Other Virtual Machine Management Tasks

vCenter Server provides a range of other virtual machine-related management tasks that you might be called upon to perform. These tasks are described in this section.

Configuring Your vSphere Environment

PART II

Change the Virtual Machine Power State

Turning on a physical server is easy—just push the power button. But where is the power button for a virtual server? And are there different options for managing the power state of a virtual machine?

The options for managing a VM's power state are found on the context menu for a virtual machine, on the Power submenu:

Power On   This option applies power to the virtual machine.

Power Off   This option removes power from the virtual machine. It can be considered the equivalent of pulling the power plug out of the back of the virtual machine—the guest operating system is not shut down in an orderly fashion, so there is a possibility of data loss or data corruption.

Suspend   This option puts the virtual machine into a state from which activities can be resumed quickly. A cold boot is not required. Instead, the VM resumes right where it left off when it was suspended. Depending on the Power Management setting on the Options tab of the virtual machine properties, this option might or might not use the guest operating system's suspend functionality.

Reset   Resets the virtual machine, as if the hardware reset button had been pushed. The guest operating system does not perform an orderly shutdown and restart, so there is a possibility of data loss or data corruption.

Shut Down Guest   This option is only available when the virtual machine is running the VMware Tools. It initiates a graceful shutdown of the guest operating system and then turns off the power to the virtual machine.

Restart Guest   Also relying on the presence of the VMware Tools, this option initiates a graceful restart of the guest operating system.

WARNING   In general, you should use the Shut Down Guest option to initiate orderly shutdowns of the guest operating system. Otherwise, you run the risk of crash consistent data corruption, file system damage, application failure, and potential data loss.

Work with Virtual Machine Snapshots

VMware vSphere's snapshots feature provides an extra layer of protection, allowing you to "roll back" to a previous virtual machine state. For example, you can take a snapshot of a virtual machine before upgrading the software in the virtual machine. If a problem occurs with the upgrade, you can revert to the snapshot and be back where you were before starting the upgrade.

However, snapshots are not backups, and should not be used as a replacement for a 1:1 backup methodology on a regular basis. The files associated with snapshots will grow in size over time and might fill your datastores. Full datastores cause all sorts of other problems.

TIP You should plan on using snapshots to provide the short-term ability to undo changes within a virtual machine, such as a guest operating system upgrade, installation of a patch or service pack, or application upgrade.

Working with snapshots involves three basic tasks:

- Taking (or creating) a snapshot
- Deleting a snapshot (which also commits the dependent delta changes)
- Reverting to a snapshot

These tasks are described in the next three sections.

Take a Snapshot

To take a snapshot of a virtual machine, follow these steps:

1. Right-click a virtual machine and select Snapshot ➢ Take Snapshot. This opens the Take Virtual Machine Snapshot dialog box.

NOTE From within the vSphere Web Client, right-click the virtual machine and choose Snapshots ➢ Take Snapshot.

---

2. Supply a name for this snapshot.
3. Enter a description of the snapshot. Ideally, this description should provide an idea of the state of the virtual machine at the time of the snapshot.

> **TIP** When creating a snapshot you may find it handy to include the date and your initials as part of the title or description. Keep in mind you may not be the only administrator taking snapshots and you might find yourself trying to determine if a snapshot can be deleted. Without adding this information in, you will need to look through the tasks and event logs in order to know the age of the snapshot and who created it.

4. To include the virtual machine's memory in the snapshot, leave the Snapshot The Virtual Machine's Memory option selected.

5. Select Quiesce Guest File System (Needs VMware Tools Installed) if the file system of the guest operating system should be quiesced before the snapshot is taken. This can help improve the consistency of the snapshot by flushing data to the virtual disks before the snapshot is taken.

> **NOTE** When running applications that take advantage of MS VSS such as SQL and Exchange, VSS offers better protection than VMware's sync driver that comes in VMware Tools.

6. Click OK to take the snapshot.

The Tasks pane in vSphere Client shows the progress of the snapshot creation. Depending on the amount of memory assigned to the virtual machine, the snapshot creation may take a few moments.

Once the snapshot is in place, additional files are created in the virtual machine's datastore, as shown in Figure 9.6.

Figure 9.6: Snapshots create additional files in the virtual machine's datastore.

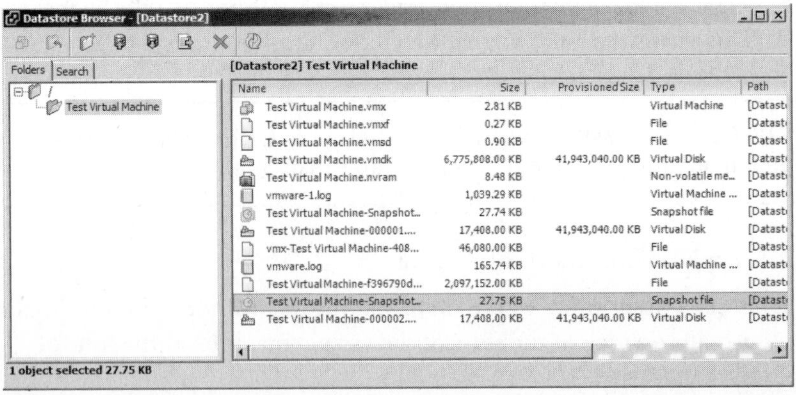

As additional snapshots are taken, additional files are created for each snapshot. To remove these files safely, you must delete the snapshot, as described in the next section.

TIP Snapshots can grow very large over time—up to the size of the virtual machine's virtual disks plus a small amount. If free space in the datastore is a concern, delete snapshot files regularly. Otherwise, the datastore could fill up and cause a number of other problems. We recommend reserving 20 percent of the disk space per Datastore for things like snapshots, VMkernel swap, swap, overhead swap, log files, etc.

Delete a Snapshot

You can delete snapshots from within the Snapshot Manager dialog box. To access the Snapshot Manager dialog box, click the toolbar button or right-click the virtual machine and select Snapshots ➤ Snapshot Manager.

In the Snapshot Manager dialog box—the title bar reads "Snapshots for *VirtualMachineName*"—simply select the snapshot to delete and click Delete. A dialog box will appear asking for confirmation, and then the snapshot is deleted. Depending on the size of the snapshot, the deletion may take some time. A task in the Tasks pane helps you gauge the progress of the operation.

So what happens to the changes stored in the snapshot when the snapshot is deleted? The answer to that question depends on whether the snapshot you are deleting is the active snapshot.

Figure 9.7 shows the Snapshot Manager dialog box.

Figure 9.7: Deleting a snapshot has different results depending on whether the snapshot is active.

This virtual machine has two snapshots.

- The snapshot labeled "You are here" (Snapshot Number 1 in Figure 9.7) is the active snapshot. This means that changes made while this snapshot is active will be written to this snapshot. When you delete an active snapshot, the changes are committed to the base disk.

- The snapshot named Snapshot Number 2 in Figure 9.7 is not active. When you delete an inactive snapshot, the changes are discarded and cannot be recovered.

Moving back and forth between snapshots is done using the Go To button, which is described in more detail in the next section.

Revert to a Snapshot

Reverting to a snapshot is also done from within the Snapshot Manager dialog box. Select the snapshot to which to revert and click Go To. A dialog box appears, informing you that the current state of the virtual machine will be lost unless it has been saved in a snapshot. Click Yes to proceed with reverting to the selected snapshot.

WARNING Keep in mind that any changes made to a virtual machine after a snapshot is taken are lost when you revert to an earlier snapshot. Refer back to Figure 9.7. If the "You are here" marker was after Snapshot Number 2 and you chose to revert to Snapshot Number 1, all changes made after Snapshot Number 2 was taken would be lost and could not be recovered.

Install or Upgrade the VMware Tools

The VMware Tools are an important part of optimizing the performance of guest operating systems in virtual machines. Although VMware vSphere has the ability to present generic hardware to guest operating systems in virtual machines—like the Intel E1000 network interface card or the LSI Logic parallel SCSI controller—the VMware Tools contain highly optimized, virtualization-aware drivers that help the guest operating system run more efficiently in a vSphere environment. By installing the VMware Tools in the guest operating system, you can reduce the performance and resource overhead of your virtual machines and thus improve the efficiency of the virtualization solution.

To install the VMware Tools into a virtual machine running a Windows-based guest operating system, follow these steps:

1. Right-click the virtual machine in the inventory tree and select Guest ➤ Install/Upgrade VMware Tools.

NOTE From within the vSphere Web Client, right-click the virtual machine and choose Configuration ➤ Install/Upgrade Tools.

---

2. A warning message is displayed indicating that the VMware Tools cannot be installed until the guest operating system is installed. Click OK.

3. An AutoPlay dialog box appears, prompting you for action. Select the option Run Setup.exe.

   If the VMware Tools installation process does not begin automatically, open Windows Explorer and double-click the CD/DVD drive icon. The VMware Tools installation should then launch.

4. Click Next on the VMware Tools installation wizard welcome page.

5. Select the appropriate setup type for the VMware Tools installation and click Next. The options are as follows:

   Typical will suffice for most situations.

   Complete installs more features than are used by the current product.

   Custom allows for the greatest level of feature customization.

6. Click Install.

7. Once the installation is complete, click Finish.

8. Click Yes to restart the virtual machine immediately or click No to manually restart the virtual machine at a later time.

NOTE Instructions for installing the VMware Tools into other guest operating systems are not included here because of the differences between the various guest operating systems.

Configuring Your vSphere Environment

PART II

Once the VMware Tools are installed, upgrades to the VMware Tools are only recommended when the ESXi hosts are patched or upgraded. Virtual machines running a Windows-based guest operating system can upgrade VMware Tools in an unattended fashion. When you choose Guest ➤ Install/Upgrade VMware Tools, the VMware Tools will install and then the virtual machine will reboot automatically. For other guest operating systems, upgrading the VMware Tools is generally the same as installing the VMware Tools.

Note that the presence of the VMware Tools running in the guest operating system is a prerequisite for a number of features within VMware vSphere. VM Monitoring, for example, relies on the VMware Tools. The Power ➤ Shut Down Guest command relies on the VMware Tools. The information displayed in vCenter Server on the Summary tab of a virtual machine relies, to a certain extent, on the VMware Tools. You are strongly encouraged to make installing the VMware Tools a mandatory part of every virtual machine build.

NOTE   Another virtual machine management task includes enabling or disabling VMware Fault Tolerance (FT). VMware FT is enabled or disabled on a per-VM basis and allows you to provide High Availability to virtual machines. This feature, as well as how to enable or disable it, is described in detail in Chapter 8, "High Availability and Business Continuity."

10

Importing and Exporting Virtual Machines

V irtualized infrastructures built using VMware vSphere exist to run virtual machines (VMs). In addition to creating those virtual machines from scratch, administrators also have the option of importing machines into the environment. These VMs can also, should the need arise, be exported out of the environment. This chapter discusses how to import and export virtual machines.

Understand the Migration Process

Migrating systems, whether they are physical systems or virtual systems, into a VMware vSphere environment is a key task that virtually every vSphere administrator will need to perform. While VMware has gone to great lengths to make the migration process as easy as possible, it is still important for vSphere administrators to understand the types of migrations that are possible and the components that are involved in these migrations.

Understand the Types of Migrations

When it comes to importing or exporting virtual machines, there are two basic types of migrations you will encounter:

Physical-to-Virtual (P2V) Migration   This type of migration involves importing an instance of an operating system running on a physical system into VMware vSphere and placing that operating system instance onto a corresponding virtual machine. Because this procedure is what brings existing workloads into your virtualization installation, it's a key task for establishing or expanding your VMware vSphere environment.

Virtual-to-Virtual (V2V) Migration   This type of migration involves importing or exporting from virtual machine format to virtual machine format. V2V is also commonly used to describe the major relocation of a VM from one cluster or datacenter to another. You might perform a V2V migration to import virtual machines from a competing virtualization solution, or even a different VMware platform. Similarly, you might perform a V2V migration to export an existing VMware vSphere virtual machine to run on a different VMware platform. Finally, you might even use a V2V migration to reconfigure an existing virtual machine, as you'll see later in this chapter.

> **NOTE** There is also a third type of migration, but it is rarely used: a virtual-to-physical (V2P) migration. VMware doesn't provide any tools for performing a V2P, so administrators who need to perform a V2P migration will have to find and acquire third-party tools.

Within these two basic types of migrations, there are two different ways of performing the actual migration. You can perform:

Hot migration In this type of migration, the source system (physical or virtual) is running and active while the migration is being performed.

Cold migration In this type of migration, the source system (physical or virtual) is shut down and inactive while the migration is being performed.

Physical-to-virtual migrations might be either hot or cold migrations, but most virtual-to-virtual migrations will be cold migrations.

In addition to understanding the types of migrations you might perform as a VMware vSphere administrator, you must also understand the various components involved in performing these migrations. Depending upon the type of migration, different components might be involved.

Review the Components in a Migration

To import virtual machines into or export virtual machines out of a VMware vSphere environment, a number of components are required.

vCenter Converter Standalone

VMware vCenter Converter Standalone is central to all the different types of migrations you might perform. You typically install vCenter Converter Standalone on the same system as VMware vCenter Server, although you can install it on a separate computer that has access to vCenter Server. Although it is easiest to use vCenter Converter Standalone in conjunction with vCenter Server, it isn't specifically required.

> **NOTE** vCenter Converter Standalone communicates with vCenter Server over TCP port 443, which is the port for Hypertext Transfer Protocol (HTTP) over Secure Sockets Layer (SSL).

vCenter Converter Standalone Agent

To perform a hot migration, vCenter Converter Standalone uses a piece of software on the source system (physical or virtual) called the vCenter Converter Standalone Agent. This software installs on the source system and assists in the process of migrating the source system while the operating system instance on that source system is still running.

vCenter Converter Boot CD

If performing a hot migration is not an option, you can use the vCenter Converter Boot CD to boot the source system and perform a cold migration. Some older operating system versions and some applications might be incompatible with hot migrations, so performing a cold migration is the only way to get these source systems into your VMware vSphere environment.

> **NOTE** Because vCenter Converter Standalone 5 does not directly support cold cloning, you must use the Boot CD from an earlier vCenter Converter edition. To obtain the Boot CD, you must download the vCenter Converter 4.1.*x* installation package.

Perform a Physical-to-Virtual Migration

Importing physical systems into VMware vSphere is a fundamental task to almost every VMware vSphere environment. Unless you are building the entire IT infrastructure from scratch, you will have physical systems that need to be imported into the virtualization solution. Performing a physical-to-virtual migration is how you will go about bringing those physical systems into your VMware vSphere installation.

A physical-to-virtual migration might be a hot migration, in which the source system is running while the migration is occurring, or a cold migration, in which the source system is unavailable while the migration is occurring. Both of these are discussed in the following sections.

Perform a Hot Migration

A hot migration, as explained earlier, is a migration that occurs while the source system is running. Hot migrations are supported for systems running Windows 2003 SP2, R2 or later, several versions of Red Hat Enterprise Linux, several versions of SUSE Linux Enterprise Server, and several versions of Ubuntu.

vCenter Converter Standalone accomplishes a hot migration by installing an agent, the vCenter Converter Standalone Agent, onto the source system. This agent enables the physical-to-virtual migration by allowing vCenter Converter Standalone to read data out of the source system while it is still running. Without the agent, a hot migration would not be possible.

To perform a hot migration of a system running Windows Server 2003 R2, follow these steps:

1. Launch VMware vCenter Converter Standalone.

2. Click Convert Machine.

3. Select Powered-On Machine from the Select Source Type drop-down and select Local Or Remote Machine, then click Next.

4. Select VMware Infrastructure Virtual Machine from the Select Destination Type drop-down.

5. Supply the IP address or fully qualified domain name (FQDN) of vCenter Server, and an appropriate user name and password. Click Next.

6. Specify a name for the new virtual machine and pick a location in the virtual machine inventory where you want to store the new virtual machine. Click Next.

7. Select the datastore where you would like the virtual machine's virtual hard disks created and stored. If you selected a cluster or a resource pool in a cluster when you initiated the import process, the Conversion Wizard will prompt you to select a specific host on which the new virtual machine should run. After selecting a specific host, click Next.

8. If you would like to resize volumes during the import process or make other changes, you can do so now (Figure 10.1). Specify a new size for each of the volumes or, to maintain the size, leave the size the same as the current size. Click Next when you are ready to continue.

Configuring Your vSphere Environment

PART II

Figure 10.1: When importing volumes, vCenter Converter Standalone offers options to selectively import certain volumes, to change the size of volumes, and to make other changes.

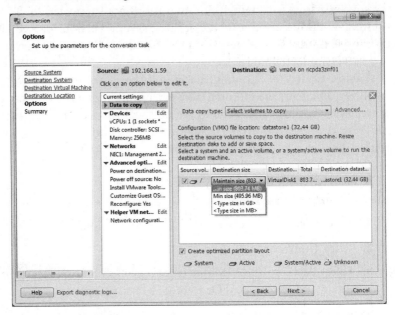

9. Review the settings for the migration. If everything is correct, click Finish. Otherwise, click Back to make changes.

vCenter Converter Standalone will create an active task for the conversion. You can use the Tasks pane in vCenter Converter Standalone to track the progress of the physical-to-virtual migration. When the migration is complete, you can start using the new virtual machine.

NOTE Since the newly created virtual machine is an exact copy of the physical source system, you must first shut down the physical source system before powering on the destination virtual machine. This will result in a small amount of downtime when the applications on that system will not be available. Be sure to plan for this downtime when conducting physical-to-virtual migrations in your environment.

A few post-conversion clean-up tasks are recommended once the physical-to-virtual migration is complete. Refer to the section titled "Clean Up After a Migration," later in this chapter, for more information.

Perform a Cold Migration

In the event you can't perform a hot migration, you can instead use a cold migration. With a cold migration, you use a boot CD to boot up the source system. The boot CD has its own operating system and also includes a version of the vCenter Converter application.

There are a number of reasons why you might want to perform a cold migration instead of a hot migration:

- The source system may have applications installed on it that are not compatible with a hot migration. Microsoft Windows Active Directory domain controllers are one example.

- You might not want users or other systems to be able to access the source system while it is being converted.

- You might not want the vCenter Converter Standalone Agent installed into the source operating system for change control or other organizational reasons.

VMware provides an .iso file that contains the boot CD image. Before starting a cold migration of a physical system, you will need to burn that .iso image to a physical CD.

To perform a cold migration of a physical source system, follow these steps:

1. Boot the source system from the CD you created with the vCenter Converter cold clone .iso file. You may need to modify the system so that it boots from the CD instead of from any local hard drives.

2. Press any key to boot the system from the CD.

3. When prompted, select the radio button labeled I Accept The Terms In The License Agreement. Click OK.

4. If you are not using Dynamic Host Configuration Protocol (DHCP) or if you need to manually adjust the network configuration, click Yes when asked if you want to update the network parameters.

5. If you chose to update network parameters, make the changes you need and then click OK.

6. When the VMware vCenter Converter window opens, click the Import Machine button in the toolbar. This launches the Import Wizard.

7. At the Source screen of the Import Wizard, click Next.

Configuring Your vSphere Environment

PART II

8. If you want to maintain the size of the disks on the source system, select Import All Disks and Maintain Size. Otherwise, select Select Volumes and Resize To Save Or Add Space and specify a new size for the volume listed. Click Next when you are ready to proceed.

9. Select vSphere Virtual Machine as the destination, and then click Next.

10. Provide the name or IP address of the vCenter Server and appropriate authentication information for that instance of vCenter Server. Click Next to continue.

11. Specify a name for the virtual machine and select a location in the virtual machine inventory where you would like to place the destination virtual machine. Click Next.

12. Select the host, cluster, or resource pool where you want the destination virtual machine to run. If you select a cluster or a resource pool within a cluster, you must also select a destination host on which to run the virtual machine.

13. Select the datastore where you would like to place the virtual machine disk files for the destination virtual machine. Use the Advanced button to place files in separate datastores. Click Next to proceed.

14. Specify the number of network interfaces for the destination virtual machine and the networks to which those interfaces should connect. Click Next.

15. Select Install VMware Tools and Remove All System Checkpoints (Recommended), then click Next. Because you will typically want the destination virtual machine to be an exact copy of the source system, don't select the check box to customize the system.

16. Review the settings for the migration. If everything is correct, click Finish. Otherwise, use the Back button to go back and change settings as necessary.

A task appears in the VMware vCenter Converter window that shows the progress of the cold migration. After the migration completes, you can shut down the source system and power on the destination virtual machine. A few post-migration cleanup tasks are recommended after the migration is complete. Some of these configuration changes are described in the next section.

Clean Up After a Migration

After you have completed a physical-to-virtual migration and the physical source system has been imported and re-created as a virtual machine on VMware vSphere, there are some additional cleanup tasks you should perform. These tasks are necessary because the migration process, by its very nature, creates a copy of the operating system instance in a VM that is identical to what was on the source physical system. However, the virtual machine is not the same as the source physical system—it has different hardware. To help optimize the performance of the operating system instance after the import has completed, you should remove unnecessary and missing hardware entries.

On a Windows-based system, you'll first need to tell Windows to show you missing hardware entries in Device Manager. Follow these steps:

1. Log on to the new Windows-based virtual machine with an account that has administrative privileges.

2. Right-click on My Computer and select Properties. If My Computer is not showing on the Desktop, use the Start Menu to open Control Panel, then double-click the System icon.

3. Click the Advanced tab.

4. Click the Environment Variables button.

5. At the bottom of the Environment Variables dialog box in the section marked System Variables, click the New button.

6. For Variable Name, specify DEVMGR_SHOW_NONPRESENT_DEVICES.

7. For Variable Value, specify 1.

8. Click OK to create the new system environment variable and return to the Environment Variables dialog box. The new system environment variable will be listed at the bottom of the dialog box.

9. Click OK to return to the System Properties dialog box.

10. Click OK to return to the Windows desktop.

Once you've completed these steps, you can use Device Manager to remove drivers and entries for hardware that is no longer present in the virtual machine after the physical-to-virtual conversion.

To remove references to missing hardware using Device Manager, follow these steps:

1. Log on to the new Windows-based virtual machine with an account that has administrative privileges.

2. Right-click on My Computer and select Properties. If My Computer is not showing on the Desktop, use the Start Menu to open Control Panel, then double-click the System icon.

3. Click the Hardware tab.

4. Click the Device Manager button.

5. Within the Device Manager console, select View ➤ Show Hidden Devices.

6. Navigate the Device Manager tree to remove missing hardware entries. These are noted with a dimmed icon in the list, as shown in Figure 10.2.

Figure 10.2: The dimmed icon for the VMware PVSCSI controller indicates that the hardware is no longer present in the virtual machine.

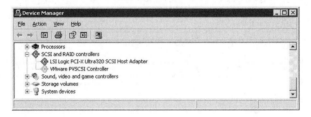

In addition, you will want to ensure that you have properly "right-sized" the new virtual machine for its needs. The physical-to-virtual migration process simply re-creates an identical virtual machine. You might need to adjust the memory configuration or the number of virtual CPUs to ensure that the new virtual machine is optimally configured.

Of course, not all physical-to-virtual migrations go smoothly, and there might be migrations that fail. In the next section, we'll provide some information on troubleshooting physical-to-virtual migrations.

Troubleshoot Physical-to-Virtual Migrations

A number of factors can contribute to problems with physical-to-virtual migrations. Insufficient memory on the source system, lack of free disk space on the source system, unrecognized hardware, missing or damaged drivers on the source system, and file system errors are all possible causes for a failed physical-to-virtual migration.

To help ensure successful migrations, follow these guidelines:

- Perform file system maintenance on the source system. Clean up files, free up disk space, defrag, and run Chkdsk (or fsck) to ensure the file system is consistent. You'll want to confirm that the source has at least 200MB free on the system volume.

- When performing a hot migration, shut down all unnecessary services.

- Avoid converting diagnostic or utility partitions.

- Ensure that you have the proper network connectivity between the source system and the destination vCenter Server system or ESX/ESXi hosts. TCP ports 443 and 902 should be open.

Perform a Virtual-to-Virtual Migration

Unlike physical-to-virtual migrations—which, by their very nature, involve importing systems into a VMware vSphere environment— virtual-to-virtual migrations might involve either importing or exporting virtual machines. In addition, almost all virtual-to-virtual migrations are cold migrations; the source virtual machine will have to be powered off in order to perform the migration.

TIP In the event you can't afford the downtime of a virtual machine in order to perform a virtual-to-virtual migration, just treat the source virtual machine like a physical system. Install the vCenter Converter Standalone Agent on the source virtual machine and perform the equivalent of a physical-to-virtual hot migration.

Virtual-to-virtual migrations are typically used in a few different instances:

- To export a virtual machine from VMware vSphere to run on a different VMware platform, like VMware Workstation or VMware Fusion

- To import a virtual machine currently running on another VMware platform, such as VMware Workstation or VMware Server, into VMware vSphere

- To reconfigure an existing VMware vSphere virtual machine by resizing its virtual machine disks or aligning its partitions

- To import a virtual machine currently configured for a competing virtualization solution, such as Microsoft Hyper-V Server

Try not to let the term "virtual-to-virtual" confuse you. You can use vCenter Converter Standalone in this sort of mode to do quite a few things. In the next few sections, we'll look at the most common uses of vCenter Converter Standalone for manipulating virtual machines.

Migrate to or from a Different VMware Platform

VMware vSphere is not VMware's only virtualization platform. VMware has a number of others, such as VMware Workstation, VMware Server, and VMware Fusion. While these products share a great deal of commonality with VMware vSphere, there are enough differences that VMs created on one platform might not run on another platform without modification. For example, VMware vSphere VMs can use virtual machine hardware version 8, but VMs on VMware Workstation 7.1 use virtual machine hardware version 7. Without modification to the VM, a virtual machine created on VMware vSphere won't run on VMware Workstation 7.1.

Fortunately, vCenter Converter Standalone can perform a virtual-to-virtual migration to resolve this issue. You can use VMware Converter Standalone to import VMs created on another VMware virtualization platform and to export VMs created on VMware vSphere so they will run on a different VMware virtualization platform. The process to import and export VMs using vCenter Converter Standalone is described in the next two sections.

Import VMs from a Different VMware Platform

If you have virtual machines created using a different VMware virtualization platform but you want to run those virtual machines on VMware vSphere 5, you can use vCenter Converter Standalone to import the virtual machine and perform the necessary reconfiguration to enable it to run in your vSphere environment.

vCenter Converter Standalone can import the following types of VMware virtual machines:

- VMware Workstation virtual machine

- VMware Player virtual machine

- VMware Server virtual machine
- VMware Fusion virtual machine

During the import process, vCenter Converter Standalone also offers the option of customizing the virtual machine so that the virtual machine you end up with might be very different from the one with which you started.

To import a virtual machine created using VMware Workstation or VMware Server, follow these steps:

1. Launch VMware vCenter Converter Standalone.

2. Click Convert Machine.

3. Select VMware Workstation Or Other VMware Virtual Machine from the Select Source Type drop-down.

4. Specify the local or Universal Naming Convention (UNC) path to the folder where the virtual machine files are stored, then click Next.

5. Select VMware Infrastructure Virtual Machine from the Select Destination Type drop-down.

6. Supply the IP address or fully qualified domain name (FQDN) of vCenter Server or an ESXi host, and an appropriate user name and password. Click Next.

7. Specify a name for the new virtual machine and pick a location in the virtual machine inventory where you want to store the new virtual machine. Click Next.

8. Select the datastore where you would like the virtual machine's virtual hard disks created and stored. If you selected a cluster or a resource pool in a cluster when you initiated the import process, the Conversion Wizard will prompt you to select a specific host on which the new virtual machine should run. After selecting a specific host, click Next.

9. On the Options screen of the Conversion Wizard dialog box, choose whether you would like to resize volumes during the import process. Also choose whether you want to install the VMware Tools, customize the virtual machine, or remove all System Restore checkpoints. Click Next when you are ready to continue.

   It's recommended to remove System Restore checkpoints. The other two options depend upon the particular circumstances surrounding this virtual machine. In most cases, you will want to install the VMware Tools and not perform any customization.

Configuring Your vSphere Environment

PART II

10. Review the settings for the migration. If everything is correct, click Finish. Otherwise, click Back to make changes.

vCenter Converter Standalone will create an active task in the Tasks pane where you can monitor the progress of the task. Once the task has completed, you will have a new virtual machine in your inventory.

NOTE   The process for importing a virtual machine created in VMware Fusion is fundamentally the same, but with some additional steps in the beginning to get the virtual machine files from the Mac OS X–based computer to a location accessible to vCenter Converter Standalone.

Export VMs to a Different VMware Platform

You can use vCenter Converter Standalone not only to import virtual machines from another VMware platform, but also to export virtual machines to another VMware platform.

To export a virtual machine for use with a different VMware platform, like VMware Workstation 7, follow these steps:

1. Launch VMware vCenter Converter Standalone.

2. Click Convert Machine.

3. Select VMware Infrastructure Virtual Machine from the Select Source Type drop-down.

4. Supply the IP address or fully qualified domain name (FQDN) of vCenter Server or an ESXi host, and an appropriate user name and password. Click Next.

5. Select the appropriate virtual machine from inventory. Click Next.

6. Select VMware Workstation or other VMware virtual machine from the Select Destination Type drop-down.

7. Select VMware Workstation 7.0.x from the Select VMware Product drop-down.

8. Specify the virtual machine name and a local or Universal Naming Convention (UNC) path to store the virtual machine files, then click Next.

9. On the Options screen of the Conversion Wizard dialog box, select whether you would like to pre-allocate disk space and whether to split volumes into 2GB increments during the export process. Also select how many network interface cards (NICs) the exported virtual machine should have, and whether each of those NICs should connect to a Network Address Translation (NAT) network, a bridged network, or a host-only network. Click Next when you are ready to continue. (See Figure 10.3)

Figure 10.3: The vSphere administrator has several options for network connectivity when exporting VMs out of VMware vSphere.

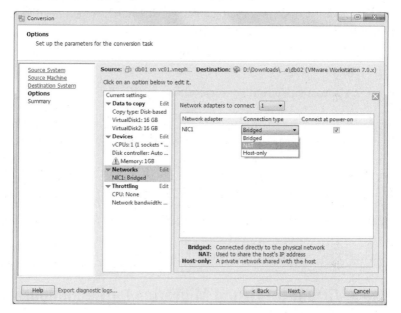

10. Review the settings for the migration. If everything is correct, click Finish; otherwise, click Back as necessary to make changes.

As with most other import and export processes we've discussed, vCenter Server Standalone will create an active task that is visible in the Tasks pane once the export actually begins. You can monitor the progress of the export using this active task. Please note that you will not be able to use or edit the new virtual machine until the export is complete.

After the export is complete, you will need to add the new virtual machine to the other VMware platform. The procedure for adding the newly exported virtual machine varies based on the specific platform.

Migrate from a Competing Product

In addition to importing and exporting virtual machines to and from VMware platforms besides VMware vSphere, vCenter Converter Standalone can import virtual machines from some competing virtualization products. This functionality is invaluable during a migration from another virtualization product to VMware vSphere. For example, perhaps you initially deployed Microsoft Hyper-V Server to perform some testing of virtual machine images, but now you want to deploy those images into your VMware vSphere environment for additional testing. You can use vCenter Converter Standalone to help with this process.

The following competing virtualization platforms are supported for import:

- Microsoft Virtual PC 2004 and Virtual PC 2007 (Windows guests only)

- Microsoft Virtual Server 2005 and 2005 R2

- Microsoft Hyper-V Server (Windows and Linux guests only)

- Parallels Desktop for Windows and Mac OS X 2.5, 3.0, and 4.0

The process for performing an import of a virtual machine created using a competing virtualization platform is the same as for importing a virtual machine created using a different VMware platform. The instructions provided in the earlier section titled "Import VMs from a Different VMware Platform" are equally applicable to importing virtual machines from a competing virtualization platform.

Use a Virtual-to-Virtual Migration for Reconfiguration

As mentioned earlier, using a virtual-to-virtual migration is one way to reconfigure an existing VMware vSphere virtual machine. Consider this situation: you have a virtual machine that has been allocated too much disk space. Using a virtual-to-virtual migration, you could resize the disk volumes during the migration to reclaim disk space.

To resize the disk volumes for a virtual machine using a virtual-to-virtual migration, follow these steps:

1. Launch VMware vCenter Converter Standalone.

2. Click Convert Machine.

3. Select Powered-on Machine from the Select Source Type drop-down and select Remote Machine, and then click Next.

4. Select VMware Infrastructure Virtual Machine from the Select Destination Type drop-down.

5. Supply the IP address or fully qualified domain name (FQDN) of vCenter Server or an ESXi host, and an appropriate user name and password. Click Next.

6. Specify a name for the new virtual machine and pick a location in the virtual machine inventory where you want to store the new virtual machine. Click Next.

7. Select the datastore where you would like the virtual machine's virtual hard disks created and stored. If you selected a cluster or a resource pool in a cluster when you initiated the import process, the Conversion Wizard will prompt you to select a specific host on which the new virtual machine should run. After selecting a specific host, click Next.

8. Because you are specifically performing this virtual-to-virtual migration to resize the virtual machine's hard disks, you can do so here. For each volume listed, use the drop-down list to choose the minimum size or to specify the size of the volume after the migration. Figure 10.4 shows the drop-down list for a virtual machine. Click Next when you are ready to continue.

Figure 10.4: The drop-down list provides the minimum size possible for a virtual machine's hard disk.

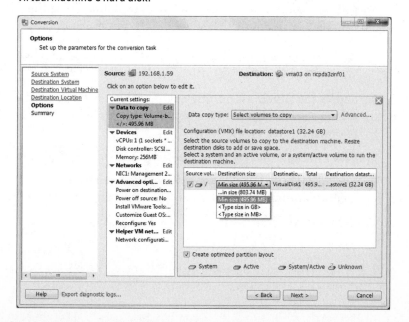

Configuring Your vSphere
Environment

PART II

9. Review the settings for the migration. If everything is correct, click Finish. Otherwise, click Back as necessary to make changes.

As you have seen in other migrations, vCenter Converter Standalone will create an active task that is visible in the Tasks pane. You can use this task to monitor the progress of the virtual-to-virtual migration. When the migration is complete, you can power on the virtual machine and start using it.

NOTE If you did not customize the virtual machine as part of the virtual-to-virtual migration, the new virtual machine created as part of the process will be an exact copy of the original virtual machine. This means that you should be sure to power down the original before powering on the new one.

In addition to resizing virtual disks, vCenter Converter Standalone can also be used to reconfigure a virtual machine in the event that an error has occurred and it is no longer able to boot. VMware provides a specific option for using vCenter Converter Standalone in this particular way.

To use vCenter Converter Standalone to reconfigure an unbootable virtual machine so it will boot, perform these steps:

1. Launch VMware vCenter Converter Standalone.

2. Click Configure Machine.

3. Select VMware Infrastructure Virtual Machine from the Select Source Type drop-down.

4. Supply the IP address or fully qualified domain name (FQDN) of vCenter Server or an ESXi host, and an appropriate user name and password. Click Next.

5. Select the appropriate virtual machine from inventory. Click Next.

6. Select the check boxes marked Remove System Restore Checkpoints On Destination and Reconfigure Destination Virtual Machine, as in Figure 10.5. Click Next to continue.

Figure 10.5: When using vCenter Converter Standalone to reconfigure a virtual machine, there's no need to install the VMware Tools or customize the VM.

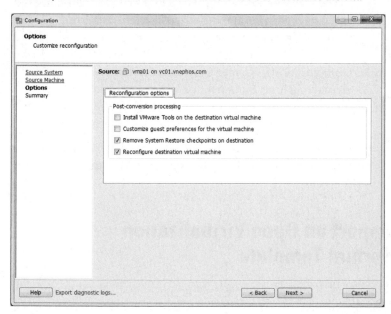

In almost all other cases, since you are simply reconfiguring an existing system, you will not want to select either of the other two check boxes.

7. Click Finish to perform the reconfiguration.

vCenter Converter Standalone will reconfigure the virtual machine so that it will boot properly. (Note that this does not fix problems with the guest operating system within the virtual machine. In these cases, the administrator must usually revert to guest OS–specific techniques, like performing a repair installation.) Like other procedures with vCenter Converter Standalone, a task is present in the Tasks pane by which you can monitor the progress of the task.

Troubleshoot Virtual-to-Virtual Migrations

While virtual-to-virtual migrations aren't the same as physical-to-virtual migrations, many of the recommendations for ensuring successful physical-to-virtual migrations, described in "Troubleshoot Physical-to-Virtual Migrations," earlier in this chapter, also apply here.

Some additional considerations for virtual-to-virtual migrations include:

- Make sure you have all the correct files necessary to import a virtual machine from a competing virtualization platform. For example, if you might have the .vhd (Virtual Hard Disk) file for a Microsoft Virtual PC virtual machine, but not the .vmc (Virtual Machine Configuration), vCenter Converter Standalone can't import the virtual machine. Similarly, for VMware virtual machines created on other VMware platforms you must have both the .vmx (virtual machine configuration) file and the .vmdk (virtual hard disk) files.

- If the source is a virtual machine created in Microsoft Virtual PC, remove the Virtual PC Additions prior to importing the virtual machine.

Import an Open Virtualization Format Template

The idea of a virtual appliance—a prepackaged virtual machine that is already installed and configured with the necessary software to perform a specific task—has been discussed at VMware for quite some time. One thing VMware needed was a standard way of packaging and deploying virtual appliances. The Open Virtualization Format (OVF) is one such standard. Ratified by the Desktop Management Task Force (DMTF) as a standard, the OVF 1.1 standard is fully supported by VMware vSphere and by several other virtualization products. Additional virtualization vendors have announced support for OVF in their products. Using OVF, creators of virtual appliances have a way of packaging and distributing their products in a format that multiple vendors will understand.

This section describes OVF templates and how to deploy virtual appliances using them.

Understand OVF Templates

This book primarily addresses OVF templates as they relate to VMware vSphere, but it is important to remember that OVF is designed to a platform-neutral, format-neutral specification.

According to the DMTF, OVF was designed to meet the following requirements:

- OVF supports both single-VM and multiple-VM configurations; the latter is key to VMware's vApp functionality.

- OVF is both vendor- and platform-agnostic, supporting multiple virtual hard disk formats. In addition, OVF does not depend upon any specific host platform, hypervisor, or operating system.

- OVF is extensible, allowing the specification to accommodate present as well as future requirements.

NOTE   Readers interested in more details on OVF are encouraged to download and review the official OVF Specification from the DMTF at `http://www.dmtf.org/standards/published_documents/DSP0243_1.1.0.pdf`.

An OVF template (sometimes also referred to as an OVF package) will consist at minimum of an OVF descriptor with an `.ovf` extension. In addition, the template may include one or more hard disk images, and may include a Manifest (`.mf` file), certificate (`.cert` file), and additional resource files (like `.iso` files).

An OVF template can be distributed as separate files, or the OVF package can be distributed as a single file using the `.ova` extension. OVF templates distributed as a single file use the standard UNIX TAR format. This means that you can both assemble and extract OVF packages using standard TAR-compliant tools.

The OVF descriptor is an XML document that contains the definitions for the number of virtual machines in the package, the virtual machine hardware for each of the virtual machines, references to other files (virtual machine disk files, for example), the operating system running within the virtual machines, network and storage configuration, and so on. The complete description of one or more virtual machines is encapsulated in the OVF XML document. It is this document that VMware vSphere and other virtualization solutions use to deploy the OVF template.

Deploy an OVF Template

Now that you have an idea of what an OVF template is, let's deploy an OVF template into your VMware vSphere environment. As an example, we'll work with the vSphere Management Assistant (vMA), a command-line interface designed for use with VMware vSphere. vMA is distributed as an OVF template.

Configuring Your vSphere Environment

NOTE The vSphere Management Assistant is available for download from VMware's website at: `http://www.vmware.com/download/download.do?downloadGroup=VMA50`

To deploy the vMA using an OVF template, perform the following steps:

1. From within vSphere Client while connected to a vCenter Server instance, select File ➤ Deploy OVF Template.

2. If you have already downloaded the vSphere Management Assistant, use the Browse button to find and select the OVF file you downloaded, then click Next when you are ready to continue.

3. Click Next at the OVF details screen.

4. Click Accept, then click Next.

5. Specify a name for the new virtual machine and select a location in the virtual machine inventory. Click Next to continue.

6. Choose a host or cluster on which to deploy this OVF template. When you are ready to continue, click Next.

7. If you selected a cluster that has DRS disabled or configured for manual automation, you must select a specific ESX/ESXi host on which to run the new virtual machine. Click Next to continue.

8. Select a datastore where the virtual machine's virtual hard disks should be stored. Click Next to continue to the next step.

9. Map the vMA's Management Network to an applicable network defined in your VMware vSphere environment. While this virtual appliance has only a single network connection, some virtual appliances may have multiple network connections. Each network connection must be mapped to the appropriate network in the destination VMware vSphere environment. Click Next when you are ready to continue.

10. Review the settings. If everything is correct, click Finish. Otherwise, click Back to go back and make any necessary changes.

11. vCenter Server will display a dialog box that shows the progress of deploying the virtual machine from the OVF template. If you chose to deploy from a URL, vCenter Server will download the necessary files from the specified URL. Depending upon the size

of the virtual appliance, this may take some time. vCenter Server will also show an active task in the Tasks pane of vSphere Client.

After the new virtual machine has been fully deployed, you can configure it in the same fashion as any other virtual machine. Depending upon the software within the virtual machine, there may be additional configuration steps necessary before it is fully functional.

Configuring Your vSphere Environment

PART II

11

Configuring Security

IN THIS CHAPTER, YOU WILL LEARN TO:

Configuring Your vSphere Environment

PART II

There's a saying in the security community: "Security is a pursuit, not a goal." In your VMware vSphere environment, security is required. This chapter presents a number of ways to help improve the security of the various components of your VMware vSphere environment.

Configure vCenter Server Access Control

Part of the security of any environment is ensuring that access to resources is controlled properly. Users should have access to only those areas necessary to do their job and should be able to do only the tasks that are applicable to that job. For example, a help desk technician might need the ability to change the power state of a virtual machine, but most likely he or she does not need the ability to create new virtual machines and should not have access to that feature.

As a key part of vCenter Server's management functionality, vCenter Server provides role-based access control (RBAC) for the VMware vSphere environment. vCenter Server's RBAC implementation provides granular control over the specific tasks users are allowed to perform on certain types of objects. This allows organizations to ensure that users are granted the appropriate level of permission on the appropriate subset of objects as determined by the needs of the organization.

There are three aspects to configuring access control, which you'll learn about in this section:

- Using the predefined roles that are available with vCenter Server.

- Customizing roles when the predefined roles don't meet the needs of your organization. You can create new roles and edit, clone, or remove roles.

- Combining users, groups, and roles into permissions that you assign to objects in vCenter Server.

Understand vCenter Server's Predefined Roles

vCenter Server comes with a number of predefined roles. These roles provide a starting point for customers to create the roles that fit their organization's administrative model. Here are the default roles available with vCenter Server:

No Access   This role denies access to an object for a user or group. It's primarily used to prevent a user or group that has permissions at some point higher in the hierarchy from having permissions on the object to which this role is assigned. You can use it to create exceptions, where a user or group has access to all the virtual machines in a folder or resource pool except for just a few.

Read-Only   Read-Only allows a user or group to see the vCenter Server inventory and the power status of virtual machines. It does not allow the user or group to interact with any of the virtual machines in any way through vSphere Client or the web client.

Administrator   A user or group assigned to an object with the Administrator role will have full administrative capabilities over that object in vCenter Server. A user or group assigned the Administrator role for a virtual machine can change the hardware assigned to the virtual machine, connect and disconnect media, start and stop the virtual machine, and alter its performance parameters.

NOTE   A user or group with the Administrator role does not have any privileges within the guest operating systems installed inside the virtual machines. Those privileges must be assigned within that guest operating system instance.

Virtual Machine Power User (Sample)   The Virtual Machine Power User sample role assigns permissions to allow a user or group to perform most functions on virtual machines. This includes things like configuring CD/DVD and floppy media, changing the power state, taking and deleting snapshots, and modifying the configuration. These permissions apply only to virtual machines. A user or group granted this role would not be able to change settings on objects such as resource pools.

Virtual Machine User (Sample)   The Virtual Machine User role grants a user or group the ability to interact with a virtual machine, but not the ability to change its configuration. Users can operate the virtual machine's power controls and change the media in the virtual CD/DVD drive or floppy drive as long as they also have access to the media they want to change.

Configuring Your vSphere Environment

PART II

NOTE   vCenter Server's permissions are granular. For instance, if you want a user who is assigned the Virtual Machine User role to be able to attach an ISO file or a floppy image to a virtual machine located on a datastore, they must also be granted the Browse Datastore permission. Otherwise, the user will only be able to change the CD or floppy media to his or her own client system's physical CD/DVD or floppy drive.

Resource Pool Administrator (Sample)   The Resource Pool administrator can manage and configure resources within a resource pool, including virtual machines, child pools, scheduled tasks, and alarms.

VMware Consolidated Backup User (Sample)   The user given this role has the privileges required for performing a backup of a virtual machine using VMware Consolidated Backup (VCB).

Datacenter Consumer (Sample)   The Datastore Consumer role is targeted at users who need only a single permission: the permission to allocate space from a datastore. Clearly, this is a very limited role.

Network Consumer (Sample)   Similar to the Datastore Consumer role, the Network Consumer role has only a single permission: the permission to assign networks.

NOTE   For environments using vSphere Client to manage ESXi hosts directly, only three roles are available: No Access, Read-Only, and Administrator. The additional roles are only present when you are using vCenter Server.

These roles can be granted on an object at any level in the hierarchy and the user or group that is assigned the role will have those permissions on that object and—if the inheritance box, labeled Propagate To Child Objects, is marked—any child objects beneath it in the hierarchy.

Customize Roles

The predefined roles might not meet the specific needs of medium to large organizations. In that case, you can customize the roles to exclude certain privileges or to include additional privileges. Or you might find that none of the predefined roles meet your needs, in which case you can create an entirely new role. vCenter Server provides the functionality to edit the predefined roles, delete roles, clone existing roles, and add new roles.

All of this functionality is found in vSphere Client by navigating to the Roles area either by using the navigation bar or by selecting View ➤ Administration ➤ Roles. The Roles area displays all the currently defined roles. Right-clicking on a role provides commands to clone, edit, or remove the role. An Add Role button is also provided just below the navigation bar.

NOTE   The No Access, Read-Only, and Administrator predefined roles cannot be edited or deleted. To customize one of these roles, you should clone the role and edit the cloned copy of the role.

Create a New Role

To create a new role, perform these steps:

1. Connect to a vCenter Server instance with vSphere Client.

2. Select View ➤ Administration ➤ Roles.

3. Click the Add Role button.

4. In the Add New Role dialog box, specify a name for the new role.

5. From the list of privileges, select the privileges you want to grant to this role. For example, if you wanted to create a role for managing distributed virtual network settings, you would assign permissions out of the Distributed Virtual Port Group and Distributed Virtual Switch categories, as illustrated in Figure 11.1.

Figure 11.1: The Add New Role dialog box allows you to specify the privileges assigned to a new role on a granular basis.

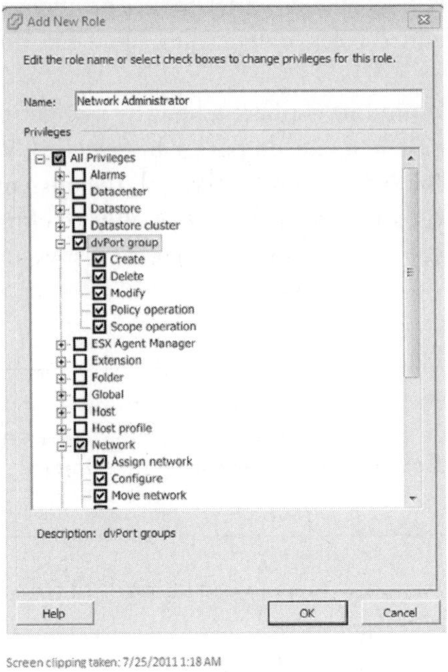

Screen clipping taken: 7/25/2011 1:18 AM

6. Click OK to save the settings and create the new role.

You've now created the new role and can use this role in assigning permissions.

Edit an Existing Role

Editing an existing role is necessary when you find that a role includes privileges that should not be included, or fails to include privileges that should be included.

To edit a role to add or remove privileges, perform these steps:

1. Connect to a vCenter Server instance with vSphere Client.

2. Select View ➤ Administration ➤ Roles.

3. Right-click the role you want to edit and select Edit Role.

4. In the Edit Role dialog box, specify a new name for the role (if desired) and add or remove privileges from the list.

5. Click OK to save your changes and return to vSphere Client.

> **TIP** You can rename the role in the Edit Role dialog box, or by right-clicking on a role and selecting Rename to rename the role.

Clone an Existing Role

Sometimes, you might find that you need a new role that is very similar to an existing role but with a few privileges added or removed. While you could create a new role and assign all the permissions manually, you will find that cloning the role is quicker, easier, and less error-prone.

To clone an existing role, perform these steps:

1. Connect to a vCenter Server instance with vSphere Client.

2. Select View ➢ Administration ➢ Roles.

3. Right-click the role you want to clone and select Clone. Alternately, select the role and click the Clone Role button just below the navigation bar.

4. A new role appears in the list of roles. Type a name for the new role, and then press Enter.

The new role is now available for you to customize as needed.

Remove a Role

When a role is no longer needed, you can easily remove it. Simply right-click on the role you want to delete and select Remove.

If the role is currently in use—meaning that one or more users have been assigned a permission with that role—vCenter Server will prompt you for the correct action to take:

- To remove the permissions, select Remove Role Assignments when prompted.

- To reassign the permissions, select Reassign Affected Users when prompted. You'll have the option to select a different role to assign to the affected users.

Manage Permissions

After you have created the necessary roles, you must then combine those roles with a user or group to create a *permission*. You'll then assign the permission to an object in order to put it into effect.

You can assign permissions from any of the inventory views: Hosts And Clusters, VMs And Templates, Datastores, and Networking. In all these different views, the process is the same.

To assign a permission to an object, perform these steps:

1. While connected to a vCenter Server instance, navigate in vSphere Client to the inventory view for the type of object on which you want to assign the permission. For example, if you want to assign a permission on a specific ESXi host, navigate to Hosts And Clusters view.

2. Select the object on which the permission should be assigned.

3. Select the Permissions tab from the content pane on the right.

4. Right-click in a blank area of the Permissions tab and select Add Permission. This opens the Assign Permissions dialog box.

5. Under Users And Groups, select the Add button.

6. Select the specific users or groups to include in the role. When you've added all the users and groups, click OK.

7. From the Assigned Role section, select the role you want to assign to the selected users and groups.

8. If you want the permission to apply to child objects, be sure to leave the Propagate To Child Objects check box selected.

9. If you need to add more users or groups with other roles, repeat steps 5 through 8.

10. When you are finished assigning roles to users and groups, click OK to return to vSphere Client.

The permissions will appear on the Permissions tab for the selected object. If you need to remove a permission, simply right-click the permission and select Delete. To change the role assigned in the permission, right-click on the permission and select Properties. vCenter Server will display the Change Access Rule dialog box to allow you to change the role assigned in the permission for the selected user or group.

With vCenter Server's role-based access control, organizations can properly secure access to the objects and resources in their VMware vSphere environment by binding to an existing directory service such as Microsoft Active Directory or LDAP. This is an important part of every organization's security efforts, but not the only part. In the next section, we'll examine some other ways to help secure vCenter Server.

Secure vCenter Server

By now, you are well aware of the central role that vCenter Server plays in the management of your VMware vSphere environment. In addition to securing user access to objects and resources within vCenter Server, it's also important to secure vCenter Server and the computer on which vCenter Server runs. In addition, you will want to lock down the default administrative access to vCenter Server, which unnecessarily exposes access to vCenter Server to users who may not need access to the virtualization environment.

Harden the vCenter Server Computer

A discussion of hardening the vCenter Server computer is really more of a discussion on hardening Windows Server. Some general guidelines to keep in mind include:

- Be sure to keep the vCenter Server computer properly patched and up-to-date on all security updates.

- Follow published best practices from Microsoft with regard to securing Windows Server when using a Microsoft hosted vCenter Server.

- Be sure to harden not only the vCenter Server computer, but also the computer running the vCenter Server database (if it is on a separate computer).

- Follow published best practices from the appropriate database vendor for the database server you are using for vCenter Server.

- In accordance with your organization's security policy, properly install and configure antivirus agents, intrusion detection systems, and other security software.

- If possible, control network access to the vCenter Server computer using a firewall or access control lists (ACLs).

- Install an Internet-facing VUM server on a separate machine.

WARNING   Using a firewall with Network Address Translation (NAT) enabled between the vCenter Server and the ESXi hosts might cause problems. Avoid the use of NAT between the vCenter Server computer and the ESXi hosts.

- If you are using Windows authentication with SQL Server, use a dedicated service account for vCenter Server. Don't share an account with other services or applications.

Configuring Your vSphere Environment

PART II

- Replace the default self-signed SSL certificates with valid SSL certificates from a trusted root authority.

- Restrict physical access to the vCenter Server computer to authorized personnel only.

These are just a few guidelines to get you started; there are many, many more hardening guidelines available for securing Windows Server 2003 or Windows Server 2008. Although many different security guidelines and benchmarks exist to help you harden Windows Server, the best place to start is with Microsoft's website at www.microsoft.com. From there, you will find documentation and references to other useful resources.

In addition to securing the operating system underneath vCenter Server, there are also some steps you can take to secure vCenter Server itself. One of these steps is removing the default administrative access to vCenter Server, as described in the next section.

Remove Default Administrative Access to vCenter Server

By default, when vCenter Server is installed on a Windows platform, the local Administrators group on the vCenter Server computer is granted the Administrator role at the datacenter object within vCenter Server. Effectively, this means that the local Administrators group is given full permission on all objects within the vCenter Server hierarchy. When the vCenter Server computer is part of an Active Directory domain, this also means that the Domain Admins group—which is, by default, a member of the local Administrators group on every member server in the domain—also has full permission on all objects within the vCenter Server hierarchy. This default administrative access exposes vCenter Server to personnel that may have no need for access within the VMware vSphere environment.

To remove the default administrative access in vCenter Server, perform these steps:

1. On the vCenter Server computer, use the Computer Management console to create a new local group. You could call the group vCenter Administrators or something similar.

2. Create a new user and place this user into the group created in step 1. Be sure not to place this user in the local Administrators group.

3. Log on to the vCenter Server computer using an account with administrative permissions.

4. Launch vSphere Client and connect to a vCenter Server instance.

5. Assign the Administrator role to the new group created in step 1 to the vCenter Server object at the top of the hierarchy. Be sure to leave Propagate To Child Objects selected.

6. Log off and log back on as the user created in step 2.

7. Log in to vCenter Server using vSphere Client and ensure that you are able to perform all tasks available for a vCenter Server administrator.

8. Remove the permission on the vCenter Server object for the local Administrators group.

9. If you are using Active Directory, create a group in Active Directory and add it to the local group created in step 1. Add domain users to the domain group as necessary.

After making this change, only the users that are members of the local group (or the Active Directory domain group, where applicable) will have administrative permissions within vCenter Server.

Secure Your ESXi and ESXi Hosts

In addition to securing access to the objects within vCenter Server and securing the vCenter Server computer, you need to appropriately secure your VMware ESXi hosts.

In each of the following sections, we'll identify configuration steps to secure ESXi. This will make it easier to identify which security configuration recommendations apply to each product.

Control Network Access to the Management Network

To help control network access to the VMware ESXi Management Network, VMware supplies a firewall for the Management Network and a command to configure the firewall. You can configure the firewall via vSphere Client or via the command line. If you choose to use the command line, use the command `esxcli network firewall` to enable or disable network services through the firewall.

To view or configure the firewall from vSphere Client, perform these steps:

1. Connect to an instance of vCenter Server with vSphere Client. If there are multiple vCenter Server instances in your environment,

be sure to connect to the instance that is managing the host you wish to configure.

2. Navigate to Hosts And Clusters inventory view using the View menu, the navigation bar, or the Ctrl+Shift+H keyboard shortcut.

3. Select an ESXi host from the inventory on the left.

4. Select the Configuration tab from the content pane on the right.

5. Select the Security Profile link under Software.

6. The current incoming and outgoing connections allowed through the firewall are listed in the content pane. If you need to make changes, click the Properties link.

7. In the Firewall Properties dialog box, check or uncheck the services whose state you need to modify. Check a service to allow it through the firewall; uncheck a service to deny it through the firewall. Figure 11.2 shows the Firewall Properties dialog box with some services enabled and other services disabled.

Figure 11.2: Firewall Properties dialog box

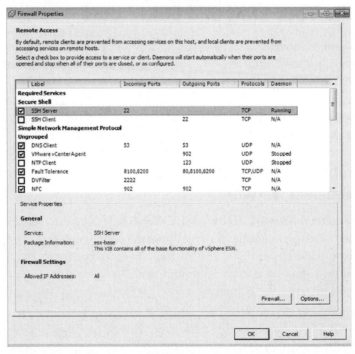

8. Click OK to return to vSphere Client.

To view or configure the firewall from the command line, perform these steps:

1. Using a terminal window, log in to the console of the ESXi host.

2. Use the `esxcli network firewall` command to view the current firewall settings:

   ```
   esxcli network firewall get
   ```

3. List the defined services that are understood by the firewall with this command:

   ```
   esxcli network firewall ruleset rule list
   ```

4. Enable a service through the firewall with this command:

   ```
   esxcli network firewall ruleset -e true -r=<service name>
   ```

5. Disable a currently enabled service using this command:

   ```
   esxcli network firewall ruleset -e false -r=<service name>
   ```

Changes made using `esxcli network firewall` take effect immediately, but may not be reflected in vSphere Client for a few minutes, or when you click the Refresh button.

NOTE For additional flexibility in controlling network access to the VMware ESXi host, you can also leverage other Linux-based network access control features, such as TCP Wrappers.

Isolate the Management Network

The VMware ESXi Management Network needs its own network connectivity to communicate with other VMware ESXi hosts and with vCenter Server. For ESXi, this network connectivity does not need to be shared with VMkernel traffic (used for VMotion, Fault Tolerance logging, or IP-based storage) or virtual machine traffic, so we highly recommend that you isolate the management network using either VLANs or a physically separate network. Redundancy of the management network is important, however, so be sure to include redundant network connections for the Management Network where possible.

Figure 11.3 shows a sample network configuration for a VMware ESXi host that places the management traffic onto a separate set of NICs. These NICs might connect to switches on a physically segregated network, or just to ports in a different VLAN on the same physical switches.

Figure 11.3: This network configuration allows for the VMware ESXi management traffic to be segregated onto a physically separate network.

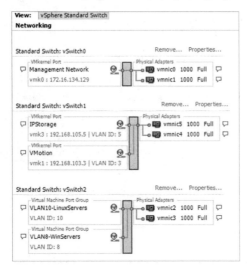

When it isn't possible to use separate ports in a different VLAN or a physically separate switch, you can run the Management Network on a different VLAN than VMkernel or virtual machine traffic. Refer to Chapter 6 for more information on how to configure VLANs.

Delete Unnecessary Local Accounts

In many environments, especially those using vCenter Server, the individual ESXi hosts will not have many, if any, unnecessary local accounts. In other environments, though, many local accounts might have been created on the ESXi hosts. When these accounts are no longer necessary, they should be disabled and removed to prevent possible unauthorized access to the hosts.

NOTE   vCenter Server acts as an authentication proxy between the end users and the ESXi hosts. Rather than passing credentials through to the ESXi hosts, vCenter Server proxies all connections using a special account named *vpxuser*. Do not modify or delete this account on your ESXi hosts or you will break vCenter Server's management functionality.

On a VMware ESXi host, you can delete unnecessary local accounts either using vSphere Client connected directly to the host, or via the Management Network with the userdel *<username>* command. If you prefer to keep the account but lock it so that it can't be used for logins, use the passwd -l *<username>* command (that's a lowercase *L* in the command). The passwd -u *<username>* command will unlock the account.

To use the vSphere Client to remove local accounts on an ESXi host, perform these steps:

1. Log in to the ESXi host directly using vSphere Client.

2. From the right content pane, select the Local Users & Groups tab.

3. Click Users.

4. Right-click the user you want to remove and select Remove.

Understand Lockdown Mode

Lockdown Mode, when enabled, prevents management of the ESXi host outside of vCenter Server. Direct connections to the ESXi host using vSphere Client are denied—all management requests must go through vCenter Server. This ensures that vCenter Server's role-based access controls come into play and are not circumvented by connecting directly to the ESXi host. Limited administrative functions can also be performed at the local ESXi console. If a root password has been specified, it will be required before these administrative functions can be performed.

NOTE   Be sure to specify a root password on all ESXi hosts.

Secure Your Virtual Machines

The fourth major component of a VMware vSphere environment that you need to secure is the virtual machines themselves.

Configuring Your vSphere Environment

Not only do you need to secure the guest operating systems installed within these virtual machines, but you must also secure the virtual machines themselves. The fact that these are virtual machines, as opposed to physical machines, does introduce new security issues that must be taken into account in an overall effort to improve the security of the environment.

Configure Virtual Machine Isolation

One specific area that is unique to virtual machines is virtual machine isolation—how and when a virtual machine is allowed to interact with the virtualization layer.

Isolation is a key benefit of virtualization. It is the isolation of one guest operating system instance from other guest operating system instances that allows you to run multiple operating systems on the same hardware. It is the isolation of the guest operating system from the underlying hardware that gives virtual machines their hardware independence.

Some of this isolation is removed to simplify things for administrators. For example, administrators expect the ability to use copy-and-paste between their local computer and the console of a remote virtual machine. Enabling this greater interaction between virtual machines and the rest of the physical environment has to be weighed with a careful eye toward security.

The next few sections describe some of these isolation settings.

Disable Copy and Paste

By default, the remote console of vSphere Client provides the ability to use copy and paste to move data to and from a virtual machine to the local workstation. To prevent this functionality, disable copy and paste by adding the following lines to the virtual machine's configuration file:

```
isolation.tools.copy.disable = "true"
isolation.tools.paste.disable = "true"
```

You can either edit the virtual machine configuration (.vmx) file directly, or you can add these entries using vSphere Client.

> **NOTE** Editing the virtual machine configuration file directly is more error-prone than using vSphere Client to modify the virtual machine configuration.

To add entries to a virtual machine configuration file using vSphere Client, perform these steps:

1. Launch vSphere Client, if it is not already running, and connect to a vCenter Server instance.

2. Navigate to an inventory view that displays the virtual machine you wish to modify. The virtual machine must be powered off to make the changes; if necessary, shut down the virtual machine first.

3. Right-click the virtual machine and select Edit Settings.

4. Select the Options tab, click Advanced, and then click General.

5. Click the Configuration Parameters button.

6. Select the Add Row button at the bottom of the Configuration Parameters dialog box.

7. Specify the name of the parameter (for example `isolation.tools.copy.disable`) and a value (such as `true`).

8. Click OK to return to the virtual machine's Properties dialog box.

9. Click OK again to return to vSphere Client.

10. Power on the virtual machine.

Don't Allow a Virtual Machine User or Process to Disconnect Devices

It's a good idea in terms of security to prevent a user or process inside a virtual machine from being able to connect or disconnect devices such as the floppy, CD/DVD drive, or network adapter. Otherwise, an unprivileged guest OS user or process could potentially connect or disconnect these devices. Keep in mind that we are not talking about preventing a properly authorized user, using vSphere Client, from connecting or disconnecting devices. Instead, we are talking about preventing the connecting or disconnecting of devices *from within the virtual machine and the guest operating system.*

To make this change, add this configuration parameter to the virtual machine configuration file:

```
<device_name>.allowGuestConnectionControl = "false"
```

You can add this parameter to the VM configuration file using vSphere Client. Follow the procedure described in the previous section,

"Disable Copy and Paste." You'll want to replace `<device_name>` with the name of the device, such as `ethernet0` or `floppy0`.

Making this change ensures that only users granted the appropriate access within vCenter Server are able to connect or disconnect devices like the floppy drive, CD/DVD drive, or network adapter. Again, this change only affects the ability of users and processes within the virtual machine or guest operating system; it does not affect users operating upon the virtual machine using vSphere Client.

NOTE Along the same lines as preventing a user or process from connecting or disconnecting devices, you should also remove any unnecessary hardware components from the virtual machine. For example, if the virtual machine doesn't need a floppy drive, you should remove the floppy drive from the virtual machine configuration.

Harden the Guest Operating System

It's important to manage the security of the guest operating system within the virtual machine. Controls placed at the virtualization layer—such as access controls within vCenter Server—don't translate into the appropriate security controls within the guest operating systems. Be sure to follow established best practices with regard to securing the guest operating systems found within the virtual machines. This includes applying all applicable security patches and updates, using firewalls where applicable, enforcing access controls within the guest OS, and exercising the principle of least privilege. The guest operating system vendors provide extensive resources with detailed recommendations on how to secure their specific products. We suggest that you refer to the recommendations from your guest OS vendors to secure the guest operating systems appropriately.

12

Managing Resources and Performance

IN THIS CHAPTER, YOU WILL LEARN TO:

Configuring Your vSphere Environment

PART II

I n a VMware vSphere environment, managing resources and managing performance go hand in hand. Performance will suffer if resources are over- or under-allocated. To avoid this situation, you need to understand how to assign resources, control allocation during times of resource contention, and identify when resource contention is occurring.

Understand Resource Allocation

Understanding how to use resource allocation effectively will help you configure virtual machines correctly and support more virtual machines with fewer resources.

So, what is resource allocation? Resource allocation is the division of a physical server's finite resources—namely, computer power, memory, network bandwidth, and storage capacity—among multiple virtual machines. This division of resources by the administrator might be static, as in the maximum amount of RAM assigned to a virtual machine, or it might be dynamic, as in controlling what percentage of CPU cycles a virtual machine gets during times of CPU contention. You must know how VMware ESXi allocates resources to virtual machines and how to modify that default behavior to achieve the desired results.

Understanding resource allocation starts with understanding the three ways in which resources are assigned to a virtual machine. First, resources such as CPU, memory, network, and storage are assigned to a virtual machine via the virtual machine configuration itself. For example, when you create a virtual machine, you must decide how many virtual CPUs (vCPUs) should be assigned to that VM, or how much memory should be assigned to the VM. These resource assignments are fairly static, but they can easily be adjusted—a core benefit of virtualization and abstraction of resources.

Second, you can apply certain controls to dynamically modify the behavior of the assigned resources by guaranteeing certain resource levels or by constraining resource usage. Specifically, you will use *reservations* to guarantee resource levels and *limits* to constrain resource usage.

Third, and finally, you can adjust how ESXi grants resource access during times of resource contention. Using a mechanism called *shares*, administrators can fine-tune how resources are granted when those resources are in short supply. When an ESXi host has plenty of memory, there is no need to control how that memory is granted—there is enough to go around, so every VM gets whatever it needs. When that ESXi host runs low on memory, though, you need a way to control which VMs get memory and how much memory those VMs get. This is where shares come into play. Shares are only active when there is resource contention; reservations and limits are always active although they can behave differently depending on the resource.

The next section discusses these controls in more detail and provides specific information on how to use these tools to control resource allocation for individual virtual machines. In the vast majority of situations, you are primarily going to be concerned with how CPU and memory are allocated, so the content in this section and throughout the chapter will focus heavily on controlling CPU and memory allocation.

Allocate Resources to Virtual Machines

Efficiently allocating resources to virtual machines is a key skill that every VMware vSphere administrator needs to master. If you allocate too many or too few resources, performance is negatively impacted. VMware vSphere provides a number of ways to help you make sure that resources are allocated and used efficiently, as you'll see in this section.

Allocate Resources in the VM Configuration

The first way in which you control resource allocation is by assigning resources in the configuration of the virtual machine. When you create a virtual machine, you assign certain levels of resources to that virtual machine. For example, Figure 12.1 shows the memory configuration for a virtual machine.

Figure 12.1: This virtual machine is configured with 4 GB of RAM, so any guest operating system installed here will never see or use more than 4 GB of RAM.

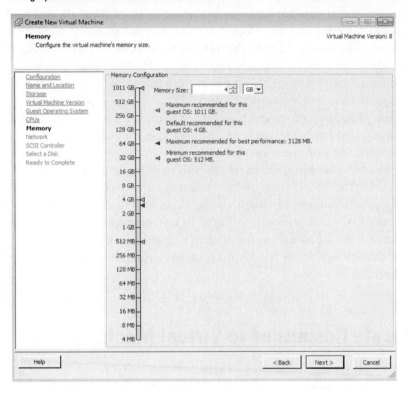

In the same way that the configuration of a physical machine establishes a limit on how many resources are available to that physical machine, the configuration of a virtual machine controls how resources are allocated to that virtual machine and the guest operating system running inside that virtual machine. If a virtual machine is configured for 4 GB of RAM, that virtual machine has only 4 GB of RAM visible to it. Any guest operating system installed in that virtual machine will not see or use more than 4 GB of RAM in the static configuration. Again, the resources can be easily adjusted, sometimes while the VM is powered on. The same is true for CPU resources as well.

Of course, one key difference between a physical machine and a virtual machine is the ease of adding resources to a virtual machine. If the 4 GB of RAM assigned to the virtual machine in Figure 12.1 proves insufficient, it is very easy for you to add more RAM to the system by modifying the configuration. In some cases, you can make this change while the virtual machine is running using the hot-add feature. Hardware hot-add is discussed in more detail in Chapter 9.

If, on the other hand, the guest operating system in that virtual machine is not fully utilizing the RAM that has been assigned to it in the VM configuration, it's also very easy to reduce the RAM assigned to the VM.

NOTE   VMware ESXi utilizes some advanced memory-management technologies that lessen, or perhaps even eliminate, the impact of assigning too much memory to a virtual machine. The same cannot be said for virtual CPUs. Assigning multiple vCPUs when the workload can't effectively use multiple vCPUs can negatively impact performance. This fact underscores the importance of "right sizing" virtual machines to give them only the resources they actually need.

This ease of modification—which allows you to quickly and easily add or remove resources assigned to a virtual machine—means that you should be sure to right size virtual machines instead of continuing to provision virtual machines the same way that physical machines are provisioned. Physical machines are provisioned with the maximum amount of resources the administrator thinks the system might need, because adding more resources is more difficult. Virtual machines should be provisioned for only what they need; should the guest operating system and application prove to need more or less than what is assigned, you can easily change it.

Guarantee Resources with Reservations

Just because you have assigned resources to a virtual machine in the virtual machine's configuration doesn't necessarily guarantee resource availability. If you need to guarantee that certain levels of resources are available to a particular virtual machine, you will need to use a reservation. A *reservation* is a guarantee of a certain amount of a certain type of resource so long as the VM is successfully powered on, so a virtual machine is assured of having at least that amount of the resource available to it.

The Resources tab of a virtual machine's properties, shown in Figure 12.2, is where you will set a reservation for a virtual machine. For CPU, the reservation is specified in megahertz (MHz); for memory, the reservation is set in megabytes (MB).

Configuring Your vSphere Environment

PART II

Figure 12.2: You can set reservations on CPU or memory on the Resources tab of the Virtual Machine Properties window.

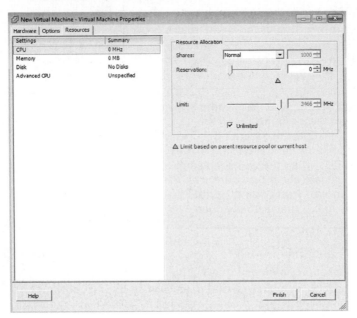

NOTE You cannot set these same types of reservations on storage (disks) or network resources.

So how do reservations work?

- When you set a CPU reservation, that amount of CPU time is guaranteed to the virtual machine *when needed*. If the virtual machine uses less than its CPU reservation, the excess clock cycles can be assigned to other virtual machines. For example, if a virtual machine with a 1 GHz reservation is using only 500 MHz of CPU time, the remaining 500 MHz in the reservation may be used by other virtual machines or the hypervisor.

- When you set a memory reservation, that memory is set aside for that virtual machine. ESXi allocates memory on-demand; that is, memory is not granted to a virtual machine until it accesses the memory. In this case, memory guaranteed by a reservation cannot be used by any other virtual machine once it has been accessed (and allocated) to the assigned virtual machine. Furthermore, VMware's advanced memory technologies, like idle page reclamation, do not reclaim idle pages that are part of a reservation. The memory is available for use only by the virtual machine to which it was assigned and reserved.

As you can see, CPU reservations and memory reservations are similar in function, but different in approach. Given the different nature of these resources, however, these behaviors make sense. If you are setting reservations on virtual machines, be sure to reserve only enough resources to guarantee a minimum level of performance. Otherwise, you run the risk of preventing other virtual machines from starting up or operating properly due to a lack of unreserved capacity.

NOTE   A virtual machine will only power on if there are enough unreserved resources—both CPU and memory— available to satisfy the reservations on that virtual machine.

To assign a CPU or memory reservation to a virtual machine, follow these steps:

1. In vSphere Client, right-click on the virtual machine to which you wish to add the reservation and select Edit Settings.

2. In the Virtual Machine Properties window, select the Resources tab.

3. To assign a CPU reservation, select CPU from the list of resources on the left and specify a reservation, in MHz, on the right.

    To assign a memory reservation, select Memory from the list of resources on the left, and then specify a reservation (in MB) on the right.

4. Click OK to save the settings and close the Virtual Machine Properties window.

Looking back at Figure 12.2, you'll note a small triangle that indicates the maximum amount of a resource that may be specified in a reservation. This limit is derived from the resources available to that virtual machine based on the ESXi host on which it is running or the resource pool in which it has been placed. Resource pools are discussed in the "Use Resource Pools" section later in this chapter.

Constrain Resource Usage with Limits

There might be situations in which you need to constrain, or limit, the amount of a particular resource that is consumed by the virtual machine.

For example, you might want to limit how much CPU time a virtual machine uses, or limit how much memory a virtual machine is allowed to use. The *limits* functionality within VMware vSphere provides this ability. By default, VMware vSphere sets the limits for CPU and memory to Unlimited; that is, there is no artificial limit. Use limits with caution, particularly with memory. Using limits might cause ballooning and/or swapping, which impacts VM operating system and application performance.

NOTE Clearly, a virtual machine does have limits to its computing power or memory. These limits are specified by the configuration of the virtual machine itself. For example, a virtual machine specified with 1 virtual CPU (vCPU) can never use more than 1 logical CPU (core or thread) at a time. Similarly, a virtual machine configured with 1 GB of RAM can never address more than 1 GB of RAM at a time. Because a virtual machine already has "built-in" limits, many vSphere administrators do not use the limits functionality to constrain resource usage.

As with reservations, limits are specified on the Resources tab of the Virtual Machine Properties window. Figure 12.3 shows a virtual machine with a CPU limit of 1200 MHz assigned.

Figure 12.3: Assigning a limit prevents the virtual machine from ever using more of that resource than is specified in the limit.

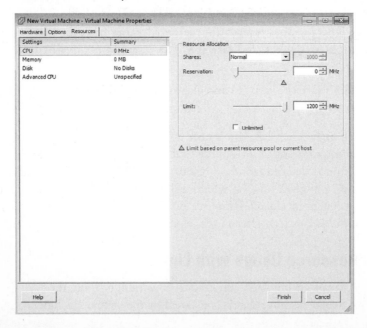

As with reservations, CPU limits and memory limits behave differently:

- With a CPU limit, the ESXi hypervisor simply does not allow the VM to use more CPU cycles than specified in the limit. Because the hypervisor controls the scheduling of VMs onto logical CPU cores, it is easy to enforce a CPU limit by simply not scheduling the VM onto an available logical CPU core.

- With a memory limit, the hypervisor uses the balloon driver—a guest OS–specific driver installed with the VMware Tools—to control guest OS memory usage. As the guest OS memory usage approaches the limit, the balloon driver starts to "inflate," or request memory from the guest OS. The balloon driver takes the memory assigned to it by the guest OS and passes that memory back to the hypervisor for use by other virtual machines or the hypervisor itself. As guest OS memory usage decreases and falls below the limit, the balloon will "deflate," or return memory to the guest operating system. In this manner, the memory usage of the guest OS within the virtual machine is kept below the specified limit.

NOTE   If the VMware Tools are not installed, VMware vSphere can still enforce the memory limit. Instead of using the balloon driver to control guest OS memory usage, the hypervisor will forcefully swap virtual machine memory pages out to the VMkernel swap file when the memory limit is reached. Because this has a dramatic impact on performance—disk access is many thousands of times slower than memory access—use limits carefully on VMs that do not have VMware Tools installed, or ensure that you have the VMware Tools installed on all VMs.

It's important to understand that you should use limits carefully. VMware ESXi will not allow access to resources controlled by limits, even when those resources are underutilized. Improper use of limits can significantly impair the performance of the virtual machines and the operating systems and applications running in them.

To specify a CPU or memory limit for a virtual machine, follow these steps:

1. In vSphere Client, right-click on the virtual machine to which you want to assign a CPU or memory limit.

2. Select Edit Settings from the context menu.

Configuring Your vSphere Environment

PART II

3. In the Virtual Machine Properties dialog box, click the Resources tab.

4. If you wish to set a CPU limit, select CPU from the list of resources on the left. Then deselect the Unlimited check box and specify a CPU limit in MHz.

   To set a memory limit, select Memory from the list of resources on the left. Deselect the Unlimited check box and specify a memory limit in MB.

5. Click OK to save the changes and return to vSphere Client.

Once the limit is set, it is enforced as described earlier, depending on whether it is a CPU limit or a memory limit.

As you've seen so far, both reservations and limits are absolute values—you can guarantee at least 2,400 MHz of CPU capacity or limit memory usage to 512 MB of RAM, for example. These controls are in effect at all times, whether the ESXi host on which the virtual machine is running has plenty of resources to allocate or is running low on resources. Alternatively, *shares* are a way for you to adjust resource allocation behavior only when resources are constrained.

Control Resource Allocation Using Shares

So far in this chapter, we have discussed how to use the VM configuration, reservations, and limits to control resource allocation for individual virtual machines. In all three instances, these controls are effective when the ESXi host has plenty of resources as well as when the ESXi host is running low on one or more of these resources (i.e., is resource-constrained). The last way of affecting resource allocation is through the use of *shares*. This control, unlike the other three controls, is only effective during times of resource contention. Shares do not impact the resource allocation behaviors of a host when the host is not running low on a particular resource.

Shares allow you to control the proportions of resources that are allocated to virtual machines when those resources are in contention. These proportions are calculated by comparing the number of shares assigned to the specific virtual machine to the total number of shares assigned overall. Consider an ESXi host with five virtual machines and the following shares assigned:

- RedVM, 2,000 shares

- GreenVM, 2,000 shares

- BlueVM, 2,000 shares

- YellowVM, 3,000 shares

- OrangeVM, 1,000 shares

The total number of shares assigned among all these VMs is 10,000 shares. That total is compared to the number of shares assigned to each VM to determine the proportion of resources that will be granted to each VM during periods of resource contention. Table 12.1 shows the results of this example.

Table 12.1: Using shares to allocate resources proportionally

VM name	Shares assigned	Total shares	Proportion of shares
RedVM	2,000	10,000	20%
GreenVM	2,000	10,000	20%
BlueVM	2,000	10,000	20%
YellowVM	3,000	10,000	30%
OrangeVM	1,000	10,000	10%

As you can see in Table 12.1, ESXi uses the shares to determine the proportion of resources allocated to each virtual machine. Keep in mind, however, that these proportions only apply when the resources are under contention. If these shares were applied to memory and the host server was running out of memory, these shares would affect how the hypervisor allocated RAM to each of the virtual machines. If these shares were applied to memory but the ESXi host had plenty of RAM to give all the virtual machines all the memory they requested, there would be no need for shares.

Because shares work only when a resource is under contention, they are a valuable addition to the use of reservations and limits. Reservations and limits are absolute; they don't change as the availability of resources changes, and they don't provide a way to determine how limited resources should be allocated among a group of virtual machines. Shares give vSphere administrators that flexibility.

You can assign shares on CPU, memory, and storage and network with Network IO Control (NIOC) enabled on the vDS. When assigning shares, you can choose from three predefined selections—Low, Normal, or High—or choose Custom, which allows you to specify a number of shares to assign to the VM. For CPU and storage, the default setting is Normal. This translates into 1,000 shares per vCPU. A 4 vCPU VM would have 4,000 shares with the Normal value. For memory, the default setting is also Normal, which is equal to ten times the assigned memory value or 10 shares for each MB of memory assigned. For a VM that is assigned 1,024 MB of memory, the default number of shares for memory is 10,240.

NOTE   The predefined High setting doubles the default Normal number of CPU and memory shares. The predefined Low setting halves the default number of CPU and memory shares. Another way to think of this is to remember that each higher tier of shares is double the previous tier. For example, the Normal setting is twice as much as the Low setting, and the High setting is twice as much as the Normal setting.

To change the number of shares assigned to a virtual machine for a particular resource, follow these steps:

1. Within vSphere Client, right-click on the virtual machine you'd like to modify and select Edit Settings.

2. Click the Resources tab.

3. From the list on the left, select the resource for which you'd like to change the number of shares assigned to the VM.

4. Change the assigned shares value to Low, Normal, or High. To set a custom value, select Custom and then specify the number of shares to be assigned for that resource to that virtual machine. Figure 12.4 shows the number of shares for CPU being set to a custom value.

Figure 12.4: The Custom setting allows you to assign the number of shares for a particular resource.

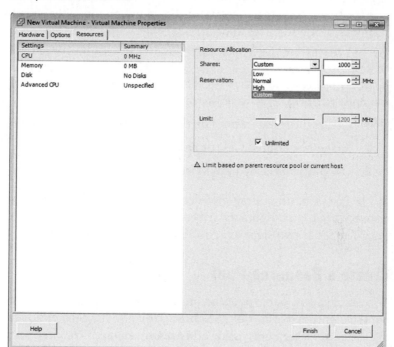

5. Click Finish to save the changes and return to vSphere Client.

For a quick review of the shares assigned to a virtual machine, select the virtual machine from the inventory and click the Resource Allocation tab. This tab will show you the reservation, limit, and number of shares assigned.

Use Resource Pools

The ability to fine-tune resource allocation settings within a VMware vSphere environment on a per-VM basis is useful, but what about when you want to control resource allocation for an entire group of virtual machines? Surely, there has to be a better way. There is, and it's called a resource pool.

Resource pools allow administrators to set resource allocation settings for CPU and memory for multiple virtual machines at the same time. Unlike setting resource allocation values on individual virtual machines, using resource allocation settings with resource pools only allows you to adjust CPU and memory. You cannot set storage shares on a resource pool.

To control resource usage for multiple VMs using a resource pool, you must perform three basic steps:

1. Create the resource pool on the appropriate ESXi host or cluster.

2. Assign the desired CPU or memory resource usage settings.

3. Use drag-and-drop to put virtual machines into the resource pool.

The last step, using drag-and-drop to put virtual machines into the resource pool, is straightforward enough that it needs no further discussion. The other two steps are covered in the next few sections.

Create a Resource Pool

You can create resource pools on individual ESXi hosts or shared resource pools assigned to clusters of ESXi hosts. You also have the option of creating nested resource pools inside other resource pools. Resource pools created within a cluster are also called *parent resource pools*. When created inside another resource pool, they are called *child resource pools*. In any case, the process for creating a resource pool is the same.

To create a resource pool, follow these steps:

1. In the Hosts And Clusters inventory view of vSphere Client, right-click on a host, cluster, or existing resource pool and select New Resource Pool.

2. Specify a name for the resource pool.

3. In the CPU Resources section, specify the settings for how CPU resources should be handled for virtual machines within this pool. More details on how these settings work is provided in the next section, "Control CPU Allocation with a Resource Pool."

4. In the Memory Resources section, specify the settings for how memory resources should be allocated for virtual machines in this pool. The next section also provides more information on how these controls work.

5. Click OK to create the resource pool and return to vSphere Client.

Now that the resource pool has been created, you can adjust its settings to modify how ESXi will allocate resources to virtual machines located in that resource pool.

Control CPU Allocation with a Resource Pool

By using a combination of reservations, limits, and shares, you can control CPU allocation for all the virtual machines within a resource pool.

Use CPU Reservations with a Resource Pool

To guarantee a minimum amount of CPU resources for a resource pool, specify a CPU reservation. The amount of the reservation, specified in megahertz (MHz) as with individual virtual machines, is guaranteed for use by *all* the virtual machines in the resource pool. This is not a reservation for each VM in the resource pool, but rather a reservation for all the VMs as a group to share.

Within the resource pool, you might wish to assign CPU reservations to individual virtual machines. This configuration is fully supported, but the behavior might be a bit different from what you expect. The key to understanding how resource pool reservations and VM reservations interact is found in the Expandable Reservation option, as shown in Figure 12.5.

Figure 12.5: The Expandable Reservation option allows a VM having a higher reservation within the resource pool to borrow resources from its parent container.

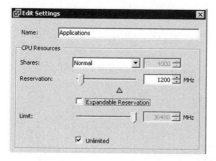

When Expandable Reservation is unchecked, as it is in Figure 12.5, the resource pool has a finite amount of CPU resources that can, in turn, be reserved by virtual machines within the resource pool. In the figure, the resource pool has a nonexpandable reservation of 1,200

MHz. This means that you can assign up to 1,200 MHz of reservations to individual virtual machines within the resource pool. If you attempt to reserve more than 1,200 MHz to individual virtual machines in the resource pool, that attempt will fail. Note that this is not a limit on how many CPU cycles the resource pool or its member VMs can *use*, but rather a limit on how many CPU cycles member VMs can *reserve*.

If, on the other hand, the Expandable Reservation option is checked, the resource pool is permitted to "borrow" resources from its parent container. Again, this "borrowing" only pertains to individual VM reservations and does not affect CPU limits. The parent container of the resource pool depends on where it was created:

- The parent of a resource pool created on an individual ESXi host is the host itself and is hidden.

- The parent of a resource pool created on a cluster is the cluster.

Figure 12.6 graphically illustrates the relationships between clusters, ESXi hosts, and resource pools with regard to how resources might be borrowed from a parent container with expandable reservations.

Figure 12.6: Expandable reservations allow objects to borrow resources from their parent object.

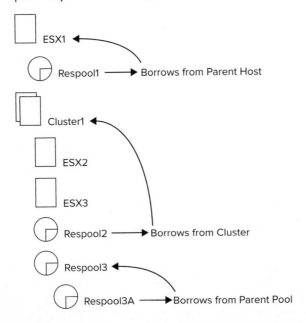

The default setting on a new resource pool is an expandable reservation of 0 MHz, which means you will be able to reserve CPU resources borrowed from the parent object, up to the maximum available in the parent host, cluster, or resource pool.

Follow these steps to assign a CPU reservation to a resource pool:

1. Within the Hosts And Clusters inventory view of vSphere Client, right-click on the resource pool to which you want to assign a CPU reservation.

2. Select Edit Settings.

3. Specify a value, in MHz, that you want reserved for the resource pool and its member VMs.

4. Uncheck the Expandable Reservation box if you want to limit the CPU reservations by member VMs to the amount assigned to the resource pool itself.

5. Click OK to save the changes and return to vSphere Client.

Use CPU Limits with a Resource Pool

In addition to using CPU reservations with resource pools, you have the option of using CPU limits with resource pools. Figure 12.7 shows an example of a resource pool with a limit specified.

Figure 12.7: Setting a CPU limit prevents the resource pool and its member VMs from using more than the specified amount of CPU resources.

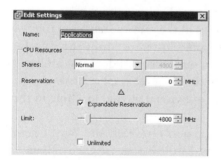

CPU limits function in much the same way when used on a resource pool as when used on a virtual machine. Of course, the key difference is that the limit applies to all the virtual machines in the resource pool rather than a single virtual machine.

To set a CPU limit for a resource pool, perform these steps:

1. Within the Hosts And Clusters inventory view of vSphere Client, right-click on the resource pool to which you want to assign a CPU limit.

2. Select Edit Settings.

3. Deselect the Unlimited check box.

4. Specify a limit, in megahertz (MHz), to which the resource pool should be constrained.

5. Click OK to return to vSphere Client.

The maximum limit that you can specify for a resource pool created on an ESXi host is the capacity of the host itself. Similarly, the maximum limit that you can specify for a resource pool created on a cluster is the aggregate capacity of the cluster. For a child resource pool—that is, a resource pool created within another resource pool—the maximum amount that can be specified for the limit is whatever limit is applied to the parent. For example, if a parent resource pool has a limit of 4,800 MHz, any child pools within it cannot have a limit set greater than 4,800 MHz.

In addition to CPU reservations and CPU limits, you can assign CPU shares to a resource pool. The next section describes that functionality.

Use CPU Shares with a Resource Pool

Using shares with a resource pool allows you to specify the priority of the resource pool for access to resources. This priority is relative to other resource pools or virtual machines in the same parent container— that is, on the same ESXi host, in the same cluster, or in the same parent resource pool. Assigning shares to a resource pool does not affect the priority of virtual machines within the resource pool relative to each other; the shares assigned to each individual virtual machine in the resource pool determine that priority.

In Figure 12.8, there are two resource pools—Green and Blue. Green has 2,000 shares assigned, and Blue has 1,000 shares assigned. When resources are allocated between the two resource pools, Green will receive approximately two-thirds of the resources and Blue will receive approximately one-third of the resources. Thus, the shares assigned to the resource pools only establish priority relative to each other. Within the Green resource pool, the VMs have equal priority relative to each other, but within the Blue resource pool, VM3 has double the priority of VM4. The shares assigned to the pools have no impact on determining the priority of the VMs.

Figure 12.8: Shares only establish priority relative to other objects at the same level in the hierarchy.

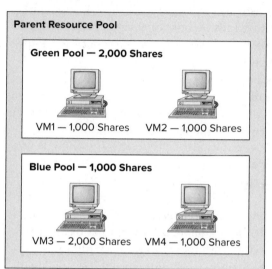

To assign shares to a resource pool to control CPU usage relative to other peer resource pools, follow these steps:

1. In the Hosts And Clusters inventory view of vSphere Client, right-click on the resource pool you want to modify.

2. Select Edit Settings.

3. From the Shares drop-down list, select Low, Normal, High, or Custom.

4. If you selected Custom, specify a number of shares to assign to the selected resource pool.

5. Click OK to return to vSphere Client.

Be sure to understand the cascading effect of using shares on both the resource pools and the virtual machines within them. Otherwise, virtual machines could end up getting drastically lower priority to resources than expected. This is true not only for CPU resources, but also for memory resources, as described in the next section.

Control Memory Allocation with a Resource Pool

In all cases, using a reservation, limit, or shares on a resource pool to control memory allocation for the virtual machines in this resource pool behaves the same way as it does for CPU resources. You assign these controls in the same way as described in the previous section. Refer to the procedures in the previous section, "Control CPU Allocation with a Resource Pool," for specific details on how to assign a reservation, limit, or shares on a resource pool. Assigning any of these controls for memory is done in the same way as for CPU resources.

Controlling resource allocation using reservations, limits, and shares is only part of the picture. The rest of the picture involves being able to identify when hosts or virtual machines are resource-constrained so that, as an administrator, you know when to use the resource allocation controls.

Monitor Performance

There's another side to resource allocation and resource management, and that's the monitoring side. It's not enough for you to know how to adjust vSphere's default behaviors with regard to resource allocation; you also need to know how to identify when virtual machines aren't getting the resources they need. Once you've identified a virtual machine that isn't getting enough resources, you can use the settings outlined earlier in this chapter to adjust how resources are allocated to that virtual machine.

Although other resources exist that could become bottlenecks—consider storage, for example—this section focuses on only two major resources: CPU and RAM.

Identify a Resource-Constrained ESXi Host

So, how do you identify when an ESXi host is CPU- or memory-constrained? Usually, making the identification is reasonably simple. Rectifying the problem, however, might be a bit more complicated, depending on the environment.

vSphere Client provides a Performance tab when an ESXi host is selected in the Hosts And Clusters inventory view. This Performance tab provides performance graphs and statistics on the ESXi host. These make it easy to identify when an ESXi host is resource-constrained.

Figure 12.9 shows the default view on the Performance tab for an ESXi host. In this particular example, the host is quite clearly not

CPU-constrained. The memory graphs aren't visible in this example, so it's not possible to tell whether the host is RAM-constrained.

Figure 12.9: The Performance tab provides enough information to identify whether an ESXi host is resource-constrained.

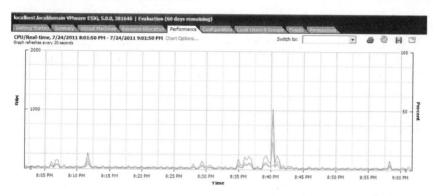

The Performance tab within vCenter Server provides the majority of the information you need to identify when an ESXi host is resource-constrained. Table 12.2 provides more information on where you should look in vSphere Client to find information on ESXi host resource constraints.

Table 12.2: Identifying resource constraints in vCenter Server

To identify ESXi constraints for this resource...	...Look in this area of vCenter Server
CPU	Summary Tab ➤ Resources Pane ➤ CPU Usage
	Performance Tab ➤ Overview ➤ CPU (%)
	Performance Tab ➤ Overview ➤ CPU (MHz)
Memory	Summary Tab ➤ Resources Pane ➤ Memory Usage
	Performance Tab ➤ Overview ➤ Memory (MB)
	Performance Tab ➤ Overview ➤ Memory (Mbps)
	Performance Tab ➤ Overview ➤ Memory (%)
Disk	Performance Tab ➤ Overview ➤ Disk (Kbps)
	Performance Tab ➤ Overview ➤ Disk (Milliseconds)
Network	Performance Tab ➤ Overview ➤ Network (Mbps)

Configuring Your vSphere Environment

PART II

While identifying when an ESXi host is resource-constrained is usually straightforward, sometimes you might need to dig deeper. In those cases, tools like esxtop or vm-support are helpful. The Advanced view of the Performance tab also exposes specific performance counters that might be necessary.

NOTE The esxtop and vm-support tools are available from the Tech Support Mode or remote SSH session of a VMware ESXi host.

Identify a Resource-Constrained Virtual Machine

All too often, administrators trying to diagnose a performance problem within a guest operating system running in a virtual machine on VMware ESXi make the mistake of using guest OS–native tools to determine resource utilization. For example, a Windows administrator might use Performance Monitor or Task Manager to observe memory or CPU utilization of a Windows Server–based virtual machine, or a Linux administrator might use top to observe resource usage on a Linux-based virtual machine. Unfortunately, while these tools are familiar, they don't provide the whole picture. Can you guess why these tools won't provide the right information?

Guest OS–native tools are only able to report on the usage of what the ESXi hypervisor *allocates to the guest*, not what is *actually available on the host*. This is a key distinction that's important for all vSphere administrators to understand. The resources that the guest OS sees are only those resources allocated to it, not the full resources actually available on the host. So, when a guest OS reports 100 percent CPU usage, that doesn't mean the host is CPU-constrained. It only means that the guest OS is using 100 percent of the cycles given to it by the hypervisor. What if the hypervisor is only giving that VM 10 percent of its available cycles because of limits or shares? Using only guest OS–native tools would provide only part of the picture. To effectively diagnose resource-related issues with a virtual machine, you must use tools both inside and outside the virtual machine.

The next two sections describe how to use tools both inside and outside the guest OS to help identify when a virtual machine might be CPU- or RAM-constrained.

Identify a CPU-Constrained VM

As mentioned earlier, vSphere administrators attempting to identify whether a VM is CPU-constrained should start by looking both *inside* and *outside* the guest operating system. From inside the guest operating system, use guest OS–native tools to determine current CPU usage. From outside the guest operating system, use vCenter Server's performance-monitoring tools to determine both how much the VM is being granted as well as how much the VM is actually using.

NOTE   The performance graphs within vSphere Client are available in environments that are not using vCenter Server. Just connect vSphere Client directly to an ESXi host to view performance information.

Here are two common scenarios that arise when evaluating CPU usage in a VMware vSphere environment:

The guest OS shows high CPU usage, but the ESXi host has plenty of spare CPU capacity.   In this situation, the guest OS in the virtual machine is using all the CPU cycles granted to it by the hypervisor and is starving for more as indicated by %RDY in esxtop or Ready MS in the vSphere Client. If application performance within the virtual machine is not at acceptable levels, then ensure that no limits have been placed on the virtual machine or the resource pool(s) in which this virtual machine resides. Adding a second CPU might help performance, if the applications within the virtual machine are sufficiently multithreaded to take advantage of the extra processing power. If not, migrating the virtual machine to an ESXi host with faster CPU cores might help improve performance.

The guest OS shows high CPU usage, and the ESXi host's CPU utilization is also very high.   In this case, the VM needs lots of CPU cycles, but the ESXi host is already heavily loaded. If application performance is acceptable, no further changes are needed; otherwise, you should also check the CPU Ready counter (available in esxtop or the Advanced view of the Performance tab in vSphere Client) to determine if the guest OS is using all the cycles it can get or if it is waiting on cycles from the host. A high CPU Ready counter would indicate that the guest OS in the virtual machine would use more CPU cycles if they were made available. In this case, using shares to grant this

Configuring Your vSphere Environment

PART II

virtual machine higher-priority access to CPU resources might correct the performance issue. Adding a second virtual CPU might not help, as the ESXi host still might not have enough cycles to provide, and the application has to be sufficiently multithreaded as to be able to take advantage of the additional CPU core. Migrating this VM to a less heavily loaded host might also help. Alternately, you can migrate other workloads to other hosts in order to free up resources for this virtual machine. If VMware DRS is enabled and configured for fully automatic operation, this process would be handled without administrator intervention.

Many of these same techniques apply when diagnosing a virtual machine that is thought to be RAM (memory)-constrained, as you'll learn next.

Identify a RAM-Constrained VM

In much in the same way as you would look both inside and outside the virtual machine to determine CPU contention, you need to look at counters and information from both sides to identify a RAM-constrained virtual machine.

Here are two common scenarios that you will encounter when dealing with memory contention issues:

The guest OS reports high memory usage, but the ESXi host shows plenty of memory capacity. In this instance, the guest operating system is using all the memory given to it by the hypervisor. If the hypervisor is not showing signs of memory pressure, adding memory to the virtual machine might resolve the issue. Also be sure that no memory limits have been applied to the virtual machine or the resource pool(s) in which the virtual machine resides. If limits have been applied, removing them might help resolve the issue and relieve memory pressure within the guest operating system.

The guest OS reports high memory usage, and the ESXi host's memory utilization is also high. When both the guest OS and the ESXi host are reporting high memory usage, identifying the real source of the problem is a bit more difficult. Adding memory won't fix the problem, as the host is also running low on memory. In this case, review reservations to ensure that memory has not been needlessly allocated in memory reservations. Recall that with memory reservations, once the guest OS has accessed reserved memory, that reserved memory is never reclaimed by the hypervisor for other purposes. This could lead to a high-memory-usage situation where some machines are being starved for memory. The Memory Swap Used (Average) counter, available in the Advanced view of the Performance tab, will provide a reasonably good idea of whether the ESXi host is actually under memory pressure. If the host is indeed under memory pressure and all other measures have been taken, you must migrate VMs to other hosts and/or add memory to the host in order to alleviate the problem.

Configuring Your vSphere
Environment

PART II

Index

Note to the reader: Throughout this index boldfaced page numbers indicate primary discussions of a topic. Italicized page numbers indicate illustrations.